The Future of Wisdom

The Future of Wisdom

Toward a Rebirth of Sapiential Christianity

BRUNO BARNHART

NEW YORK • LONDON

2008
The Continuum International Publishing Group Inc
80 Maiden Lane, New York, New York 10038

The Continuum International Publishing Group Ltd
The Tower Building, 11 York Road, London SE1 7NX

Copyright © 2007 by Bruno Barnhart

All rights reserved. No part of this book may be reproduced, stored in a retrieval system, or transmitted in any form or by any means, electronic, mechanical, photocopying, recording or otherwise, without the written permission of the publishers.

Continuum is a member of Green Press Initiative, a nonprofit program dedicated to supporting publishers in their efforts to reduce their use of fiber obtained from endangered forests. For more information, go to www.greenpressinitiative.org.
Printed in the United States of America

Library of Congress Cataloging-in-Publication Data

Barnhart, Bruno, 1931-
The future of wisdom : toward a rebirth of sapiential Christianity / Bruno Barnhart.
p. cm.
Includes bibliographical references and index.
ISBN-13: 978-0-8264-2767-0 (hardcover : alk. paper)
ISBN-10: 0-8264-2767-7 (hardcover : alk. paper)
ISBN-13: 978-0-8264-1932-3 (pbk. : alk. paper)
ISBN-10: 0-8264-1932-1 (pbk. : alk. paper)
1. Spirituality. 2. Wisdom—Religious aspects—Christianity. I. Title.

BV4509.5.B3735 2007
230—dc22

2007003506

Contents

Sapientiás adj
relating to wisdom

say'pee'entiás
sounds like end of Essentiás

[latin sapientia wisdom]

Acknowledgments

My thanks go to Alessandro Barban, from whose suggestion the book originated; to Prior Raniero Hoffman and the community of New Camaldoli, who have encouraged me throughout the course of the project; and to Robert Hale for his helpful comments on the manuscript. I am grateful to Frank Oveis of Continuum for his warm support and expert guidance, and to Lynne Clarkin for her fine, expressive cover drawing.

Quotations from the Revised Standard Version of *The Bible,* 2nd edition, copyright 1952, by the Division of Christian Education of the National Council of the Churches of Christ in the United States of America. Used by permission. All rights reserved.

Quotations from *The Liturgy of the Hours,* volume II, copyright © 1970, 1973, 1976 by International Committee on English in the Liturgy, Inc. All rights reserved. © 1976 by Catholic Book Publishing Company, New York.

Quotations from Ewert Cousins, *Christ of the 21st Century,* Element Books, Rockport, Massachusetts, © 1992.

Quotations from Bede Griffiths, *Return to the Center,* © Bede Griffiths, 1976. First published in Great Britain by Collins, London. U.S. edition published in 1977 by Templegate Publishers, Springfield, Illinois. © The Bede Griffiths Trust.

Quotations from Bede Griffiths, *New Vision of Reality: Western Science, Eastern Mysticism and Christian Faith,* edited by Felicity Edwards. © Bede Griffiths, 1989. Published in the U.S. in 1990 by Templegate Publishers, Springfield, Illinois. © The Bede Griffiths Trust.

Quotations from the *Tao Teh Ching,* by Lao Tzu, translated by John C. H. Wu, © 1961 by St. John's University Press, New York. © 1989 by Shambhala, Boston and Shaftesbury. Used by permission. All rights reserved.

Quotations from Thomas Merton: "Baptism in the Forest: Wisdom and Initiation in William Faulkner," in *The Literary Essays of Thomas Merton,* copyright © 1960, 1966, 1967, 1968, 1973, 1975, 1978, 1981 by the Trustees of the Merton

Legacy Trust, copyright © 1959, 1961, 1963, 1964, 1965, 1981 by The Abbey of Gethsemani, Inc. Copyright © 1953 by Our Lady of Gethsemani Monastery. Used by permission of New Directions Publishing Corp., New York.

Quotations from Karl Rahner, *Theological Investigations,* vol. 4, Darton, Longman & Todd, London, 1966; vol. 5, Darton, Longman & Todd, London, 1966; vol. 20, Seabury, New York, 1981.

Quotations from Pierre Teilhard de Chardin, *The Future of Man,* copyright © 1959 by Editions du Seuil. English translation copyright © 1964 by William Collins Sons & Co., Ltd., London and Harper & Row, Inc., New York. Originally published in French as *L'Avenir de L'Homme.*

Quotations from Simone Weil on pages 160-61 are from *The Simone Weil Reader,* edited by George A. Panichas. David McKay Company, Inc., New York, © 1977 by George A. Panichas. All rights reserved. Reprinted 1981 by Dorset Press, a division of Marboro Books Corporation. The texts were originally published in French in 1950 in *L'Attente de Dieu* by La Colombe, Paris. English translation of this book, by Emma Craufurd, was published in the U.S. by G. P. Putnam's Sons, New York, as *Waiting for God,* copyright 1951.

1

Introduction

1. A Preliminary Overview

The kingdom of heaven is like treasure hidden in a field. . . . [1]

IT MAY SEEM IMPROBABLE THAT "CHRISTIAN WISDOM" CAN MEAN SOMETHING quite specific, and even less likely that these words denote something actual, emerging, and full of promise. This book recalls, first of all, that a *sapiential* (wisdom) consciousness is central to the New Testament writings and remained the dominant mode of theological understanding in both the Eastern and Western Christian traditions for more than twelve centuries. Further, it proposes that the recovery of a truly experiential relationship to the event of Christ in our time involves the rediscovery—or, better, a new birth—of sapiential understanding and sapiential theology, with a new scope and power. As we work toward rediscovering the wisdom and the power of God in the Christ-event today, we are on the threshold of a *sapiential gospel.*

From another perspective, the book is about something alive and growing, vigorously present in multiple forms but hardly recognized and therefore hardly aware of itself; something waiting to be named so that it can awaken in its unity and truth. The intellectual history of Christianity could be written in terms of a series of awakenings—and, alas, of forgettings and long slumbers. The second half of the twentieth century, which began for Roman Catholics with the historic event of the Second Vatican Council, was a privileged time of awakening and even of self-discovery for Western Christianity. Much that had been lost was rediscovered and brought together at this time. Evidences of an earlier, deeper, and more profound vision and of a more unitary theology were brought forth abundantly by the liturgical movement, the biblical movement, and the renewal of patristic studies. We still await, however, a further awakening. The common world of thought and the common theological language that characterized much of the New Testament, the early liturgical tradition, and the patristic traditions of both East and West have rarely been recognized and named.[2] This consciousness, way of thinking, and literary language are best described as "wisdom," and historically as the *sapiential* tradition. A specific, self-conscious sapiential awakening has not yet taken place in contemporary Christianity. This is still more paradoxical since we are surrounded by spiritual "wisdoms" in today's world[3]—many of them deriving from the ancient traditions of Asia.

During this same twentieth century, Christian thinkers found themselves faced with what seemed a new world, requiring fresh perspectives and new methodologies. The phenomenon exploded within the Roman Catholic Church at the time of the same council, with far-reaching consequences. The church suddenly awakened, it seemed, to find itself stretched between the fullness of its primitive origins—seen with a new clarity—and a new and larger world requiring a new theological language, at once unitive and dynamic.

In this book I shall argue not only that a sapiential consciousness and theological perspective are the key to the inner meaning of the Christian mystery (expressed in the New Testament, the liturgy, and the patristic theological writings) in its beginnings and its unfolding but, further, that it is a sapiential approach—reconceived with a new breadth and vitality in the larger context of our world of today—that offers the best hope for a unifying theological and spiritual vision in our own time. A renewed sapiential consciousness and method offers , I believe, a privileged path toward the renewal of Christian theology itself. The resources for a radical renewal of sapiential theology are at hand, and the beginnings of such a birth can already be discerned. I shall point to the work of Karl Rahner and Thomas Merton, in particular, as evidence of this fact.

This study envisions a re-emergence of Christian wisdom in a contemporary context, which includes a profound interaction with the Asian traditions, a continuing modern Western personalism, and the historical moment of postmodernity and globalization. Our exploration, therefore, will proceed in four movements, which suggest four possible phases of the rebirth of wisdom today: (1) the sapiential awakening itself: the recovery of the basic perspective of Christian wisdom, followed by three major developments in the sapiential tradition that are called for today; (2) an Eastern turn: a recentering of spirituality and theology in baptismal identity, conceived in terms of nonduality; (3) a Western turn: an integration of the dynamic and creative element of Christianity, which is expressed in the liberation and realization of the human person in Western history; and, finally, (4) a global turn: active participation in the movement toward one world: a united humanity aware of its communion with earth and cosmos. These four movements are oriented toward an expansion of the mystery of Christ from its confinement within a *logos*-container toward its intrinsic fullness.

2. The Bias

I shall not attempt impartiality, whatever that might mean. The book is obviously written from a Roman Catholic perspective within the Christian tradition, and it was written by a monk. Further, the approach will be slanted in at least three directions: (1) toward an epistemology: the sapiential bias. I shall propose that a first key to a new Christian wisdom is the broadening and deepening of our consciousness and of our "knowing of knowing": of the way that we understand our consciousness; (2) toward "unitive consciousness": the Asian bias. The first direction in which consciousness is to be deepened is that of unity or nonduality, as we rediscover it today in our interaction with Hinduism, Buddhism, and Taoism; (3) toward "person": the modern Western bias. What I shall present will be mostly from the side of the personal rather than the collective, the individual and subjective rather than the institutionally "objective." But the mystery of Christ and its sapiential participation embrace both the objective world and the world of personal experience; in this, indeed, is the distinctiveness of the sapiential tradition.

3. The Taste

At this point, I must call upon personal experience. Like many young Catholics, I took an extended vacation from religious practice starting with my first years away from home, at college. During this time I recall reading very little of a religious nature; science and poetry were more interesting. One spiritual book, however, caught and held me. It was Aldous Huxley's *The Perennial Philosophy*,[4] that wondrous anthology of mystical and ascetical texts from the world's great religious traditions. Huxley's brief selections from the Vedanta and Meister Eckhart and St. John of the Cross and William Law fascinated me, drawing me into their circle of quiet light again and again. That glowing book was a sapiential island in a world of scientific rationality and confident literalism; it spoke—often sang—of another level of reality, another world which awakened deep longings within me. Now, before embarking on what may seem at times a long journey of abstraction, of reading *about* the wisdom that is our subject, I cannot think of a better way to convey the scent and flavor, the taste and interior experience that belongs to the world of sapiential thought and writing than with some texts from Huxley's collection. Here is the thing itself, as close to life as words can bring it. First, let us hear a bit of Huxley's introduction to the book, in which he summarizes his conception of the perennial philosophy—which owes much to the Hindu Vedanta. This philosophical basis has determined the choice and limited the breadth and variety of the extracts. The sampling is not representative of the whole of sapiential literature nor, of course, of the Christian sapiential traditions. But Huxley's choices have the essential taste.

> PHILOSOPHIA PERENNIS—the phrase was coined by Leibniz; but the thing—the metaphysic that recognizes a divine Reality substantial to the world of things and lives and minds; the psychology that finds in the soul something similar to, or even identical with, divine Reality; the ethic that places man's final end in the knowledge of the immanent and transcendent Ground of all being—the thing is immemorial and universal.[5]

And now the texts themselves, as they began to light up for me—and for many other readers—from the the first pages of Huxley's book.[6]

> Man as he now is has ceased to be the All. But when he ceases to be an individual, he raises himself again and penetrates the whole world. (Plotinus[7])

> Supreme, beyond the power of speech to express, Brahman may yet be apprehended by the eye of pure illumination. Pure, absolute and eternal Reality—such is Brahman, and "thou art That." Meditate upon this truth within your consciousness. (Shankara[8])

> Behold but One in all things; it is the second that leads you astray. (Kabir[9])

> To gauge the soul we must gauge it with God, for the Ground of God and the Ground of the Soul are one and the same. (Eckhart[10])

> The spirit possesses God essentially in naked nature, and God the spirit. (Ruysbroeck[11])

> When the Ten Thousand things are viewed in their oneness, we return to the Origin and remain where we have always been. (Sen T'sen[12])

> The farther one travels, the less one knows. (Philo[13])

> Sell your cleverness and buy bewilderment;
> Cleverness is mere opinion, bewilderment is intuition. (Rumi[14])

Were Huxley compiling his anthology today, he might quote some contemporary authors as witnesses to his *philosophia perennis.*

> It is the Ground of consciousness just as it is the Ground of existence. It is that from which all thought springs but which cannot be thought. Yet there is a point beyond thought, where this becomes known, not as an object of thought, nor even as a subject as distinct from an object, but in an identity of subject and object, of being and knowing. This is the experience of the Self, the Atman, beyond being in so far as being is an object of thought, beyond thought in so far as thought is a reflection, a concept of being. It is pure awareness of being, pure delight in being—*saccidananda,* being, knowledge, bliss. It is Nirvana, the ultimate State, the supreme Wisdom, beyond which it is impossible to go. (Bede Griffiths[15])

> The character of emptiness, at least for a Christian contemplative, is pure love, pure freedom. Love that is free of everything, not determined by any thing, or held down by any special relationship. It is love for love's sake. It is a sharing, through the Holy Spirit, in the infinite charity of God. And so when Jesus told his disciples to love, he told them to love as universally as the Father who sends his rain alike on the just and the unjust. "Be ye perfect as your Heavenly Father is perfect." This purity, freedom and indeterminateness of love is the very essence of Christianity. (Thomas Merton[16])

In a world of consciousness seemingly far distant from these explicitly spiritual texts, a sapiential current flows through much contemporary Western literature, and its enchantment can often be experienced in the words of a poem.

> The poem refreshes life so that we share,
> For a moment, the first idea. . . . It satisfies
> Belief in an immaculate beginning.[17]

4. Thinking about Wisdom

What, then, is this wisdom? We may already know what it is without knowing its name or hearing a definition, if we have encountered writings like those just quoted. Anyone conversant with *The Liturgy of the Hours* knows it: those liturgical readings are full of it, from the New Testament through the fathers and the medieval theological writers. Once pointed out and named, it is easily recognized, in contrast to mainstream Western religious thought and language today. Outside Christianity, it surrounds us today in a hundred forms—from the venerable Asian traditions of Hinduism, Buddhism, and Taoism to the esoteric currents of the West.[18] If we require a definition, let us call it *participatory knowing*: a knowing that is personal, experiential, and tending toward union with that which is known; ultimately centered in "identity." While we shall be concerned with forms of *Christian* wisdom, we shall find the Christian sapiential world broadening exponentially in our own time.

First of all a mode of consciousness and a way of knowing, this becomes an explicit theology and a form of literature. I will be focusing primarily on theological wisdom, because it is more accessible to us and lends itself to study and discussion. Implicit in this theological wisdom, however, is a contemplative or sapiential consciousness and a corresponding personal commitment and way of life.

This is an experiential knowing, a loving knowledge, as the medieval Western spiritual writers would say.[19] In this it differs from the objective and purely rational knowing of science, which has become the epistemological standard in recent centuries. In this sapiential knowing which is not purely objective but participatory, one shares in that which one knows, and knows it in the sharing. Ultimately—at the most interior level of this knowledge—it is a knowing by union, by identity. Here, in the language of antiquity, the knower, the knowing, and the known are one.

This knowing is *affirmative*; the knowing itself is an affirmation. In Christian tradition, it is *faith* that is the fundamental way of knowing, and faith with hope and love—the three are phases or modalities of a single act—is an affirmation. The whole person is opened and extended forward in affirmation. The affirmation and the knowing are themselves inseparable from the identity of the person. It is as if the person awakens to his/her true identity in this affirmation and this knowing, as can be seen in the "recognition" scenes in the Gospels; someone awakens to his or her true being in the moment in which, through the gift of faith, they are suddenly able to affirm the divine reality that is in the man Jesus.

Faith, the fundamental mode of sapiential knowing, is a knowing in darkness, an affirmative cognition of mystery. What is known is "the mystery," and the knowing is consequently obscure even as it is certain. Sapiential knowing ranges from a dark awareness in faith through various forms of symbolic understanding to the pure nondual experience of contemplation, a simple awakening to the unitive light.

"Wisdom" can easily sound like an elitist specialization. The orientation of the wisdom we shall be concerned with—as consciousness and as theology—is the opposite of specialization; it moves toward an opening of the full spectrum of consciousness, as we find it in the New Testament and the ancient literature, before the imposition of the dogmas of rationalism. To attempt to understand a sapiential text of the New Testament—let us say the prologue of John's Gospel—purely by the scientific methods of modern historical criticism (despite the great usefulness of these methods)—is much like trying to render a Beethoven piano sonata on a typewriter. With the machine you may succeed in bringing forth something *about* the music, but not the music itself—and between the two lies an immense gap. For the classical sapiential writers, in the light of spiritual understanding,[20] the Scriptures opened to bring forth something like the polyphony of a string quartet, and they proceeded to bring forth the music of the biblical word in its vibrant fullness, from the cello's sonorous depths to the nimble interplay of twin violins. The metaphor is not unjust; this wisdom at its best is a theological music resounding through the whole of the human person.

To propose a study of Christian wisdom may sound like the announcement of an archaeological expedition to the ruins of a long-abandoned city. The challenge that faces us is that of demonstrating that our quest opens a way into the *future.* I will propose that the sapiential approach comes to life today as a *historical* wisdom, and as such offers a privileged way of understanding the theological continuity of Christianity through its historical journey of twenty centuries and of orienting us toward its further unfolding. Hidden within this legacy of theological wisdom are secrets of the world's future.

5. The Christian Wisdom Tradition

i. Patristic Wisdom

Wisdom Christianity is rooted in the sapiential writings of the New Testament, particularly the Pauline and Johannine texts.[21] The classical Christian wisdom was invariably centered in the word of God, in the sapiential event of Christ—the mystery of Christ as presented in the letters of Paul—and at its best retains the simplicity and power of that event. Space will permit inclusion of only a few samples of the patristic and the later monastic literature.[22]

> We should understand, beloved, that the paschal mystery[23] is at once old and new, transitory and eternal, corruptible and incorruptible,

mortal and immortal. In terms of the Law it is old, in terms of the Word it is new. In its figure it is passing, in its grace it is eternal. It is corruptible in the sacrifice of the lamb, incorruptible in the eternal life of the Lord. It is mortal in his burial in the earth, immortal in his resurrection from the dead.

The Law indeed is old, but the Word is new. The type is transitory, but grace is eternal. The lamb was corruptible, but the Lord is incorruptible. He was slain as a lamb; he rose again as God. *He was led like a sheep to the slaughter*, yet he was not a sheep. He was silent as a lamb, yet he was not a lamb. The type has passed away; the reality has come. The lamb gives place to God, the sheep gives place to a man, and the man is Christ, who fills the whole of creation. (Melito of Sardis, second century)[24]

The Church recognizes two kinds of life as having been commended to her by God. One is a life of faith, the other a life of vision; one is a life passed on pilgrimage, in time, the other in a dwelling place in eternity; one is a life of toil, the other a life of repose; . . . one is active, involving labor, the other contemplative, the reward of labor.

The first kind of life is symbolized by the apostle Peter, the second by John [see John 21:15-24]. All of the first life is led in this world, and it will come to an end with this world. The second life will be imperfect till the end of this world, but it will have no end in the next world. And so Christ says to Peter: *Follow me;* but of John he says: *If I wish him to remain until I come, what is that to you? Your duty is to follow me.*

You are to follow me by imitating my endurance of transient evils; John is to remain until my coming, when I will bring eternal blessings. A way of saying this more clearly might be: Your active life will be perfect if you follow the example of my passion, but to attain its full perfection John's life of contemplation must wait until I come. . . .

. . . Yet we should make no mental separations between these great apostles. Both lived the life symbolized by Peter; both were to attain the life symbolized by John. . . .

Nor were they alone in this. They were one with the whole Church, the bride of Christ, which will in time be delivered from the trials of this life and live for ever in the joy of the next. (Augustine, 354–430)[25]

Therefore the mystery of the Incarnation of the Word contains in itself the whole meaning of the riddles and symbols of Scripture, the whole significance of visible and invisible creatures. Whoever knows the mys-

> tery of the cross and the tomb knows the meaning of things. Whoever is initiated into the hidden meaning of the resurrection knows the purpose for which God created everything in the beginning. (Maximus the Confessor, 580–662)[26]

This patristic theology centered in the Christ-mystery reappears in our time in the documents of Vatican II.[27]

ii. Limitations of Patristic Wisdom

At this present moment, as we experience signs of a rebirth of Christian wisdom, we have also become conscious of the limitations of the old wisdom. These often corresponded to the limitations of classical (Greco-Roman) culture itself.

1. Biblical interpretation (patristic theology was customarily expressed in the form of biblical commentary) was often naive, either in the direction of an uncritical and literalistic use of the Scriptures or of a quasi-mechanical, over-systematic use of symbolism. Allegorical interpretation sometimes operated almost independently of the literal meaning and intent of the scriptural word; an *a priori* exegesis would apply an inventory of standard principles, structures, and concepts under the guise of finding them in the scriptural word. Spiritual interpretation, exempted from rational criticism, sometimes extended to idle fantasies.
2. The Platonic (and Neoplatonic) philosophical views adopted by most of the church fathers tended to introduce a quasi-gnostic vertical dualism (spirit or intellect opposed to body and matter) into theology, suppressing the radical bodiliness of the mystery of Christ.
3. Along with the tendency toward a spiritualizing other-worldliness went, of course, a lack of respect for the realities of human earthly existence, for positive human values in this world, for secular endeavors.
4. From our contemporary point of view, patristic theology did not give sufficient value or freedom to the individual human person, often considering the individual as object among other objects in the world rather than as transcendent subject.[28]
5. The social structures of the ancient world, with their hierarchies of class, of role and status, wealth and power were often taken for granted and not confronted with the challenge of the gospel.
6. While the fathers habitually thought in terms of sacred history, a sense

of *contemporary* history was often lacking—considered unnecessary—since salvation had arrived finally and definitively in Jesus Christ and in the church.

7. The undervaluation of woman, of the feminine, which characterized Greco-Roman society remained virtually unchanged in the patristic writings.
8. A dualistic sense of religious and cultural identity was often expressed in a lack of compassion for the other, for those outside, for unbelievers, and particularly for enemies.

iii. Monastic Wisdom

Monasticism, traditionally, has been inseparable from a culture of wisdom; Western monasticism, however, has not been at home and freely creative in its own sapiential context for centuries. Since the end of the Middle Ages, Western monks have increasingly lived in cultural and theological exile. During the patristic age Christian theology was almost entirely a sapiential theology. In the medieval West, the monks became the principal custodians of both streams of the theological tradition, in the more objective ecclesial theology of the black monks (Benedictines) and the more personal or spiritual theology which became the province particularly of the white monks (Cistercians).[29] Both currents, as they continued to develop, were informed by the sapiential perspective. Why are monasticism and wisdom related? Both aspire to something more than the common goals of human striving. Both, one might say, attempt a vertical penetration of the ground of human life and experience. Both are essentially unitive in their orientation: one primarily on the existential and the other on the intellectual plane. Monastic wisdom draws its light and life from the mystery of Christ; at the same time, it offers to Christians a particular depth perspective on the mystery and its personal participation, and on their own faith and identity. It began among the monks of the East in patristic times, moved to the West[30] and developed as a Western tradition, which reached its culmination in the twelfth century. The following two texts are from the twelfth-century Cistercian writers Isaac of Stella and William of St. Thierry. While Isaac's homily stands solidly in the more objective (yet participatory) tradition of the church fathers, William's *Golden Letter* to the early Carthusians represents a specialized contemplative orientation.

> Just as the head and body of a man form one single man, so the Son of the Virgin and those he has chosen to be his members form a single

man and the one Son of Man. *Christ is whole and entire, head and body,* say the Scriptures, since all the members form one body, which with its head is one Son of Man, and he with the Son of God is one Son of God, who himself with God is one God. Therefore the whole body with its head is Son of Man, Son of God, and God. This is the explanation of the Lord's words: *Father, I desire that as you and I are one, so they may be one with us.*

And so, according to this well-known reading of Scripture, neither the body without the head, nor the head without the body, nor the head and body without God make the whole Christ. When all are united with God they become one God. The Son of God is one with God by nature; the Son of Man is one with him in his person; we, his body, are one with him sacramentally. Consequently those who by faith are spiritual members of Christ can truly say that they are what he is: the Son of God and God himself. But what Christ is by his nature we are as his partners; what he is of himself in all fullness, we are as participants. Finally, what the Son of God is by generation, his members are by adoption, according to the text: *As sons, you have received the Spirit of adoption, enabling you to cry, Abba, Father.* (Isaac of Stella, twelfth century)[31]

41. As one star differs from another in brightness, so cell differs from cell in way of life: there are beginners, those who are making progress and the perfect. The state of beginners may be called "animal,"[32] the state of those who are making progress "rational" and the state of the perfect "spiritual." . . .

43. . . . There are the animal, who of themselves are not governed by reason nor led by affection, yet stimulated by authority or inspired by teaching or animated by good example they acquiesce in the good where they find it and like blind men, led by the hand, they follow, that is, imitate others. Then there are the rational, whom the judgment of their reason and the discernment that comes of natural learning endow with knowledge of the good and the desire for it, but as yet they are without love. There are also the perfect, who are led by the spirit and are more abundantly enlightened by the Holy Spirit; because they relish the good which draws them on they are called wise. They are also called spiritual because the Holy Spirit dwells in them as of old he dwelt in Gideon [see Judges 6:34].

44. The first state is concerned with the body, the second with the soul, the third finds rest only in God. Each of them makes progress after its

own fashion and each of them has a certain measure of perfection proper to itself. (William of St. Thierry, twelfth century)[33]

iv. Limitations of Monastic Wisdom.

The monastic wisdom of patristic and medieval times developed within a set of presuppositions, limitations, and confinements. The monastic option implied a theological principle of separation and containment, corresponding to the structure of monastic life itself: separation from the world and from the church in the world, and containment within a cloister of several diverse layers.

1. The separation from the world, the "choice of God" which set the monk apart in a distinct class within the church, easily generated an anti-incarnational and one-sided vision, in which the goal of life was seen "vertically" in terms of pure interiority, as the spiritual union of the individual with God.
2. A voluntary juridical and institutional containment quickly supplanted the openness of the "wilderness": personal freedom was totally renounced in view of spiritual transformation. Implicit here is a negative vision of the world and the person.This juridical containment of monastic life becomes a microcosm of the same dominant monarchical, authoritarian, and institutional structure in the Roman Catholic Church.
3. In the theological wisdom of the monks, we find a very strong Platonic influence which supports the vertical and interiorizing monastic option and sanctions an ascending crystal tower of spiritual theology.
4. The Augustinian theological container, which came to prevail in the Western church, was also largely accepted by the monastic theologians: (1) pessimism with regard to humanity, the human person, and the world; pessimism with regard to history; (2) a rationalized faculty psychology and anthropology which came to focus almost entirely on the conscious mind and will, while body and psyche were largely ignored; (3) a dualistic view of Christianity in which "religion" returned to replace the unitive Christ-mystery, baptismal divinization was forgotten, and divine union, too often, was hardly envisioned within this present life.
5. Monastic wisdom remained within a cloister of the biblical word. The Christian wisdom of the patristic and medieval monastic periods was not only centered in the revealed word of God but often confined within the word: it was almost entirely a biblical exegesis until the time of the

> scholastics, when a systematic theology with a Platonic-Aristotelian conceptual structure was erected alongside (or upon) the Scriptures. This is a point of delicate discernment, for a Christian wisdom must always remain centered in the Christ-mystery, the mystery of the incarnate Word. Yet gradually in the postmonastic ages, and with an insistent, even climactic force in our time, the human person emerges into the center as both a primary *locus theologicus* and as a universal "language."[34] Behind this progression from biblical word to Word-in-the-person we may sense the operation of a theological principle: a law of incarnation, of personalization.

The monastic wisdom of the Middle Ages, from our contemporary viewpoint, can be seen as fixed in an intermediate position between the nondual Self (*Atman* or its equivalent) of the Asian traditions and the individuated person of the modern West. On the Eastern side, the door to pure interior realization, to the One, had been nearly closed in a dualistic theological climate. On the Western side, the energies of the person were still concentrated within an enclosure of physical separation, of interiority, and of a biblical-classical consciousness.

6. The Eclipse of Wisdom in the West[35]

Sapiential theology was the theology of Christianity throughout the patristic age. In the medieval Western church, the monks became the custodians of this theological heritage and developed it further, particularly in an Augustinian direction. During the twelfth and thirteenth centuries, in the intellectual climate of the universities, a new, more purely rational theology developed. It would be known as scholasticism. Before long, the new theological method had displaced sapiential theology as the dominant mode of Christian thought.

Monasticism and the sapiential tradition went into recession together. As monastic life survived at the edges of the Western church, sapiential theology was nearly forgotten in the increasingly rationalistic and scientific cultural climate of the modern West, surviving in conservative enclaves and in some esoteric groups—and as a subject of scholarly study. It is a striking fact that toward the end of the Middle Ages monasticism and its wisdom were adapting to a phase of decline while the individual person was beginning to emerge in the West. The new religious orders, as by a natural process of differentiation, came quickly to prevail over the older monastic order. Soon, further centrifugal waves of change would split the church itself. As the new wine of personal freedom proved too vigorous for the old wineskins, the skins burst and the wine was spilled to give birth to a modern secular world.

Today, eight centuries later, we may begin to understand the eclipse of sapiential theology as a necessary phase of evolution—a transformation of consciousness in the direction of personal autonomy. But now, after centuries of confinement within the narrow epistemological limits of rationalism, we are experiencing a reopening of the spectrum of consciousness in the individualistic climate of the modern West and—at the prophetic edge of society—from a free personal center.

It may be illuminating to pause for a moment to look at that time of sapiential eclipse and transformation as embodied in several well-known individuals,[36] in whom we can behold a process of differentiation taking place: a separation and independent development of elements which had been held together within the enclosure of an undifferentiated monastic consciousness. In Thomas Aquinas we observe the differentiation of human reason and something like the moment of conception of an autonomous secular order. In Meister Eckhart we see the differentiation of pure spirit or explicit nonduality, many centuries before our present interaction with the Asian spiritual traditions. In Dante Alighieri, personal experience and creative intuition come into their own, and theology finds a poetic expression which, in an exodus from the biblical Word, finds embodiment in the concrete secular history of the poet's time and place.

In the archetypal figure of Francis of Assisi[37] (though he is chronologically the first of our four figures), we seem to see a consummation of the movement which these figures trace. Francis appears at the sunset of medieval monasticism and the dawn of the new evangelical movements. It is also the dawn of the "awakening of the person" and of human freedom in the medieval West. It is as if he sums up in himself what is to follow. At the same time, he sums up what went before—including the Christian and monastic sapiential tradition—but not in the same cultural form, rather in a simple, existential—indeed incarnational—way. Monasticism gives way to an apostolic life among people in the world (although Francis, like Jesus, continues to retire into solitude periodically), and wisdom disappears into the simplicity of an embodied human life. In this simplicity, Christianity rediscovers its universality.

7. The Time of Vatican II: Toward a Rebirth of Christian Wisdom

The Second Vatican Council signifies an epochal turning point for the Roman Catholic Church. After centuries of defensive confinement, we witness at this time a positive opening toward the world, toward modernity and its values, toward the various Christian churches, and toward the other religions of the world. The church begins to adopt a positive attitude toward the movement of history and toward human progress. At the same moment Catholic spirituality is opening in the same directions, to a positive encounter with historical progress, with the modern secular world of the West, and with the Asian religions and their millennial spiritual traditions. This is an unprecedented moment of change for the Christian spiritual tradition and its wisdom: that which had been strenuously resisted, opposed, reluctantly adapted to, or simply unknown is now to be accepted as valuable, perhaps integrated as part of one's own heritage.

The church has been confronted by modernity and globalization for centuries, but the conscious opening to these realities—the turning point—occurs only with the council. Since Vatican II, the church has been consciously—though often hesitantly—adapting to the reality of the "age of the person." Virtually for the first time, the work of inculturation and of interreligious dialogue has been encouraged.

In the Second Vatican Council, we experience the recovery of the mystery of Christ, or the Christ-event (virtually synonymous with the paschal mystery), as the vital center of theology. With the documents of Vatican II, the church commits itself to the recovery of the sapiential core of Christian faith. This recovery is our starting point and the basis of everything else we shall do.

In addition to the first step of recovering a sapiential consciousness, we have outlined our journey toward the rebirth of wisdom in terms of three successive movements.All three confrontations—Eastern, Western (modern), and global—take place at the same time, in this era of the Second Vatican Council. Suddenly the doors are opened on all sides, and a positive response is called for on all sides. This sudden, very confusing, predicament evidently calls for a deep and comprehensive change of attitude, indeed for a new consciousness. We may speak of a theological *metanoia*, corresponding to the ecclesial conversion of Vatican II.

There is a great need, at this moment, for a theological framework or matrix in which this complex historical situation can be understood and responded to. It is here, particularly, that the urgency of a new sapiential consciousness and theology is most apparent. Only from this sapiential perspective, I believe, can the whole situation be comprehended in one vision, centered in the historically unfolding Christ-event. Then our sapiential vision must confront the continuing newness of this event.

The turn toward a positive theological appreciation of these encounters, like the opening of the church of Vatican II toward person, world, and history, is something much deeper and more significant than an adaptation: it is a new self-discovery, a rebirth,. One finds oneself anew, more largely and deeply, in that which one had rejected; in the very space of the difference, the unitive light is freshly experienced.

8. The Way of Wisdom

Turning away from the established churches and the rationalist-materialist culture of the modern West, many people in our time have set out on a personal spiritual quest. They experience no attraction to a Catholicism that has all the answers and no questions, nor to a religious life that is completely programmed. Their quest is, in some way, a search for wisdom. Like Bede Griffiths, they have begun to trace the path of the "golden string."[38] The way of wisdom was prominent throughout the cultures of classical antiquity,[39] as it still is today in Asian cultures. In earlier centuries, Christian wisdom was a way of life. St. Augustine offers an excellent example of this vocation and this mentality; for him, Christ is preeminently *Wisdom*.[40]

This way of wisdom—as a recognized path—is conspicuously absent from our contemporary Christianity. The gap in our contemporary Christian life comes clearly into view in the light of the four yogas of Hinduism,[41] which constitute a kind of comprehensive map of human spiritual life. *Raja yoga* is the way of contemplative practice, centered in meditation. *Jnana yoga* is the way of the intellect, of wisdom. *Bhakti yoga* is the way of devotion, and *karma yoga* is the way of active service. We have seen, in our time, a *raja* Christianity in the meditation movement, a new *bhakti* Christianity in the charismatic movement, and a new *karma* Christianity in the social justice movement. We still await a

the appearance of a new *jnana* Christianity, the way of Christian wisdom. Beyond the Bible study movement—which offers a basis for a resurgence of wisdom Christianity—the time is ripe for a sapiential awakening and the development of a contemplative theology that is not confined to a treatment of the individual spiritual life.

It is not difficult to account for this paradoxically meager presence of sapiential theology in contemporary Christianity. The sapiential ground has been overlaid many times—paved, fought upon, built upon. The very strength of the Judaeo-Christian tradition—its authoritative revelation—seems to become transformed, in the course of the centuries, into an obstacle to its sapiential development. The field of Christian thought has become a battlefield in the course of the dogmatic controversies that have marked the centuries; rival authorities claim the ground even today: institutional orthodoxy and scientific rationalism, the armored giants of fundamentalism and reductionist historical criticism. Most effective in suppressing sapiential consciousness has been the rational empiricism of the modern West.

With postmodernity comes an opportunity for clearing the ground, a new chance for wisdom. In the time of Vatican II, the invisible container within which these battles have been fought is opened, a space of reflection and contemplation appears; the ancient depths once again become accessible, and we experience the expansive freedom of new perspectives. In our time, a first generation of new Christian *jnanis* has already appeared, including Thomas Merton, Abhishiktananda, Bede Griffiths, and Sara Grant.[42]

Sara Grant

9. Four Historical Moments

Before we look over the stages of our sapiential journey, it will be useful to establish a large-scale historical framework. I shall propose a simple scheme of four historical moments as background to our study. From time to time I shall refer to these great turning points.

1. **The Axial Period**, a period embracing roughly the first millennium before Christ, with its center about 500 B.C.E. It was during this time, according to Karl Jaspers,[43] that the self-conscious individual person emerged in five distinct areas around the world: India, China, Persia, Greece, and Palestine.[44]
2. **The Christ-event**, as recorded in the New Testament. This will be the central point of reference in our quest for a new Christian wisdom. We shall focus specifically on the Christ-event in chap. 2.
3. **A Western Axial Period,** (ca. 1100–1500 C.E.), the time of the emergence of the individual person in the West.[45]
4. **Postmodernity and Globalization** (from about 1918 to the present and beyond). The present moment of history is marked particularly by our transition from a Eurocentric to a global consciousness.[46]

With the Second Vatican Council—which occurs at the present moment of globalization—both church and monasticism are invited to open themselves toward a larger emergent reality, which can itself be seen as a fruit of continuing incarnation—of the working of the Christ-mystery in the earth of humanity.

10. Four Movements

In this time of Vatican II, doors are opened on all sides at once. The church suddenly realizes an urgent need to move both back and forward at the same moment to recover the origins and to appropriate as well the present with its dynamic movement.[47]

The council represents an epochal change in orientation on the part of the church. From a fortified immobility, a defensive and superior withdrawal from the world, a rejection of modern individualism, and a categorical opposition to the movement of history in the modern West, the church turns toward the world, toward the human person, and toward human activity and the historical progress that flows from it. The Augustinian age of Catholic consciousness appears to come to an end, as if we were crossing a threshold from childhood into maturity. This historical shock, however, presents a rare moment of opportunity. It is a time for radical reflection, for a new self-definition. It is as if the curtain of the New Testament had once again been lifted; suddenly, the length and breadth, height and depth lie before us.

Against the historical background that we have sketched, we can imagine a new unfolding of Christian sapiential theology taking place in four movements.[48]

1. A sapiential awakening. Our journey begins with an epistemological step: the opening of our consciousness to the deeper and wider dimensions of the sapiential traditions. This is for us a recovery of the basic perspective of Christian wisdom, centered in the mystery of Christ. This sapiential consciousness had been nearly forgotten, buried under the sediment of many centuries of institutionalized and rationalized Christianity.
2. An Eastern turn. In the new contact with the Asian religions, we find that our own internal "East" is called forth. Further, we discover the reality of nonduality and of the nondual Self within our own tradition; a new unitive opening of Christian theology from within itself becomes possible. Theology and spirituality are recentered in a baptismal identity which is interpreted with the key of unitive or nondual reality, experience, and knowledge.
3. A Western turn, to modernity. In catching up with history after five hundred years and more of rejecting the movement of history, of adapting to it, of enduring a cultural exile within its flow, sapiential theology encounters the opportunity to understand and affirm the basic continuity between the Christ-event and historical progression, between

Christ and the autonomous individual person, between Christ and the secularity and critical rationality that mark the modern world. This dramatic mutation in Christian wisdom corresponds to the mutation of Catholic consciousness expressed in the Second Vatican Council. Sapiential theology begins to integrate the dynamic and creative element of Christianity, which is expressed in the liberation and realization of the human person in Western history and in the humanizing transformation of society and of nature.

4. A global (or postmodern) turn. In the bewildering world of postmodernity, everything is questioned, every affirmation is radically deconstructed and relativized—particularly those of the Western and the Christian traditions. At the same time, despite the continual violent conflicts, the world begins to become one world—one humanity—before our eyes. We are called to verify our ground in its simplicity and unity, and then to comprehend from within our sapiential perspective the ripening of earth and its humanity; to read Irenaeus together with Teilhard and discover a new depth and breadth of meaning in incarnation and in eucharist. A new Christian wisdom will imply an active participation in the movement toward one world—toward a united humanity aware of its communion with Earth and cosmos.

These four movements are oriented toward an expansion of the mystery of Christ from its confinement within a *logos*-container toward its intrinsic fullness. While the four movements are obviously related to the four historical moments that we outlined earlier, they do not correspond to them exactly; nor does any one of these quaternities correspond precisely to the quaternary expression of Christianity which is implicit in the New Testament and explicit in Irenaeus.[49]

11. Spirit and History

Two great principles will be present throughout our study; we shall continually encounter fresh aspects of their interaction. Following Henri de Lubac in his study of the sapiential theology of Origen,[50] we might call them *history and spirit.* Spirit is to be understood here not as the Holy Spirit of Christian tradition, however, but as the transcendent "third dimension" of the human person, beyond body and mind/psyche[51]—or simply as the interior or spiritual or divine aspect of humanity. These two principles correspond approximately to transcendence and historicity (or the categorial dimension) in the anthropology of Karl Rahner,[52] to which I shall frequently refer.

Spirit and history, understood in this way, correspond loosely to the Asian spiritual traditions, on the one hand, and to Israel, on the other hand; to East and West, to ancient and modern. The two dimensions intersect as vertical and horizontal axes within the human person. They intersect ultimately, however, in Jesus Christ, in whom divine Spirit enters newly and decisively into the human person and into human history. The Christ-event—or incarnation—thus becomes the center of history, the decisive meeting point of God and creation, at which is initated a new human history, impregnated with the unitive divine Reality.

Our sapiential interpretation of life and of history will, correspondingly, involve two ambitious claims, both of which are rooted in the New Testament writings: first, a principle of unitive divine immediacy or identity, and, second, a principle of radical historical Christocentricity.

2

Movement I

The Sapiential Awakening

1. Wonder and Awakening

WISDOM BEGINS IN WONDER. SOMETHING PROFOUND AWAKENS WHEN A child opens a book and finds its pages full of light, the words radiant even though their meanings remain indistinct. A light awakens within the young mind. The enchantment returns again and again at each new discovery, as a new world of knowledge is disclosed to the eager spirit. Always, much more is promised than is realized; the light continues to burn at the center of the mind, its thirst never satiated. Spiritual wisdom remains, at its core, a simple luminous fullness, and is always a beginning (see 1 Cor 13:9-12).

In the cold clarity of the modern West, it is often the poets who catalyze the awakening of a sapiential consciousness. The English Romantic poets played this role for Bede Griffiths;[1] Blake and Wordsworth and Shelley showed him the golden string that would determine his path.

> I give you the end of a golden string;
> Only wind it into a ball,
> It will lead you in at heaven's gate,
> Built in Jerusalem's wall.[2]

The young Thomas Merton, like young Alan Griffiths, was attracted by the sapiential aura of the work of William Blake.[3] Both men, finding themselves between poetry and art, on the one hand, and the Thomist philosophy of orthodox Roman Catholicism on the other, worked toward a first integration under the influence of Jacques Maritain.[4]

2. The Sapiential Event and Its Eclipse

That which was from the beginning,
which we have heard, which we have seen with our eyes,
which we have looked upon and touched with our hands,
concerning the word of life—
the life was made manifest, and we saw it and testify to it,
and proclaim to you the eternal life which was with the
Father
and was made manifest to us . . . (1 John 1:1-2)
. . . to have all the riches of assured understanding and the
knowledge of God's mystery, of Christ, in whom are hid
all the treasures of wisdom and knowledge. (Col 2:2-3)

The event of Christ, according to the Pauline and Johannine New Testament traditions, was the coming of the divine Wisdom to humanity as a human person. It was understood as a sapiential event by many of the Christian teachers and writers of the first centuries[5]: they saw Christ as the incarnation of divine Wisdom. Gradually, however, the mystery began to be confined and objectified. The process continued through the course of the centuries until, during recent centuries, the sapiential character—the ineffable unity, simplicity, and luminosity—of the mystery became almost completely lost to view.

The mystery is larger than theological wisdom too: such is its depth, comprehensiveness and power that it is distorted by every rendering, every objectification. As soon as Christians have travelled some distance from the Big Bang, the original event, they begin to objectify, to rationalize, to compartmentalize and institutionalize the mystery, and the result is always a reduction and division of the original fullness. Christian wisdom is a way that leads back through history, upstream toward the Source, but it too becomes a betrayal when it pretends to contain the mystery, rather than awakening us to our participation in the mystery.

We have already noted some of the principal ways in which the old wisdom—whether ecclesial or monastic—tended to distort or reduce the mystery. By the twentieth century, Western Christianity had become divided and militarized to such an extent that it was hardly possible—whether from the Catholic or the Protestant side—to discern the unity and fullness of the mystery. Rationalization, objectification, and the devitalization and rigidification produced by defensive polemics had carried theology very far from the sapiential perspective.

3. The Sapiential Awakening of the Twentieth Century

In the decades before the Second Vatican Council,[6] the unity and fullness of the mystery of Christ began to come once again to the surface of theological consciousness. Movements of renewal in the fields of patristic and liturgical studies converged upon the re-emerging mystery. The effort required intellectual courage, in a climate polarized between a reductionist rationalism on one side and an immobile institutional dogmatism on the other side. In the midst of the continuing war between scientism and fundamentalism—biblical, traditional, or institutional—it has never been easy to imagine and to develop a third, sapiential possibility. Individuals who rebelled against the dogmatic rationalism of the European Enlightenment were likely also to shun a Christianity that appeared to be closed within its dogmatic ramparts. They were more likely to choose the religion of romanticism. The romantic poets and philosophers sometimes catalyzed a sapiential awakening which only later would find its theological home.

The documents of Vatican II open the way to a sapiential renaissance first of all by a change of attitude and style; underlying the verbal articulations is a spirit which, confidently embracing the mystery of Christ, steps out of the habitual defensive posture with its authoritarian, juridical style to allow the mystery to express itself in the language and imagery of the New Testament and the early church. The words "mystery," "sacrament," and "unity," as they recur in the doctrinal sections of the great constitutions, take on a fresh and expansive meaning. Despite the density and nuanced complexity of these laboriously crafted texts, they breathe the air of freedom. As the mystery reveals itself again, we recognize its native language as that of Christian wisdom.[7]

> The wonderful works of God among the people of the Old Testament were but a prelude to the work of Christ Our Lord in redeeming mankind and giving perfect glory to God. He achieved this task principally by the paschal mystery[8] of his blessed passion, resurrection from the dead, and glorious ascension, whereby "dying he destroyed our death, and rising restored our life." For it was from the side of Christ as he slept the sleep of death upon the cross that there came forth "the wondrous sacrament of the whole Church."[9]

In the more directive sections of the council documents, we can often sense the internal conflict between this emerging sapiential awareness and more conventional institutional attitudes, as in the chapter of the decree on the training of priests, which sets forth principles for seminary education:

> The main object to be kept in mind is a more effective coordination of philosophy and theology so that they may supplement one another in revealing to the minds of the students with ever increasing clarity the Mystery of Christ, which affects the whole course of human history, exercises an unceasing influence on the Church, and operates mainly through the ministry of the priest.[10]

The document laudably directs attention first of all to biblical and patristic studies.[11] It has proven very difficult, however, for a student who has been nurtured in today's cultural climate to surmount the epistemological barrier and acquire a sense of the mystery in its unity and simplicity.

4. Henri de Lubac: The Anatomy of Christian Wisdom

It was the Jesuit scholar Henri de Lubac who, in the era of Vatican II, made the most extensive study of the Christian sapiential tradition, from its roots in Origen and the Greek fathers through the Middle Ages to the dawn of scholasticism.[12] Moreover, he studied this tradition *theologically;* that is, in its understanding of the mystery of Christ, the "fact of Christ" against the biblical background. The central structures of Christian wisdom come into bold relief: the continuity and radical change between Old Testament and New Testament, coordinated with the movement from a literal to a spiritual understanding of the Scriptures. This spiritual understanding is differentiated into its three phases—allegorical (or christological), tropological (or personal), and anagogical (or final: whether understood in the eschatological or in the mystical sense). The scheme of these senses of Scripture became the enduring theological backbone of Christian sapiential theology. De Lubac traces the early patristic origins, the various developments, and the final decline of this theological vision. His work offers us the differentiated characterization and theological understanding of the old wisdom that we shall need as we move forward, as well as a penetrating look into that New Testament understanding of the Christ-event which must remain the core of any future Christian wisdom.

The mystery of Christ, and the sapiential theology in which it unfolded through the centuries, is excavated from beneath two later strata: first, the analytical scholastic and positive scholastic articulation of Christian doctrine and, second, the historical-critical scholarship of the past two centuries. These movements, while very different, both tended to replace the mystery with rationalizations—whether philosophical (Aristotelian-Thomistic) or empirical (scientific). Reading de Lubac and the other twentieth-century scholarly pioneers today, we find ourselves leafing quickly through arguments against views and positions which, while no longer quite so menacing, endure in their fundamental attitudes and arguments.

The basic strength of this old wisdom—the spiritual understanding of the Scriptures—is encapsulated in the maxim *Novum Testamentum in Vetere latet, Vetus in Novo patet.*[13] The development of spiritual understanding—a movement from letter to spirit—is, de Lubac points out, parallel to development of the personal spiritual life. On the other hand, rejection of spiritual understanding is frequently connected with a more general bias against mysticism and the rejection of belief in a true union with God, at least in this present life.[14]

Again and again in the course of de Lubac's patient labor, the factuality, the actuality, the sheer newness of the New Testament breaks forth—with respect to the Old Testament and to everything else.

> The *Verbum abbreviatum* which gathers into the unity of his Person all the *verba* which had been uttered until he came surpasses them all as he fulfills them all. Through him, "the old has passed away, behold, the new has come."[15]

And finally, in Irenaeus's unsurpassable words, *"Omnem novitatem attulit, seipsum afferens,"*[16] de Lubac sets clearly before us both the strengths and the weaknesses of the medieval monastic theology. We can feel the depth and vitality, the power and experiential actuality of this wisdom when it is close to the living heart of the New Testament and the event of Christ. Then we can experience the swing toward decline and death as the structures become more important than the one central event and the vision recedes more and more from the actuality of history and life in this world, into a mechanical system or a purely individual, ascending interiority. De Lubac traces the separation of the mystical from the doctrinal understanding of Scripture from the time of Origen to that of the great Carmelites of the sixteenth century.

> We also see that the meaning which relates to the spiritual life acquires a kind of independence in the measure that the doctrine becomes more firmly established in its least details. There is a much more rapid progress through the obscurity of "allegories" toward a penetration of the "sacred delights" promised by them. Mystical exegesis is no longer much of an aid in reflecting on mystery; in this respect, it no longer has an active role; but it is still a marvelous springboard for interior

élan. The spiritual meaning of Scripture becomes the special preserve of the contemplative.[17]

As the understanding of the anagogical sense of Scripture becomes more and more individual and purely interior, mystical understanding withdraws from eschatology, resulting in a loss of social and historical significance. Eventually, "the great dogmatic vision became blurred":[18]

> The historical and social character of the Christian synthesis, which had stood out so dramatically in the exegesis of the Fathers, was in immediate danger of being compromised. For all practical purposes, morality and spirituality, though still referred to as tropology and anagogy, split into two, and this was at the expense of eschatology. The Jerusalem of the Book of Revelation becomes more or less assimilated to the contemplative soul.[19]

Further, the specific meanings of the text receive little attention as they become merely the starting point for personal reflections.[20] One further comment, referring to the tradition of spiritual exegesis exemplified by St. Bernard and St. John of the Cross, is worth quoting.

> And yet, what a world of difference there is between such works and the passages from St. Paul in which they originate! What a long road has been travelled since the time when Christian liberty was affirmed and vindicated through a renewed understanding of ancient Scripture![21]

Indeed, we may wonder at times whether one or another monastic theologian has not in effect rescinded the event of incarnation, humbly refusing the gift of Christian liberty and turning back to a theological Old Testament more easily conformable to his monastic ideal.

In the same chapter de Lubac had considered the possibility of a *new* spiritual exegesis and the essential elements that it must embody.[22] It must be christological, embracing all the dimensions of Christ. It will bring together our modern sense of history with the theological sense of history that emerges from the spiritual exegesis of the fathers. A simplified and more sober symbolism will remain closer to history and will thus be stronger. In this reborn spiritual exegesis, "the symbolic function of our intelligence may unfold anew and produce new fruits in the unforeseeable freedom of the Spirit. . . ." [23] Much of de Lubac's attention is given to the renascence of a symbolic consciousness after our age of rationalism. His concluding hope is for a new union of spiritual exegesis and historical science.[24]

5. Jean Leclercq: The Two Medieval Theologies

Benedictine scholar Jean Leclercq[25] describes the monastic theology of the late Middle Ages in contrast to the theology of the town and urban schools—the clerical schools of the same period. He sketches the two distinct milieux—monastery and town school—in which the two theologies developed.

> In general, the monks did not acquire their religious formation in a school, under a scholastic, by means of the *quaestio*, but individually, under the guidance of an abbot, a spiritual father, through the reading of the Bible and the Fathers, within the liturgical framework of the monastic life. Hence, there arose a type of Christian culture with marked characteristics: a disinterested culture which was "contemplative" in bent. Very different from this are the schools for clerics.[26]

Here he places us at the fork in the road, nearly a thousand years ago, where the separation of sapiential and scientific mentality in the West began.[27] Leclercq insists that Catholic theology is one, and that the two traditions, developing within this basic unity, are complementary. Both combine faith and speculation. The difference is largely one of method.

Leclercq had already pointed out, in the same introduction, that which most typically characterized the scholastic method: not so much the use of Aristotle as "the teaching procedures, principally the *quaestio* applied to the *sacra pagina*."[28] The learning of the clerics, then, takes place in a climate of discussion, of dialectic, of *sic et non*, which prepares one to encounter the problems of the church in the world, while the learning of the monks proceeds in a milieu devoted to the seeking of the "one thing necessary," and consequently resembles a process of unquestioning absorption, of interior assimilation, in an attitude of quiet listening and of a simple, contemplative regard.

Leclercq has noted two closely related characteristics of the theological literature produced by the monks: "on the one hand, the 'literary' character of monastic writings; on the other, their mystical orientation."[29] Here we can see another distinction appearing: between literature, or arts, and the sciences; but a third dimension asserts itself as well—the mystical—which associates itself with the literary or aesthetic rather than with the scientific.[30] We are reminded of the situation of Western culture in recent centuries, polarized between

Enlightenment scientific rationalism with its claim to objectivity, and a personalist romantic reaction, which becomes the refuge of spiritual and sapiential aspirations.

The contrast between the two methods is centered in the difference between two goals: *clarity*, the primary aim of the scholastics, and *union*, or participation in the mystery, which was the goal of the monks. While the clerical masters attribute authority not only to Scripture and the fathers, use abstract terms, and readily coin new words, ever seeking rational clarity, "The monks speak in images and comparisons borrowed from the Bible and possessing both a richness and an obscurity in keeping with the mystery to be expressed." This is the basic difference between the scholastic and the monastic theological styles.[31]

Today we may be able to imagine ourselves on either side of the divide—with Bernard or with Abelard—feeling on the one hand a deep identification with that unitive interiorizing of the mystery that proceeds through an absorption in the Word, and on the other hand experiencing within ourselves the thrill of personal discovery, of a new rational autonomy, of the divine spark of freedom and creativity which is eager to participate actively in the birth of a new world.

Jean Leclercq identifies the monastic theology with true Christian *gnosis:* "that kind of higher knowledge which is the complement, the fruition of faith, and which reaches completion in prayer and contemplation."[32] This spiritual knowledge, and the theology in which it finds expression, is characterized first of all by personal *experience,* while scholastic thought deliberately excludes personal experience—the subjective dimension—in its striving for scientific objectivity and for metaphysical universality.[33] It was the new scholastic theology that would become dominant and then obligatory in the Roman Catholic tradition, enduring in the form of a late Neothomism until the Second Vatican Council in the middle of the twentieth century.

6. Cipriano Vagaggini: Between Two Wisdoms

Another Benedictine scholar, Cipriano Vagaggini, rendered a valuable service in bringing the sapiential form of theology (*gnosis-sapientia,* he calls it) into more distinct visibility, and locating it in the history of development of Christian theology. In *The Theological Dimensions of the Liturgy*[34] he identified the theology of the patristic writers as corresponding to this model of *gnosis-sapientia*[35] and brought to light some of its basic features, particularly in relation to sacred history, to the central mystery of Christ, and to the liturgical mysteries. Later he developed further this vision of the historical development of theology and studied the more recent movements in depth.[36]

Vagaggini distinguished three successive phases of Catholic theology from the patristic era to the present:[37]

1. The sapiential model of the biblical, patristic, and high-medieval tradition: this is the Christian theology to which our "sapiential awakening" brings us.
2. The scholastic model: in the Aristotelian manner, concerned with the "entitative order of things," with an ontological analysis of the various objects of theological study.
3. The positive scholastic model, which arose in the struggle with Protestantism. Its function was polemical, apologetic: to prove that the doctrines of the Roman Catholic Church are founded in Scripture and maintained throughout the centuries by a consistent tradition.

Vagaggini finds the theology of the late twentieth century in a transitional phase, groping toward a new model. In the future—this is important for our own inquiry—he foresees the emergence of a new sapiential theology that will differ from that of the early church and the Middle Ages in several important ways. The deeper attitudes underlying these changes are, first of all, a basic anthropocentrism; second, a critical historical sense joined with a dynamic evolutionary perspective; and, third, a complex of dislikes and negative judgments, most of which are characteristic of contemporary postmodernism. These include an aversion for ontology and metaphysics, for institution, for "religion," for tradition as historical past, for the juridical, the clerical, for every religious theory that can be suspected of ideology in support of power.

The first and fundamental characteristic of the new model of theology which Vagaggini sees emerging is, therefore, a subjective, immanent, anthropological perspective,[38] which constrasts sharply with the predominantly objective, heteronomous, theocentric, and transcendent perspective of the past theologies. Second, in opposition to the defensive, apologetic stance of the positive scholastic theology, the new theology adopts a positive attitude toward the values of the modern world, toward the other Christian confessions, toward the other religions and cultures. Its defense of Catholic identity will be positive rather than negative. Third, the new theology abandons the Aristotelian perspective—metaphysical, dialectical, ontological, essentialist, and deductive—which had characterized scholastic theology.

The new sapiential theology, then, will differ from the patristic and medieval wisdom theology in three principal ways: first, by its anthropocentric, subjective approach; second, by its historical-critical sense; and, third, by the philosophical resources that it utilizes. These resources will have an "eclectic anthropocentric" character, in contrast to the Platonic-Neoplatonic philosophy that had informed the old Christian wisdom.[39]

Vagaggini's own thought seems to have evolved, during the years between *Theological Dimensions* and the *Dizionario* article, from a still largely Thomist scholastic position, which insisted on the central and enduring importance of the entitative understanding of reality, toward a distinct preference for the sapiential model. While this shift is in keeping with the centrality of the mystery of Christ and its liturgical expression in his theological vision, it also corresponds to the recovery of an understanding of this sapiential tradition at this moment within the church.

The sapiential awakening in our time is, first of all, a recovery of *unity*: the original unity of the mystery of Christ. We find ourselves involved in a movement of *return* on several levels at once. It is a return to the theological vision of the undivided church—before the separation of East and West and the subsequent division of Western Christianity. In this return to the unity of the Christ-mystery, we discover once again the intimate union of mysticism—and spirituality—with the mystery. We return—but with a modern personalist perspective—to a unitive vision that had prevailed before the separation of liturgy, spirituality, dogmatic theology, and moral theology, and before the modern polarization of person against institution.

7. The Quaternary Unfolding of the Christ-Mystery

As Henri de Lubac brought our attention to the central mystery of Christ and its essential structure, the context of this vision was a study of *spiritual understanding,* which articulated itself into the four senses of Scripture. This quaternary pattern is deeply rooted in the mystery itself and manifests itself already in the New Testament (see Eph 2:11-16; 3:17-19; Col 1:19-22). It is also to be found in early Christian writers such as Irenaeus.[40]

The figure of the cross, as Irenaeus saw, is inscribed in the cosmos and in the history of salvation.[41] The mystery of Christ—temporally centered in his cross and resurrection—can be understood as the fusion of God and creation, of Trinity and humanity.

God

Word + Spirit

Humanity

It has been very difficult to preserve the integrity of this mystery in the church. The Christian history of the past two thousand years has been characterized by a continual tendency to reverse the event of incarnation and separate once again the divine and the human, Trinity and humanity,[42] God and creation. This separation is then made permanent in theological and institutional structures. Christian sapiential theology, however, begins and ends in this unitive mystery of the cross and looks toward its eschatological fulfillment in a eucharistic plenitude.

8. The Revolution of Jesus

Sapiential thought has often taken the path of traditionalism and failed to recognize the dynamic newness of the Christ-event. This can easily happen under the gravitational attraction of the Asian traditions. Before setting forth on our Eastern turn, therefore, let us look at the mystery of Christ from a perspective that accents both its distinctness and its dynamic quality. "The revolution of Jesus" is a response to the question: What is *distinct* about Christianity? Or, What is really *new* in the Christ-event that was not already present beforehand, either in the biblical tradition or in other religious traditions of the world? Its central idea is that Christianity is most clearly understood as an *event*, standing out against a pre-existing background. The term *revolution* is chosen to underline the contrast, for the sake of this clarity. The emphasis, therefore, is on distinctness rather than similarity and relationship, on discontinuity rather than continuity with the religious and cultural traditions that historically preceded Christianity.

We shall imagine the revolution—or the full manifestation of the event of Christ in its consequences—as proceeding through a series of seven phases. The first two are preliminary: steps in one's personal approach to the mystery of Christ. There follow the three central phases, which correspond to the personal rebirth or new creation of baptismal initiation and to the new structure of life that follows from it. Finally there are two phases of wider consequences or implications of this central transformation. Phases I and III will be found to have particularly strong resonances with the Asian traditions.

Phase I is the awakening to transcendence—to a more-than-human presence—in the encounter with Jesus. This first spiritual awakening may simultaneously be a recognition of a deeper level of reality in Jesus, in oneself, and in the world.

Phase II is a recognition of "the center" in Christ. This has several levels: experiential, existential (or moral), and intellectual (or theological). One awakens to the realization that Jesus is somehow the center of reality; one finds that one's life must be reordered to correspond to that realization; and, finally, one unfolds the implications of this centrality intellectually, along the various dimensions and levels of reality. Phases VI and VII (if understood as further stages of personal awakening) will continue this Christocentric intellectual development.

Phase III, corresponding to baptismal initiation, is the basic personal revolution. In Christian tradition it has been understood as rebirth (John 3:3-8), or new creation (Gal 6:15). Through the gift of the Holy Spirit, the divine life is now experienced within oneself rather than only within Jesus as "other." In the light of the Asian traditions today, it can be understood also as the realization of nonduality or of *Atman* as a nondual divine identity. This is the closest point of encounter of the revolution with Hindu Vedanta or Buddhism or Taoism. It is also the basis of Christian contemplative experience and contemplative life. We shall focus on this phase particularly in the Eastern turn of chap. 3.

Phase IV, immediately consequent to III, is a reversal, which can be regarded from several aspects. I shall mention three of them. First, human life changes its course from an ascending to a descending direction. (This reversal will be found frequently in Jesus' teaching.) Second, the course of life reverses as one lives no longer "from outside" but "from within." Third—and this, especially, is evident on the wider cultural level—we pass from a pre-personal, dependent, and relatively passive "old participation" in God, in human society, and in the universe to a "new participation" on these three levels which is individualized, free, and creative. This third reversal has been developed by Owen Barfield.[43] Phase IV, with its reversals, is the central and pivotal stage between the peak of divinization in III and the descending way of embodiment in V. Divinization and embodiment correspond to baptism and eucharist in the Christian theological system.

Phase V, embodiment, reproduces the descending path of incarnation (see Phil 2:1-11) in the life of an individual and in the life of a community or society. The distinctiveness of Christianity appears clearly here: first, in this departure from the traditional ascending paths of spirituality, and, second, in the "scandal of particularity," which is characteristic of the biblical revelation and history, of the concrete event of incarnation and of the church, its juridical institutions, and its ministers. In the revolution of Jesus, spiritual reality—divinity—enters into earthly matter to initiate a new *sacramental* creation. A parallel descending movement can be perceived in the history of the West since 1300 or so; that historical drama belongs to phase VI.

Phase VI is the unfolding of the revolution—in its phases II, III, IV, and V—in the history of the church and of the world. The pattern can be seen with particular clarity in the history of the West, since the West is a culture and civilization that has been generated and consolidated principally by Christianity. Further, the West occupies a historical space corresponding to the period between the Christ-event and the emergence of a global humanity in the post-modern age. This position has a theological importance; it is related directly to the Christ-event. The historical effects of the revolution come about primarily through (1) a new creative freedom of the individual person and (2) a new center and *plenum* of embodiment—the body of Christ. This body of Christ, ultimately, is to correspond to the whole of humanity brought into unity.

Phase VII is a final concentric circle, which regards the effects of the revolution of Jesus not only on the scale of human history but on the scale of the evolution of the universe. Here (in chap. 5 of this book) the thought of Teilhard de Chardin and Ewert Cousins is to be invoked. As in the case of history, in phase VI, the revolution is shown to influence the path of evolution through these two factors: (1) a new creative freedom of the individual person (and consequently of humanity as a whole, as it becomes a new creative source within cosmic evolution), and (2) a new center and totality of embodiment—the body of Christ.

9. Rationalization of the Mystery

"Humankind cannot bear very much reality."[44] Our inveterate tendency is to grasp the experience, the mystery, in such a way as to reduce and denature it. The event of Christ begins very soon to become objectified in conceptual and institutional structures which then take the place of the uncontainable mystery itself. As these structures become more and more clearly defined, personal participation in the mystery diminishes. While the structures are usually imported from outside the biblical tradition—Greek philosophical structures, Roman legal structures—they represent a return to a kind of Old Testament in which the personal relationship with God is mediated by authoritative institutions. While Christianity could hardly maintain its identity through the centuries without elements of institution and of theological definition, the sheer actuality of the mystery has been, again and again, thoroughly suppressed by these forms.

The mystery is rationalized, objectified, rendered intelligible, and defensible—nearly, indeed, domesticated and controlled. The event of Christ becomes "the Christian religion" alongside the other religions while holding itself aloof from them. What has been lost in the process? The words that come to mind are diverse: mystery, participation, unity, actuality, freedom, variety, dynamism, development, openness, universality—and bodiliness, sacramentality, incarnation. As the mystery was rationalized and contained, it was also split—and thereby severely mutilated—for it is a mystery of unity. In responding to one challenge after another, the official church moved to higher ground and left behind and below the embodied church, the people of God, the body of Christ. In the act of defending the privileged divinity of Christ and of his church, Christ and church were elevated above humanity—believing humanity included—and the event of incarnation was partially rescinded.

Again and again, religious superstructures have been erected above the bodily reality of the church—that is, the people—effectively reversing the event of Christ. Jesus, referring to the Jewish religious leaders, announced that "the stone which the builders rejected has become the cornerstone" (Luke 20:17). Within Christianity lurks a perennial temptation to reject the stone which is the mystery and event of God incarnate. God was restored to his Heaven, and the three Persons withdrawn from the economy of sacred history into the "immanent Trinity." Mysticism was detached from the sacramental mystery and elevated into an interior tabernacle of pure spirit. Eucharist contracted from its cosmic, human, and ecclesial dimensions into a devotional ritual. "The church" was no longer known as the body of Christ, the people of God, but as the infallible hierarchical authority. We have found ourselves back in the situation of institutional Judaism into which Jesus came—and which his death and resurrection were to transform.

10. Thomas Merton: Opening Christian Wisdom (I)

The writings of Thomas Merton will continue to play an important role in the emergence of a new Christian wisdom, at least in the English-speaking world. To distill the sapiential Merton into a few pages, however, is an impossible task. First of all, this singularly gifted writer is truly encountered only in his own words, and most of his voluminous writing can be called sapiential. Second, he has become part of us. For an American of my time, it was Thomas Merton who brought spiritual tradition to life for us in our own language, with our own sensibility—a Catholic perennial philosophy in twentieth-century vernacular. He was the lampstand upon which the light of spiritual realization—of contemplation—burned most brightly within our own field of view. Merton is the contemporary Christian sapiential writer who, for many of us, played a central part in our own spiritual awakening.

In turning to Thomas Merton and his writings, we turn first of all from scholarly studies of sapiential thought to the thing itself, a creative sapiential mind; second, we turn from the patristic and medieval tradition to a *contem-*

porary sapiential thought. We encounter "the love of learning and the desire for God" in a new and ever-evolving realization. Jean Leclercq recognized in his friend Merton a further development of the tradition that he had helped to bring to light. Recalling the letters that he had received from Merton, he wrote,

> From the very first one of those I had kept, dated 1950, he expressed his hope of seeing formed in his country's monasteries men capable of "cultivating in their souls the grain that is the Word of God" and of bearing fruit in the field of spiritual theology. He himself never ceased to work toward this goal.[45]

In the same introduction, Leclercq ranks Merton "with the Fathers of the early Church and those of the Middle Ages." "Just as they drew from the cultures of their own times in order to make it a part of their inner experience, so did Merton work in our times toward bringing 'the good news' to the world, less by converting individuals than by christianizing cultures."[46]

Merton's wide and enduring popularity has been due largely to a combination of three factors: to the pivotal moment of history in which he lived, to his personal spiritual experience, and to his singular power as a writer, through which this experience was able to reach millions of people. The voice that we hear in Merton's writings is a subjective voice, the voice of the first person. He is in the tradition of the White Monks before him, who developed the tropological (or moral, personal, subjective) sense of the Scriptures.[47] But the voice of Merton speaks not only out of the medieval tradition but out of the highly developed individuality of a modern Western person. And this modern subjectivity is further intensified by his artistic personality, sensibility—he is a musical instrument vibrating with what he encounters, discovers, ponders.

Yet at the same time Merton continually re-orients himself toward the center of the contemplative vocation. This is, in his own language, the True Self, with its Asian overtones—the absolute Self in its classical Eastern sense, marked by the experience of unitive contemplation. Merton, then, confronts us with a fusion of two selves: the classical Asian nondual Self and the modern Western personal self, a subjectivity-in-this-world. This duality can find expression in different terms: monk and poet, for example, with the two corresponding worlds of Merton's mind and thought: monastic/contemplative and secular/humanistic.

It is difficult to separate the writer from the contemplative in Merton, though at times he himself experienced a strong tension between the two.[48] The peculiar power of his writing lives at the boundary between the two worlds;

there is already a sapiential quality in the texture and flavor of his writing. His prose becomes, at moments, poetry. And the peaks of this poetry reflect a spiritual, a contemplative, light. In his explicitly spiritual writings, it is often impossible to discern the boundary between imaginative writing and contemplative experience, between the luminous ideal and the actuality.

This intense subjectivity, this supple intelligence, is a string that quivers with every impression. The tone varies from luminous transparency to shaded implication, from clear to obscure, pungent to poignant and hauntingly evocative. As Merton thinks, he feels; and as he writes he communicates this feeling along with his meanings. He feels everything and he communicates his feeling of everything. In the country of Merton's subjectivity, clear structures and sharp boundary lines are often hard to find—except for one wide black line running through the center of his often polarized vision: between real and unreal, light and darkness, secular[49] and sacred, surface and depth. The one distinctive structure that can be extracted from Merton's thought is the axis between false self and true self, and between the other pairs of polar terms that cohere with these two.[50] Otherwise, reality is seen vitally, organically, and always within an open and undefined space of mystery rather than a rational framework.[51] Merton's theology is elusive, implicit, seldom precisely objectified. Beyond the basic duality with its shifting terms, one cannot schematize it on a blackboard. Theology disappears into the subject, the universal person which is the center of this vision. Robert Lowell had remarked on Merton's early poetry, "The poet would seem to be more phenomenal than the poetry."[52] After his death, fellow Cistercian Armand Viellieux wrote, in a similar vein,

> Merton did not elaborate a new system of spirituality. There is nothing particularly new in the things he thought. My impression is that he will remain known in history not so much by the things he wrote as by what he was. His gift seems to have been the ability to integrate into a unified personal experience not only the different currents of tradition, but also the deep spiritual movements of our time, and to share that experience in a unique manner.[53]

Merton often appears to be the observer and commentator who borrows everything from outside, from someone else. Sometimes he writes as a kind of contemplative journalist, and in that relaxed mood he is often at his best.[54] What we get from Merton is not a structured, objective vision but the light of his brilliant and sensitive subjectivity, opening the things of this world which we share with him to the beauty, depth, and simplicity within them. Everything is experienced in the music of this spirit. We have left behind the theological score to enjoy the sapiential music itself, the communicated experience.

Early Merton: A Contemplative Gospel

In his early years of monastic life, Merton must have been favored with extraordinary graces of contemplative experience. It was from this height that he proclaimed his probably impossible gospel of pure contemplation.[55] The vision is that of a perfectionist, radically polarized; between the true self and the false self no place is left for the ordinary, mortal human being; we feel little compassion in this rigorous young contemplative. Yet his writing is luminous, powerful, deeply evocative, and drew hundreds of young Americans into monasteries.

While contemplation will continue to be Merton's central preoccupation,[56] his doctrine of *pure* contemplation will gradually yield its exclusivity, and we shall feel a different spirit and rhythm, a new freedom and humanity in his writing. As we follow the trajectory of Merton's writings over the years from "morning knowledge" to "evening knowledge"[57] it is natural to assume that we are following the evolution of his own spiritual experience as well.

Broadening: A Sapiential Humanism

During the last decade of his life, Merton himself began to use the word "sapiential" with some regularity, and he applied the term with a broad inclusiveness which might seem at first unrelated to the classical Christian wisdom tradition that we have reviewed. In an essay on William Faulkner, he wrote:

> I might say at once that creative writing and imaginative criticism provide a privileged area for wisdom in the modern world. At times one feels they do so even more than current philosophy and theology. The literary and creative current of thought that has been enriched and stimulated by depth psychology, comparative religion, social anthropology, existentialism, and the renewal of classical, patristic, Biblical, and mystical studies has brought in a sapiential harvest which is not to be despised. Let me mention some of the more obvious examples: T. S. Eliot both as critic and as poet, Boris Pasternak, St.-John Perse, D. H. Lawrence,[58] and William Butler Yeats. Jacques Maritain's *Creative Intuition in Art and Poetry* illustrates what I mean, as do D. T. Suzuki's

> *Zen and Japanese Culture* and William Carlos Williams's *In the American Grain*. A great deal of what I call "sapiential" thinking has come out in studies of Melville and of the American novel in general, as well as in some of the recent Milton and Shakespeare criticism. I was fortunate to study in college under "sapiential" teachers like Mark Van Doren and Joseph Wood Krutch. In the classics Jane Harrison, Werner Jaeger, and F. M. Cornford have left us "sapiential" material.[59]

In this essay Merton departs from the explicit sapiential language of the Christian tradition, adopting a language of symbol, myth, "efficacious sign-situations," and such archetypal realities as initiation, and presenting Faulkner as a contemporary wisdom writer. He crosses two boundary lines at once: from explicit to implicit sapiential writing, and from Christian to secular. Wisdom is now a human, a *personal* thing for Merton: it is not simply unitive experience. And he insists that wisdom is *creative*, expressive: it is in the line of imaginative literature that he finds the richest veins of sapiential thought and writing today.

Merton's distinctive personalism[60] and his confessed existentialism are evident as he continues,

> The "wisdom" approach to man seeks to apprehend man's value and destiny in their global and even ultimate significance . . . sapiential thought resorts to poetic myth and to religious or archetypal symbol. . . .[61]

Merton distinguishes two aspects of wisdom:

> . . . metaphysical and speculative, an apprehension of the radical structure of human life, an intellectual appreciation of man in his human potentialities and in their fruition.
>
> . . . moral, practical, and religious, an awareness of man's life as a task to be undertaken at great risk, in which tragic failure and creative transcendence are both possible . . . a peculiar understanding of conflict, of the drama of human existence, and especially of the typical causes and signs of moral disaster . . . beyond the conscious and systematic moral principles which may be embodied in an ethical doctrine and which guide our conscious activity. Wisdom also supposes a certain intuitive grasp of unconscious motivations, at least insofar as these are embodied in archetypes and symbolic configurations of the psyche.[62]

So far we have identified two dimensions of Merton's expanding spiritual universe, which can be imagined as perpendicular axes: the vertical line of his quest for pure contemplative experience or union with God, and the horizontal line of this sapiential breadth, which extends to everything of truly human significance.

The Emerging Direction

"The young poet is a god; the old poet is a tramp."[63]

Wallace Stevens's words would seem to apply to contemplative monk as well as poet; Merton was both. His story, in retrospect, resembles a parable of incarnation. As the years in the monastery pass, we can discern in the evolution of his writing a double movement: (1) *downward*, from pure spirit to embodied spirit, from pure contemplation to a divine immanence in human existence; (2) from rational clarity and limpid prose *"off the road"* into deliberately elliptical, obscure, and ironic forms of writing, in the company of "anti-poets" and the more difficult modernists.[64]

The movement of Merton's life can be observed in relation to the polarity of monk and poet, or contemplative and creative artist. Drawn first to the sapiential poetry of William Blake, he emigrated—after his conversion and entry into monastic life—into the country of the "old Christian wisdom," plunging himself into the writings of the church fathers and the medieval monks. "Contemplation" had become the obsessive center of his interest and his quest. He would explore further in this contemplative direction as he studied the Asian traditions. But at the same time—roughly during the last decade of his life—he began to move back toward the modern world which he had left behind, particularly through those of its thinkers and writers with whom he felt a great affinity.[65] He was moving further into the country of imagination, and at the same time apparently discovering the wide ecumenical territory of the sapiential, in which he was able to rediscover everything that he loved. The sapiential world, in the new sense in which he was coming to conceive it, included the mystery of Christ and the archetypal contemplative East; but it also included everything of value that had been left outside the walls of his earlier theological enclosure, labeled "Toxic-Secular." Merton was awakening to a new Christian wisdom in which the immanent force of incarnation has awakened divinity within the human person in the active, creative mode.

Gradually the early Merton's Catholic and monastic triumphalism—and the subtle self-contentment of the favored contemplative and adulated author—gives way to a more sober experience of the life of faith and a deeper awareness of solidarity[66] in the human condition and in a collective guilt.[67] The sunlit morning ascent has become a descending journey on the shadowed slope of maturity in which Merton joins his fellow Westerners.[68] This is the threshold of postmodernity, of the post-Western mind, of global consciousness and global participation on every level. Here once again, with his passionate intuitive mind, his continual struggling toward truth and his expressive genius, Merton's voice becomes prophetic. Now, however, he writes often in the language of paradox and enigma, arriving at a poetry of such high acidity that it becomes antipoetry. In this sarcastic inversion of his earlier romantic exaltation, few of his readers are inclined to follow him. Perhaps, however, he is faithfully reproducing, once again on the finely tuned strings of his own subjectivity, the corresponding "evening" phase of the life of Jesus in the Gospels, of every human life, and of his own Western world at this global threshold.

In his emigration from explicit conceptual theology to the shadowy country of embedded meanings which is modern imaginative literature, Merton seems both to be finding his own most natural voice and to be learning the universal *language of the person,* which he calls "existentialism" or "sapiential writing."

If we often seem, with the late Merton, to be descending into a gathering darkness, just as often we experience the excitement of discovery and the glimmer of an imminent dawn. We feel this when we share his exhilaration at the sudden new hope of a liberation of the Christian spirit in his time—and again when he beckons us toward the enchanted sapiential world of one of his favorite poets.

> All really valid poetry (poetry that is fully alive and asserts its reality by its power to generate imaginative life) is a kind of recovery of paradise. Not that the poet comes up with a report that he, an unusual man, has found his own way back into Eden; but the living line and the generative association, the new sound, the music, the structure, are somehow grounded in a renewal of vision and hearing so that he who reads and understands recognizes that here is a new start, a new creation. Here the world gets another chance. Here . . . the reader discovers himself getting another start in life, in hope, in imagination. . . . [69]

Merton remains, as ever, the preacher of the unitive divine light within the individual self, the personal subject. But that light has now become a transformative spark within the world. He has become a prophet of the new, creative wisdom that is beginning to awaken out of centuries of sleep and the violence of revolution.

Armand Viellieux, concluding his brilliant evocation of Merton's charism, imagines him as a spiritual dancer who gradually moves from stiffness to grace and freedom until finally (no longer "teaching"), he

> is able to embrace every person from every horizon and carry them away in the whirl-winds of a dance that could be more and more daring, yet sure and peaceful, because the dancer was solidly rooted in the Source of the Dance.
>
> Except for the point, the still point,
> There would be no dance, and there is only the dance.[70]

Within this lovely image of the wildly whirling dancer rooted unfailingly in the Ground, the invisible Source, is hidden a truth of Merton's era as well as of his own unfolding. In his development we can feel the liberating expansive energy of the epochal event of Vatican II in the world of Catholicism. Breaking out of the container of absolutized institutional and doctrinal structure, the Christian spirit was simultaneously freed to move *inward,* eastward—to the Source, the naked divine Mystery—and *outward,* westward—toward the hitherto forbidden *other,* into the world and its religious traditions, into the depths of the modern and postmodern secular. As in few other figures, we can observe in Merton both directions of this expansive movement: inward, eastward to the absolute pole of nondual experience, and outward, westward to the unconfined dynamism of the modern and postmodern person and world—from the light of the ancient East to the fire of the modern West. If we have not found the structure of a new spiritual theology in Merton, it may be because he prefers to invite us to grow into these two dimensions of Christian freedom—inward, as it were, to the depths of the Father, outward in the unbounded movement of the Holy Spirit. Merton opens to us a sapiential space beyond the *apparent* boundaries of Christian faith in both these directions.

11. Karl Rahner: Opening Christian Wisdom (II)

Since Karl Rahner will be quoted more extensively in this book than any other author, some indication of his significance for our project is in order here. The incisiveness and scope of his thought will only become really apparent, however, as we proceed. I am aware of no one who has integrated the theological process of two millennia—from the biblical wisdom of the fathers through the centuries of rationalized theology to our present "age of the person" and of global consciousness—into a vision of such depth, such liberating breadth, and such power as has Rahner.

Thomas Merton and Karl Rahner, in their wide and very evident difference, are complementary. The difference is discovered immediately in the experience of reading their work. Rather than the spontaneous and intimate satisfaction of sharing in Merton's personal experience—at once spiritual, intellectual, and aesthetic—reading one of Rahner's major theological pieces is like working through a brilliant scientific text which, after a hundred intricacies and precisions, brings us suddenly to a vantage point—a new idea, a synthetic intuition—from which a wide field of reality is freshly illuminated. And yet the perspective is always, somehow, the same.

Both men belong to the time of the Second Vatican Council, and both express the expansive movement out of the closed "second order" both eastward and westward: on one hand, toward unitive interiority and, on the other hand, toward the personal awakening into this world that characterizes the modern West. Merton, the artist-monk, conveys to us with grace the spiritual luminosity and resonance of a life of faith, reflecting the experience of God or of concrete things of the world. Rahner, the theologian's theologian, in his abstract, laborious prose, trains us to a way of seeing and reflecting from which come forth as if by magic the great structural principles, the joints and members of a new sapiential edifice, situated firmly in our own time at the threshold of a global era. Both open to us the same broad yet unified field of vision: one through personal resonance and the other through conceptual clarity and the force of the idea.

The synthetic power of Rahner's thought derives primarily from his transcendental method,[71] which brings each theological question into the light of personal subjectivity and the infinite *transcendence* of the human spirit.[72]

> Rahner's use of transcendental categories has given him a common framework within which to link the past with the present, and also to link the variety of religions and cultures in our own contemporary world, and, finally, to unify the "religious" and "secular" moments within our single human existence.[73]

The transcendental categories are practically equivalent to the existentials which recur continually in Rahner's writing: self-presence, freedom, transcendence, and grace as *supernatural* existential.[74] These existentials are the "general structures which necessarily characterize all human existence, and which therefore constitute the philosophical foundations upon which theology can build."[75]

Rahner's thought recalls the sapiential theological vision of the church fathers in its intuitive boldness and synthetic sweep, in the magnitude and power of his central ideas. After centuries of a more cautious, land-bound Catholic theology fettered by an anxious concern for material orthodoxy (or conformity), we experience in Rahner's work the exhilaration of intellectual flight once again—and, at the same time, a liberation of Christian understanding to a Pauline magnitude. Rahner's theology develops, however, not directly from the patristic or medieval sapiential tradition, but rather from the scholastic and academic "scientific" tradition of Catholic theology. His contribution to a new sapiential theology comes from "the other side," and thus brings with it much of what had been missing in the wisdom tradition itself; a new breadth and power are offered. What we observe in Rahner, I believe, is the reconvergence of the two theological streams that had separated at the end of the medieval period—beginning in the twelfth and thirteenth centuries—the monastic sapiential thought, which derived directly from that of the fathers, and the new philosophy and theology of the schools, which followed a more conceptual and analytical, critical, and dialectical course. In Rahner this abstract and analytical theology opens once again to the intuitive sweep of the New Testament and the patristic theologians and to the participatory quality of the wisdom tradition. The two long-separated streams come together here in a powerful new synthesis of wisdom and science, of unitive *intellectus* and systematic, analytical *ratio.*

Rahner's theology and his vision of a future theology remain clearly distinct from the sapiential tradition, however; he insists repeatedly that theological thought remain *abstract*, rather than rely on image and metaphor, and that it avoid a continual citation of scriptural passages. Christian sapiential theology has, until now, been distinguished precisely by its poetic, imaginative, and symbolic language and by its frequent use of biblical texts and expressions. In Thomas Merton's broadening of sapiential consciousness, we have also seen the boundary of an explicit Christian and scriptural language crossed, but into the country of imaginative literature and concrete human experience rather than into an abstract theological language. It becomes clear that the comprehension of the term "sapiential" must be expanded to embrace all three of these modes of thought and expression. The new Christian wisdom will be pluriform.

Rahner's thought, as it unfolds, embraces within itself the four movements that form the structure of our study. In outlining his contribution to our projected new wisdom theology, therefore, I shall follow the order of these four movements.

Sapiential, But New

While those who have recognized Rahner's magnitude resist attempts to circumscribe his thought within a particular category, school, or current of theological tradition, the traditional term *sapiential*, with its breadth and depth, fits him well.

> Rahner not only explained critically and precisely what the Christian faith is, but he also sought to unite people with it. To Rahner, theology is more than faith seeking understanding; it is as well a mystagogy that gives the people of God experiential union with the faith by leading them into their own deepest mystery. Thus, he was more a "sapiential" than an "academic" theologian.[76]

Rahner's *mystagogy*, like that of the early Christian theological writers, is a distinctly *participatory* theology, which aims to interpret for the reader or listener that which they have experienced in their personal participation of the mystery.[77] Rahner leads the Catholic theological tradition back across the border into the country of participation. This is evident in the shift in vocabulary which he subtly urges upon theology: toward *mystery* (he prefers to speak of God as "the holy mystery") and mystagogy, toward a personal *transcendence* in which the human consciousness breaks through the envelope of its contingency to touch God; toward a recovery of the concept of *divinization*, and toward a translation of the divine salvific action into the *self-communication* of God. Rahner clears the mediatory partitions of scholastic theology out of the way to reopen the divine Trinity—as well as incarnation—to a participatory understanding. Finally, this participatory revolution relativizes the distinction between the particular Judeo-Christian saving history and universal human history. While the essential distinctions remain, the boundaries have become permeable, and theology has become once again an interaction of *totalities:* God, person, humanity, the created universe.

Rahner has very deliberately opened the container of Western theology by relocating *mystery* at the center of vision. This return to a sense of mystery, he writes, corresponds to an exigency of the contemporary person, who is no longer captivated by a rationalistic interpretation of reality. This suggests that we are crossing a historical threshold into a new era which is once again hospitable to the sapiential consciousness. Rahner finds the *new* situation of the Western person demanding, once again, a unity and simplicity in Christian doctrine.

> As long as men find it [doctrine] a highly complicated collection of arbitrarily linked assertions, their readiness to believe will be inhibited. And this is not because they abhor the incomprehensible. . . . They sense and revere the nameless and inexpressible. And for that very reason, they find a complicated dogmatic system too knowledgeable by far, too clever, rationalistic and positivist, too ready to lay down the law. . . . Men find the mystery of God so all-embracing that they can-

> not easily bring themselves to accept a multitude of mysteries which look very much like the complications of human reasoning which has tied itself up in knots.
>
> . . . . Is Christian doctrine, where it covers real mysteries, really a highly complicated system of orderly statements? Or is it rather a mysteriously simple thing of infinite fullness, which can be propounded in an immense variety of statements, while its mysterious and simple unity remains unchanged? So that man, faced with this multiplicity of assertions, need not be the victim of modernistic simplifications of religion if he finds himself as he really is, the being in face of the nameless mystery.[78]

This unity and simplicity, we shall find, must be in the form of a *new* wisdom; it is here particularly that Rahner will help us.

Transcendence and Nonduality

The meaning and centrality of *transcendence,* as Rahner employs the term, emerge from his lapidary statements in *Foundations of Christian Faith.* "Being a person, then, means the self-possession of a subject as such in a conscious and free relationship to the totality of itself."[79]

"What is meant more precisely by the subjectivity which man experiences becomes clearer when we say that man is a transcendent being."[80] Transcendence is the foundation of the distinctness of being a person and is the infinite ground of human consciousness; it is an immediate though inaccessible knowledge of God; through transcendence the human person is open to all reality, whether to God or to created things. "Man is a transcendent being insofar as all of his knowledge and all of his conscious activity is grounded in a pre-apprehension *(Vorgriff)* of "being" as such, in an unthematic but ever-present knowledge of the infinity of reality. . . ."[81] "The infinite horizon, which is the term of transcendence and which opens us to unlimited possibilities of encountering this or that particular thing, cannot itself be given a name."[82] And yet, " . . . this term and source by which transcendence is borne can be called "God." We can also speak of being, of ground, of ultimate cause, of illuminating, revealing logos, and we can appeal to what is meant by a thousand other names."[83] "Transcendence strictly as such knows only *God* and nothing else, although it knows him as the condition which makes possible categorical knowledge, history and concrete freedom."[84] Rahner's understanding of transcendence and its relation to the multiple objects of categorical knowledge carefully avoids the two deviations of pantheism and "a more popular form of *dualism* which places God and the non-divine simply as two things alongside of each other, a dualism which is also found in religion."[85] This human participation in God which Rahner calls transcendence is the source of every truly personal or spiritual act. It is the ontological basis not only for the specific history of salvation but for all history. It locates human life—as well as human consciousness and thought—on a plane of divine immediacy which is implicitly *sapiential.*

Rahner has very little to say specifically about the Asian religious traditions. Nevertheless, I believe that he opens the way to a theological understanding of the relationship between Christianity and the traditions of Hindu Vedanta, of Buddhism, and of Taoism. With David Loy, I will propose that at the core of these three great traditions is the same reality of nonduality.[86] It is Rahner's anthropological concept of *transcendence* which, I believe, becomes, at the "eastward" end of its comprehension, practically identical with the Asian concept of nonduality. This relationship between the two conceptions becomes more credible when we imagine a third term—"the unbounded"—which mediates between them. Rahner's transcendence can be understood as the Western or "extensive" understanding of the unbounded, while Asian nonduality is the Eastern or "intensive" (or reflexive or internal) version of the unbounded. I am aware that it will not be possible to prove this equivalence of transcendence and nonduality; it is further supported for me by the continual manifestation in Rahner's own thought—particularly around the subject of transcendence—of a unitive consciousness.

It is through this universal existential of the transcendence of the human subject that the seemingly magical junctures of Rahner's synthetic vision are made. For example, I believe that the four existentials listed above—self-presence, freedom, transcendence, and grace—can be seen as facets or corollaries or synonyms of nonduality. It is *transcendence,* however, which is the central term mediating this unity. The universal human experience of God through transcendence (which appears most clearly and purely in the Asian Axial religious traditions) finds its perfect historical objectification in the event of Christ.[87] Here is the key that Rahner offers to an understanding of the relationship—the continuity and the essential difference—between Christianity and the great Eastern traditions.

The starting point of Rahner's conception of the transcendence of the human subject is to be found in the writings of Thomas Aquinas; more specifically, in Aquinas's principle that the human subject, in every act of knowledge of a particular being, implicitly knows absolute Being, that is, God.[88] This conviction is the origin of the "double vision" which is distinctive of Rahner's own theological thought. At every point, the discourse is opened to the unbounded mystery by this "vertical" of transcendence, which is present within the thinking subject.

The Eastern pole of Rahner's thought, then, is this concept of anthropological transcendence. The pure or quasi-unmediated experience of this transcendence would be a contemplative experience of unitive or nondual consciousness, an enlightenment like the *samadhi* or *satori* of Hinduism and Buddhism. In the second movement of our study (chap. 3), I shall relate this experience also to Christian baptismal initiation. Rahner's "transcendence" offers an anthropological, natural basis for this supernatural event. The Western pole of Rahner's theological world, on the other hand, will involve historical movement and the awakening of the human person in this world.

Awakening in This World: The Inner Sun

Christianity originates from and remains ever centered in a historical event, and for Rahner historicity—along with transcendence—is an essential dimension of the human person. After sketching the synthetic scope and power of the transcendental categories, William Dych turns to the other side of Rahner's theological world.

> Now there is one further step he must take to prevent the misuse of transcendental method and an idealistic misunderstanding of it. Because human beings are historical and social beings, transcendental structures of knowledge and freedom must be actualized in the world and in history.[89]

The two all-pervading principles of Rahner's anthropology, his Christology and his theology as a whole, then, are *transcendence* and *historicity.* His notion of the historicity of the human person embraces the person's "intrinsic situation in the world, . . . corporeality, . . . the racial unity of humanity . . . sexuality, . . . social orientation (family, state, and church), . . . the character of [one's] existence as a test, as historically conditioned and incalculable. And there is the incalculable pluralism of [one's] nature. . . .[90]

At this point it may be helpful to return to the brief treatment of *spirit and history,* which concluded the introduction to this book.[91] Rahner's transcendence and historicity correspond to these two great dimensions—vertical and horizontal—which will run through the whole of our study, and Rahner has opened a new way of theological reflection in these terms—embracing, as they do, the whole of the reality that we know—which will be very useful for our sapiential project.

Rahner has been steeped in the modern Western (especially German) philosophical tradition from Kant and Hegel to Heidegger, but his grasp of the essential spirit of the West and of modernity is deeper and simpler than particular systems or ideas. Perhaps the one word that best expresses it is "freedom." Much of his theological thought has been directed toward an expression of Christianity appropriate to the worldview and exigencies of a modern person in the West. The movement of his thought has, accordingly, been in the direction of the "turn to the subject," which he discerns in the history of Western culture; Rahner's theology is centered in an anthropological perspective. Here is to be found much of what a new sapiential theology can learn from Rahner; here is the radical *newness* that belongs to the unprecedented *awakening of the person in this world,* which has been proceeding in the West from the age of scholasticism to the present. If Rahner likes to write of "the free history of God in this world,"[92] this history of God is a history of human awakenings, of the realization of freedom and creative powers on the part of human persons, and of the transformation of the human environment which—with its huge shadow—has resulted from this awakening.

The newness of Rahner's *mystagogy*—the step that he has taken away from the sacramental mystagogy of the church fathers—is indicated in the words of Harvey Egan that were quoted at the beginning of this section: "a mystagogy that gives the people of God experimental union with the faith by leading them into their own deepest mystery." The mystagogical initiation penetrates into the mystery of *personal existence*, rather than moving directly and explicitly into a participatory experience of the mystery of Christ. This shift corresponds to the "turn to the subject." If Charles Taylor's words concerning the receptiveness of our modern contemporaries to objective truth first call to mind Merton's writings, they apply equally if less obviously to the mystagogical project of Rahner:

> something has undoubtedly changed since the era of the great chain of being and the publicly established order of references. I have tried to express this by saying that the metaphysics or theology comes indexed to a personal vision, or refracted through a particular sensibility.[93]

Beneath the particular insights that one may experience in the company of Rahner, there is a single, general awakening of the person—an inner quickening, a self-realization in freedom, a sudden magnitude, a new awareness of the unbounded scope of the human spirit—which may be the master's greatest gift (and challenge) to the sapiential project. This experience corresponds to the historical awakening of the person (seldom mentioned in a climate of critical postmodernity) in the West.[94] Rahner's transcendental anthropology—and his theological world which is centered in this anthropology—contains within itself implicitly the essential movement of this Western emergence as well as the Eastern light of the transcendence of the human spirit.

Sapiential theology, opening to Rahner's prophetic vision, arrives at the transcendent awakening of the person *in this world*. This Copernican revolution is the greatest challenge for a Christian sapiential tradition that has faithfully and humbly remained within the enclosure of the given—whether biblical revelation or classical wisdom—rather than awakening to the autonomous subject, the self, the person free and responsible in this world. Responsible—for the person is not alone in this world.

One Church, One Humanity

Karl Rahner was aware of the historical threshold of globalization, and understood it—beneath its economic and other visible phenomena—in terms of the deep and broad movement of unification of humanity, of the collective awakening of one human race. He wrote of the separate histories of the different peoples becoming a single history, and he saw this epochal event as a further unfolding of the event of Christ which has operated in history through the unique development of Western culture and civilization.[95]

Rahner's universalizing of the Christian reality through his transcendental anthropology, opening toward an "anonymous" participation in the mystery of Christ by every human person, may be motivated partly by an awareness of the great human convergence in our time. It is certainly related to his awareness of the dramatic change in the expressed attitude of the church in the time of Vatican II toward those outside: its turn toward the other with respect and in a spirit of dialogue. Rahner was attuned to the movement of the Holy Spirit which more widely than ever impels human beings anew toward dialogue in our time. He powerfully drew out the implications of this global threshold for the church in his articles on the Second Vatican Council as the historical moment of the inception of the world church.[96] He saw the third age of the church as beginning with Vatican II, after (1) the short period of Jewish Christianity and (2) the many centuries during which Christianity and church remained confined within a single cultural container—the Greek-Latin-Germanic or European cultural complex. With Vatican II and the abolition of Latin as the obligatory uniform and universal liturgical language, the church was opened to a diverse inculturation among all the peoples of the earth. At the same time, the awakening world church began to address the world itself with respectful recognition, and—after so many centuries—to affirm the positive value and graced existence of that which lies outside its own visible boundaries: the other Christian churches, the secular efforts and achievements of human beings, and even the other great religious traditions of the world. In his prophetic understanding of this new openness of the church, Rahner has brought to expression a confident and expansive sense of Christian freedom, which is indispensable to a new Christian wisdom.

Rahner's characteristic double vision—at once phenomenal and transcendent—and his corresponding mystagogical approach reflect the spiritual understanding or *gnosis* of the classical sapiential theology of the church fathers,[97] but with a major difference which is related to Rahner's distinctive personalism, or turn to the subject. The progression from patristic wisdom through the rational-critical phase that began with scholasticism to a new sapiential theology may be conceived in terms of a succession of three "ages" or phases of Christian thought, exemplified by Augustine, Thomas Aquinas, and Karl Rahner. In the first age—let us say of biblical revelation or of the Word—a Platonizing theology remains confined within the enclosure of the biblical word. In the second age, of Reason or of Being, under the influence of Aristotle, the edifice of a rationalized and objectifying, nonparticipatory theology is erected alongside the Scriptures. In the third age, of the Person or Subject, the divine mystery is known once again in a participatory way, but through the existence and experience of the personal subject. The movement from the first to the third age can be seen—ideally at least—as reflecting a progressive *embodiment* of the divine Word in the human person and in humanity more generally, which reflects the incarnational Christ-event.

I am reminded forcefully, from time to time, that the new sapiential vision that I have been working to develop is likely, so far, to be intelligible and acceptable only to people living within the circle of Christian faith. And gradually I am becoming convinced that our new wisdom must also be meaningful to "those outside," to every human person. Rahner's universalization of Christian truth through his philosophical anthropology and pastoral mystagogy suggests a way to achieve this transition from "interior" intelligibility to "exterior" intelligibility, to a sapiential vision which is also capable of intelligent dialogue and interaction with the other wisdoms of the world. While Christianity can never be reduced to a perennial philosophy, a sapiential gospel may include an anthropology that brings light to every human existence. In this age of the person, the human person itself becomes the primary language of faith.

Like Merton but more clearly and coherently, Karl Rahner has opened for us again the mystery of Christ, which had for so long been imprisoned within conventional structures. He has sketched in bold strokes the larger world in which a new sapiential vision must realize itself and has demonstrated that the vitality and intellectual potency of the gospel is adequate to this challenge.

12. The Paradox of Christian Wisdom: The Word of the Cross

Sapiential theology itself has not avoided the flight from incarnation into superstructures, ascending ladders, conceptual containers, and mediatory dualism. In fact, under the influence of Platonism and Neoplatonism—and of the common Augustinian legacy of the West—the sapiential tradition has quite consistently developed in the direction of ascending constructions rather than in the descending direction of incarnation. Wisdom has sequestered itself, cultivated itself, elevated itself, left behind—as if outside and beneath—the human body and the body of Christ. Wisdom has eluded the Christian paradox of incarnation and cross.

The antidote for this hereditary malady has been ever near at hand in the New Testament: in the life and teaching of Jesus and of Paul.

> For Christ did not send me to baptize but to preach the gospel, and not with eloquent wisdom, lest the cross of Christ be emptied of its power. For the word of the cross is folly to those who are perishing, but to us who are being saved it is the power of God. For it is written, "I will destroy the wisdom of the wise, and the cleverness of the clever I will thwart." Where is the wise man? Where is the scribe? Where is the debater of this age? Has not God made foolish the wisdom of the world? For since, in the wisdom of God, the world did not know God through wisdom, it pleased God through the folly of what we preach to save those who believe. For Jews demand signs and Greeks seek wisdom, but we preach Christ crucified, a stumbling block to Jews and folly to Gentiles, but to those who are called, both Jews and Greeks, Christ the power of God and the wisdom of God. For the foolishness of God is wiser than men, and the weakness of God is stronger than men. (1 Cor 1:17-25)

Christian wisdom reduces itself to Jesus Christ—this bodily human being who is divine—and his cross: the physical death of this human being at the center of humanity, history, and cosmos. The mystery of Christ in its actuality is known as one finds oneself at the central point of the cross—and Paul vividly describes his life in this place of the cross (2 Cor 4:7-12; 6:3-10). Here higher and lower have disappeared or exchanged places. There is no place to climb to, and nobody resides on a privileged height. Hierarchies and other structures, from this viewpoint, are functional and provisional supports, external to the mystery that they serve: the mystery which is union, communion, the divine *koinonia.* The fullness is known in emptiness, in unknowing, as the forms and ideas give way to participation: "to know nothing among you except Jesus Christ and him crucified." The mystery is beyond reason, unknowable by the rational mind, yet in its dark density is the very core of meaning.

Wisdom is loving faith, and Christian faith is the dark knowing of embodied light, of incarnation. Wisdom, as faith, is union, identity with Christ. The true apophatism of Christianity is this union with Christ in the darkness of embodied human life, of incarnation. This is not a specialization, nor does it bring into being a contemplative or sapiential elite. As we shall see, the shape of Christian life corresponds to the pattern of Jesus' own life on this earth. This is a descent from baptism to eucharist, a giving to the world of the divine-human self to which one has awakened.

13. Conclusion

Our first movement—the sapiential awakening—brings us home to the traditional heart of Christianity. The following movements, however (in chaps. 3, 4, and 5), will lead us into strange, new regions which we may not immediately recognize as belonging to Christ. This sapiential initiation, breaking the conventional container of our Christian and Western consciousness, begins to open us toward these worlds. The challenge that a new Christian wisdom must confront again and again is to integrate these new realities with Jesus Christ, with the Christ-event, as their center and fullness. The mystery of Christ, as we have found it in the New Testament, will provide the template for this integration—across the length of the centuries and the breadth of human experiences and cultures.

The integration will involve several different kinds of magic—metaphysical and theological transformations—sudden leaps and turns which may remind us of the metaphors of a modernist poem or of the equations of contemporary physics which join disparate realities in a quantitative relationship. These transmutations and migrations will come to birth in the light of nonduality, which emerges in the course of our next movement, the turn to the East.

3

Movement II

The Eastern Turn

1. The New East-West Relationship

i. Contact and Dialogue

DURING THE SECOND HALF OF THE TWENTIETH CENTURY, AND ESPECIALLY since the Second Vatican Council, a new interaction between Christianity and the Asian spiritual traditions developed. Christians have gone East, and Hindu and Buddhist teachers have come to the West. In this new climate, Christian spirituality begins to understand itself in a new way. The change in perspective is, in some cases, revolutionary. Common elements appear and differences become clearer. Gradually we arrive at a more precise differentiation between meditation and prayer, between a universal level of contemplation and a Christian mystical experience—while all of this is envisioned within the single universe of human spiritual realization.

ii. Redefinition of Meditation and Contemplation

Our understanding of meditation, under Asian influence, evolves from the conventional Western conception—a process of reflection on revealed realities—to that of a silent descent into the depths of the person. Contemplation is reconceived in a similar way. Rather than as a quiet gazing—a mode of intentionality—we begin to think of contemplation as an experience of *nonduality* or of pure consciousness. This, in fact, is the direction of each of these Eastern redefinitions: understanding shifts from the key of relationship and intentionality to the key of identity or pure interiority. At this point we are confronted with the challenge to integrate this unitive understanding into our Christian theological vision.[1]

iii. A Map of Totality[2]

Our interaction with the Asian traditions promises to open our theology and spirituality to dimensions of development that have remained largely unrealized until now—or which emerged only to be subsequently forgotten. In a chronic climate of institutional overmediation, Christian consciousness has often remained confined within the security of a *logos*-container. Hinduism, as we have seen,[3] confronts this one-sided Christianity with its full spectrum of paths—*margas* or *yogas*.

I. *Dhyana* or meditation yoga, or less strictly, the *Raja* yoga of Patanjali, corresponds to a first archetypal pole of nonduality. The eight stages of Raja yoga culminate in *dhyana* (meditation oriented toward nondual experience) and, finally, in *samadhi*, the nondual realization itself.
II. *Jnana* yoga is the way of abstract thought, discriminating phenomena from reality and arriving finally at nondual consciousness.
III. *Bhakti* yoga is the way of devotion. At this third pole we might place also *kundalini* yoga and other paths that are centered in the ascent or sublimation of energy.
IV. *Karma* yoga, the path of selfless action or service, corresponds to the moral teaching that is central to the Christian tradition.

In Christian tradition, each of these four paths has been cultivated in some way, but their unity and relationship have not been perceived with comprehensiveness and anthropological balance. In the context of Christian faith, the particular ways rarely maintain the distinctness and intensity with which they are found in the Asian traditions. Integrative disciplines of body[4] and energy, in particular, have been little developed in the West.

We have already seen a quaternary expression of the mystery of Christ in early Christianity.[5] The four principal *yogas*, or Hindu spiritual paths,[6] correspond to four dimensions of the human person[7] and also to the four poles of this theological quaternity, which we may call the Christian mandala. The mandala, or quaternary figure, represents the mystery of the cross,[8] which is realized as Trinity and creation become one in Christ. The figure described by the representation of this mystery in the Pauline letters, however, is based on and inseparable from a particular historical occurrence—the paschal event of Jesus' death and resurrection. In contrast to a figure of cosmic and human wholeness which would correspond to the perennial philosophy, this Pauline figure visually symbolizes an event that has become the center and pivot of history and represents the progressive consummation of history as an integration—or recapitulation—of all reality around that center.[9]

The Christian mandala, however, also has an ontological level of significance. The ultimate quaternity, as we find it in the New Testament and in theological writings of the second century, is that of God, Word, Spirit, World. The Word is that divine Word, Wisdom, or Son which has become a human person in Jesus Christ.

I—God (or the Unitive Absolute)
Word—II + III—Holy Spirit
IV—Cosmos

This quaternary vision, as we find it already in Irenaeus,[10] offers itself today as the structural framework of one possible new Christian wisdom.[11] Christian theology has been until now—quite understandably—largely confined to the dimension of the Word (II). This pluralistic paradigm, on the other hand, presents all reality gathered together at its center (which is first of all the risen Christ) and unfolding into four dimensions. It is our contact with the Asian traditions—and our consequent awakening to the absolute unitive principle (I) in its autonomy and purity—that opens our theological consciousness to this wider view. I shall return to this quaternary perspective from time to time as we continue our journey.

iv. The Internal East of Christianity

We can see these revisions of perspective as facets of a single great emergence: the rediscovery in the modern West of the "interior East" of Christianity. This recovery of the archetypal or theological East accompanies and further develops the great theological recovery of Vatican II, which we examined in chap. 2: an awareness of the dynamic mystery of Christ, which is the center and fullness of Christianity. Our Eastern turn brings the further recovery of a *unitive* interpretation, opening our theological vision to the depths of the mystery's Pauline and Johannine expressions.

These fruits of the Asian-Christian interaction should not be dismissed as importations from Hinduism or Buddhism. Rather, the Asian traditions offer a luminous mirror in which Christianity rediscovers itself, its origins, its fullness—and its distinctness—with a new clarity. Perhaps the global confrontation of our time is a sign of the *ripening* of Earth, the planet of humanity. If so, it is not suprising that rapid mutations occur everywhere at once, as in the transition of a single, comprehensive process into a new phase. Nor should we be greatly surprised to experience a sudden ripening within Christianity at the same time. The Christ-event, center of the faith of Christians, is also the dynamic center of the overall historical process.

The words "East" and "West" have more than a geographical and historical meaning; they have an archetypal meaning as well. On the one hand, East connotes mystery, wisdom, origins, a primordial revelation and primordial tradition. East, also within Christianity, suggests a deeper kind of knowing, a vision of all things in one single light, a unitive life and experience, a luminous innocence. West suggests, on the other hand, movement, a journey, an eclipse of the first light, exile, alienation, traveling in the common light of day, by the everyday way of knowing. East suggests nonduality and West duality; East implies spirit and the eternal, while West implies history and mutability.[12] To the East belongs a contemplative monastic life with its practices of solitude, silence, and meditation facilitating the awakening of the interior self; active ministry belongs to the Christian West.

East, Orient, is "beginning" (Greek *archē*), and at the beginning there is light. In the New Testament this *archē*, or first principle, has multiple levels of meaning. It is God, Father, ultimate Source. It is the moment of first creation (see Gen 1:1ff.). It is the second creation, which commences with the coming of Jesus Christ. The beginning is the written gospel. And it is initiation, baptism. This will be important for our study. Fullness is present at the beginning, at this Eastern pole, this Orient and origin of Christianity. Around this metaphor of "the beginning" cluster other resonant images: the boundary of night and early morning, with its recalling of the first creation and of Easter morning, nocturnal vigil as a diurnal baptism, a participation in the new creation which is also a rebirth in the absolute beginning.

2. Nonduality

Implicit in our general approach is a conviction that reality, while complex, is ultimately one, manifesting its inner structure and movement in large and simple shapes. Sometimes an apparently shameless inattention to scholarly detail and nuance will result, and this will be noticed particularly as we turn to the Asian traditions. Further, the language with which we grope for these simple but elusive forms is continually that of analogy and metaphor; we walk forward over the surface of reality with the qualification "it is as if. . . ."

From the perspective of our Eastern turn, then, it is *as if* we observe in the event and mystery of Christ an encounter between the unitive perennial philosophy and the decisive saving act of God. The divine Wisdom has become a historical event. This historical embodiment of divine Wisdom is also, from below, the historical realization of human transcendence.

Our study will often proceed through a series of unproven assertions. In this section I shall propose (1) that the three great Asian traditions of Hindu Vedanta, Buddhism, and Taoism are centered in the same principle of *nonduality*, and (2) that the most promising starting point for discovering the theological potential of these three traditions for a fuller self-understanding of Christianity (and hence for a new sapiential theology) lies in the correlation of Asian nonduality with Christian baptismal initiation. From this point we can proceed to explore the implications of the concept of nonduality for our understanding of the mystery of Christ more generally, focusing finally on the central and germinal relationship between nonduality and incarnation.[13] From a dynamic historical perspective, the incarnation can be understood as a continuing nondual event.

Now let us return to the first of our two assertions. Here I shall rely upon the work of David Loy, who has persuasively set forth the thesis that the three great Asian traditions are centered in the same principle of nondual reality, nondual experience, and nondual consciousness, that "Buddhism, Vedanta and Taoism are basing their worldview on the experience of subject-object nonduality."[14] As vivid illustrations, rather than as proof, I shall offer a few texts from these three traditions. The texts are representative of Indian Vedanta, Chinese Taoism, and Japanese Zen Buddhism.

i. Vedanta–Atman

The extensive lexicon of nonduality in Hindu Vedanta includes the Sanskrit terms *Brahman* (absolute being and consciousness), *Atman* (the absolute Self), *advaita* (nonduality), *sat-chit-ananda* (being-consciousness-bliss as attributes of Brahman), *samadhi* (contemplative absorption), *nirvikalpa samadhi* (ultimate nondual consciousness), *prajna* (wisdom, nondual consciousness), and *jnana* (ultimate knowledge). The spiritual teaching of the Vedanta, which appears for the first time in the *Upanishads*, points to a way of absolute interiority, focused on the realization of the absolute Self, or Atman.

1. Because when there is duality, as it were, then one smells something, one sees something, one hears something, one speaks something, one thinks something, one knows something. [But] when to the knower of Brahman everything has become the Self, then what should one smell and through what, what should one see and through what [repeated for hearing, speaking, thinking and knowing]? Through what should one know That owing to which all this is known—through what, O Maitreyi, should one know the Knower?[15]

2. To the seer, all things have verily become the Self: what delusion, what sorrow, can there be for him who beholds that oneness?[16]

Adi Shankara (ca. 788–ca. 820 C.E.) distilled the doctrine dispersed through the Upanishads into a compact, explicit, and single-minded spirituality of nonduality: *Advaita Vedanta.*

> When the mind is completely absorbed in the supreme Being—the Atman, the Brahman, the Absolute—then the world of appearances vanishes. Its existence is no more than an empty word.
>
> The world of appearances is a mere phantom; there is but one Reality. It is changeless, formless and absolute. How can it be divided?
>
> There is neither seer nor seeing nor seen. There is but one Reality—changeless, formless and absolute. How can it be divided?
>
> There is but one Reality—like a brimming ocean in which all appearances are dissolved. It is changeless, formless and absolute. How can it be divided?[17]

ii. Taoism–Tao

Chinese Taoism is a tradition of spiritual freedom based on a realization of nondual consciousness. This finds objectification in the doctrine of the Tao, or "the Way." The writings of Taoism have a supple, humorous charm, a music of freedom that is all their own. The nondual language includes, first, the Tao, or the pivot of the Tao, the One or great One, then *wu* (non-being) and *yu* (being), *chih* (intuitive knowledge), *wu-wei* (non-action), *wu-ming* (the nameless) and *yu-ming* (the named), *te* (power, virtue), *yu* (wandering), and the True Man, the sage, the embryo or infant, (original) chaos, simplicity, and purity of mind.

1. Lao Tzu: *Tao Te Ching* (fourth century B.C.E.)

    1. Tao can be talked about, but not the Eternal Tao.
    Names can be named, but not the Eternal Name.
    As the origin of heaven-and-earth, it is nameless;
    As "the Mother" of all things, it is nameable.[18]

    2. The Tao is like an empty bowl,
    Which in being used can never be filled up.
    Fathomless, it seems to be the origin of all things.
    It blunts all sharp edges,
    It unties all tangles,

It harmonizes all lights,
It unites the world into one whole.
Hidden in the deeps,
Yet it seems to exist for ever.
I do not know whose child it is;
It seems to be the common ancestor of all, the father of things.[19]

2. Chuang Tzu (369–286 B.C.E.)
    1. If there is no other, there will be no I. If there is no I, there will be none to make distinctions.[20]
    2. For this reason, whether you point to a little stalk or a great pillar, a leper or the beautiful Hsi-shih, things ribald and shady or things grotesque and strange, the Way makes them all into one. Their dividedness is their completeness; their completeness is their impairment. No thing is either complete or impaired, but all are made into one again. Only the man of far-reaching vision knows how to make them into one. So he has no use [for categories], but relegates all to the constant. The constant is the useful; the useful is the passable; the passable is the successful; and with success, all is accomplished. He relies upon this alone, relies upon it and does not know he is doing so. This is called the Way.[21]
    3. The sage leans on the sun and moon, tucks the universe under his arm, merges himself with things, leaves the confusion and muddle as it is, and looks on slaves as exalted. Ordinary men strain and struggle; the sage is stupid and blockish. He takes part in ten thousand ages and achieves simplicity in oneness. For him, all the ten thousand things are what they are, and thus they enfold each other.[22]

iii. Mahayana Buddhism

Nondual reality and experience find many different verbal expressions in the various languages of the Mahayana Buddhist traditions, including the Sanskrit terms *nirvana* (extinction), *sunyata* (emptiness, the void), *prajna* (wisdom), *tathata* (suchness), the Japanese term *satori* (enlightenment), and other expressions equivalent to the English terms "true nature," "original nature," "Buddha-nature," "Buddha-mind," "Dharma-mind."

1. Suchness: Asvaghosha[23] (first century C.E.)
    1. In the one soul we may distinguish two aspects. The one is the soul as suchness, the other is the soul as birth-and-death. Each in itself consti-

tutes all things, and both are so closely interrelated that one cannot be separated from the other.

What is meant by the soul as suchness is the oneness of the totality of things, the great all-including whole, the quintessence of the doctrine. For the essential nature of the soul is uncreated and eternal.

Therefore all things in their fundamental nature are not nameable or explicable. They cannot be adequately expressed in any form of language. They are without the range of apperception. They are universals. They have no signs of distinction. They possess absolute sameness. They are subject neither to transformation, nor to destruction. They are nothing but the one soul, for which suchness is another designation. Therefore they cannot be fully explained by words or exhausted by reasoning.[24]

2. Enlightenment is the highest quality of the mind. As it is free from all limiting attributes of subjectivity, it is like unto space, penetrating everywhere, as the unity of all.[25]
3. When the oneness of the totality of things is not recognized, then ignorance as well as particularization arises, and all phases of the defiled mind are thus developed. But the significance of this doctrine is so extremely deep and unfathomable that it can be fully comprehended by Buddhas and by no others.[26]

2. *Satori:* D. T. Suzuki (1879-1966)

The Zen tradition of Buddhism focuses on the realization of *satori,* nondual consciousness. Japanese Buddhist scholar Daisetz T. Suzuki brought the heart of this tradition to the twentieth-century Western world with clarity, freshness, and force.

1. So we see that Enlightenment is not the outcome of an intellectual process in which one idea follows another in sequence finally to terminate in conclusion or judgment. There is neither process nor judgment in Enlightenment, it is something more fundamental, something which makes a judgment possible, and without which no form of judgment can take place. In judgment there are a subject and a predicate; in Enlightenment subject is predicate, and predicate is subject; they are here merged as one, but not as one of which something can be stated, but as one from which arises judgment. We cannot go beyond this absolute oneness; all the intellectual operations stop here; when they endeavor to go further, they draw a circle in which they for ever repeat themselves. This is the wall against which all philosophies have beaten in vain.[27]

2. Satori may be defined as an intuitive looking into the nature of things in contradistinction to the analytical or logical understanding of it. . . . The world for those who have gained satori is no more the old world as it used to be; even with all its flowing streams and burning fires, it is never the same once again. Logically stated, all its opposites and contradictions are united and harmonized into a consistent organic whole. . . .[28]
3. . . . Satori as the Zen experience must be concerned with the entirety of life [e.g., not just the intellectual aspect]. For what Zen proposes to do is the revolution, and the re-valuation as well, of oneself as a spiritual unity.[29]

We have found, at the center of these different expressions of the three great Asian spiritual traditions, a single multifaceted reality: nonduality. In the next section we shall focus upon the nonduality *(advaita)* of the Hindu Vedanta. Several contemporary sapiential thinkers have sought a Christian counterpart to *advaita.*

3. Christian Nonduality I

Again and again, Christian theologians and spiritual teachers encountering the Asian traditions have recognized that the central problem for theology and spirituality that emerges from this encounter is that of a Christian nonduality or *advaita.*

i. Three Positions

The three fathers of Shantivanam[30]—Henri Le Saux (Abhishiktananda), Jules Monchanin, and Bede Griffiths—responded to this challenge in three ways which differ from one another as, respectively, (1) audacious and one-sided, (2) cautious and conservative, and (3) optimistic and synthetic.

1. Abhishiktananda's pursuit of *advaita* was bold and absolute. Influenced by the contemporary *advaitin* mystic Ramana Maharshi, he related the Vedantin realization of the nondual Self to the "I am" statements of Jesus in John's Gospel and to the baptism of Jesus—theologically one with Christian baptism. Thus the realization of Christian baptismal identity is the experience of Jesus' baptism and of the nondual divine identity in which Jesus could appropriate to himself the divine Name revealed to Moses at the burning bush: "I AM," or Yahweh. The revelation of both Testaments is consummated in the realization of this nondual Self.

> Deep in his heart, the Indian seer heard with rapture the same "I AM" that Moses heard on Mount Horeb (Exod 3:14); it was enough for his contemplation, his peace and joy for ever. India become Christian would surely feel a quite special attraction to silent meditation on the name of Yahweh. . . . For the ineffable Name cannot be truly understood except in the "innermost depth of man's heart," where it lies concealed in its own mystery. . . . In this most secret centre of man's being the only means of illumination is the purest awareness of the self; and this self-awareness is in fact nothing else than the reflection, the mirror, of the unique "I AM," the very Name of Yahweh. . . .[31]

> This whole mystery is Jesus, the "I AM", ego eimi; my name is "I am" *(ahamasmi namakah).*[32]

Again and again, Abhishiktananda emphasizes the transconceptual quality of this experience.

> The discovery of Christ's I AM is the ruin of any Christian theology, for all notions are burnt within the fire of experience. Perhaps I am a little too Cartesian, as a good Frenchman. And perhaps others might find a way out of the atomic mushroom.[33]

After Abhishiktananda's heart attack in July 1973, his experience attained a further degree of ineffability.

> I feel too much, more and more, the blazing fire of this I AM, in which all notions about Christ's personality, ontology, history, etc., have disappeared. And I find his real mystery shining in every awakening man, in every *mythos.*[34]

For Abhishiktananda, the two great experiences or "visions" of Christianity are, first, the experience of Jesus at his baptism in the Jordan, and, second, the experience of the apostles who discovered him to be alive after his resurrection. Very likely, he understood these as two successive realizations of the same nondual Self: first by Jesus himself and then by his disciples.

2. Jules Monchanin, while a pioneer in the Indianization of Christian monasticism, was theologically cautious, refusing to break with the Greek formulations of Christian dogma. While Abhishiktananda emphasized the importance of a spiritual experience that transcended intellectual concepts, Monchanin distrusted this "experience beyond thought." Becoming increasingly aware of a gulf between the two religions, he became pessimistic about

dialogue between Christians and Hindus.[35] Recalling the evolution of his relationship with Abhishiktananda, he wrote

> Serious divergences between us have cast a shadow over these last years; I think he goes too far in his concessions to Hinduism, and it seems to me more and more doubtful that the essence of Christianity can be recovered on the other side of *Advaita. Advaita,* like yoga and more than it, is an abyss. Whoever in the experience of vertigo throws himself into it does not know what he will find at the bottom. I am afraid that he may find himself rather than the living, trinitarian God.[36]

Monchanin found it impossible to reconcile the Hindu concept of *advaita* with the trinitarian God of Christianity.[37]

3. Bede Griffiths, decidedly more optimistic than Monchanin concerning the possibility of a Christian *advaita,* stops short of Abhishiktananda's radical acceptance of Hindu nonduality. Remaining securely on the Christian side of the divide, he finds the Christian experience of nonduality in a participation of Jesus' communion of love with the Father.

> Jesus can say, then, "I and the Father are one." He knows himself as one with the Father, and yet, as we saw, in distinction from the Father. He does not say, "I am the Father," but "I and the Father are one." This is unity in distinction. This mutual interpenetration combining unity and distinction developed . . . in the whole course of Christian mysticism, as one of its fundamental elements. This is what distinguishes the Christian experience of God from that of the Hindu. The Hindu in his deepest experience of advaita knows God in an identity of being. "I am Brahman." "Thou art that." The Christian experiences God in a communion of being, a relationship of love, in which there is none the less perfect unity of being.[38]

ii. Conclusions

What can we understand from these divergent responses to the challenge of a Christian nonduality? I believe that the models of Christian nonduality proposed by Abhishiktananda and by Bede Griffiths are both valid. The basic Christian experience of baptismal initiation or "illumination" (*photismos* in the Greek of the patristic writers) is an experience of divine-human identity, of the divine nonduality at the core of the person. The experience of a new *koinonia* among Christians is also an experience of divine nonduality; this communion is a participation in the divine communion or unity. The experience of "identity" in baptism is an experience of the nonduality of the "beginning," of the root or ground, the Source, the Father, while the experience of communion in love can be understood as an experience of the "end," the final fulfillment in the Holy Spirit.[39] We may speak of these two aspects of our participation in divine nonduality as *radical* and *interpersonal,* respectively.

I think that Abhishiktananda has located the decisive point of contact between Hinduism and Christianity, the point at which the central contemplative experience of the Vedanta meets the divine identity of Jesus—which is communicated to us in baptism. While the French monk's insight is deeper and more revolutionary, he tends to absolutize this experience of "initial nonduality" at the expense of an integral Christian theological vision. Bede Griffiths maintains a better balance, though in cautiously excluding a Christian nonduality of identity, he rejects a key that will prove extremely fruitful for the revisioning of Christian theology and spirituality in a unitive perspective. While the question of a Christian nonduality finds a partial resolution at this point of baptismal identity, it remains still far from closed. There will remain for us to consider, later in our study, the relation of nonduality to incarnation.[40]

4. Baptismal Initiation: Point of Contact with the East and Pivot of Identity

I propose, then, that the first pivotal meeting point of Hindu Vedanta (or, in different terms, of Buddhism) with Christianity is to be found in bringing together the realization of the nondual Self (or, paradoxically, of *Sunyata* or *Satori*) and baptismal initiation. This becomes evident when we consider our question in the light of the New Testament, where our beginning is to be found. The Vedantin doctrine of nonduality and of the nondual Self is a teaching about the beginning, after all: a beginning in which reality is still undifferentiated, one. In the biblical tradition, God is One (Deut 6:4; Mark 12:29). In the New Testament, God and creation, God and humanity become one in Jesus Christ. This oneness, then, is transmitted to us in our baptism.

> There is one body and one Spirit, just as you were called to the one hope that belongs to your call, one Lord, one faith, one baptism, one God and Father of us all, who is above all and through all and in all. (Eph 4:4-6)

While the Gospels and letters of the New Testament contain many different teachings, the whole of this revelation concludes in a single communication of divine life through the death and resurrection of Jesus and the gift of the Holy Spirit, which is received by the believing person in baptism. Jesus makes this simplicity and unity of the gift very clear in his response to Nicodemus, the Pharisee who seeks him out. He has come to communicate not this or that teaching but the gift of new life.

> Jesus answered him, "Truly, truly, I say to you, unless one is born anew, he cannot see the kingdom of God." Nicodemus said to him, "How can a man be born when he is old? Can he enter a second time into his mother's womb and be born?" Jesus answered, "Truly, truly, I say to you, unless one is born of water and the Spirit, he cannot enter the kingdom of God." (John 3:3-5)

Here we step back from the analytical faculty psychology which we have inherited from the Greek philosophical tradition and from St. Augustine; it is the *whole person* that is reborn.

At the beginning of Mark's Gospel we encounter the baptism of Jesus by John in the Jordan (1:9-11)) and in the scene that originally concluded that Gospel (16:1-8) we are present at the tomb, within which the women find a young man clothed in white. Beginning and end are chiastically related; this symmetry identifies the empty tomb with Jesus' baptism. Since, in the early rite of Christian baptism the font was often identified with the tomb of Jesus and the newly baptized person was clad in a white garment, the meaning of Mark's very deliberate structural symmetry is this: Christian baptism is an immersion, a participation, in the baptism of Jesus (as well as in his death and resurrection), and in this rite of initiation the believer is identified with Jesus himself.

> Do you not know that all of us who have been baptized into Christ Jesus were baptized into his death? We were buried therefore with him by baptism into death, so that as Christ was raised from the dead by the glory of the Father, we too might walk in newness of life. For if we have been united with him in a death like his, we shall certainly be united with him in a resurrection like his. (Rom 6:3-5)

I believe that the same baptismal meaning is concealed beneath the surface of John's Gospel. It is a very striking and curious fact that the Fourth Gospel contains no account of Jesus' institution of the eucharist and no narrative of his baptism. Instead, we find a full five chapters of supper narrative, which consists mostly of Jesus' discourse and his prayer, and we encounter at the beginning of the Gospel a long prologue resembling a liturgical hymn. Rather than excluding the sacramental dimension of Jesus' story, the author of this Gospel is translating it from literal language into *sapiential* language. John's supper narrative expresses the eucharistic reality in terms of its actualization within the disciples: indwelling, communion of life, new birth, and a participation in the divine oneness. John's prologue (into which two narrative verses about John the Baptist are crosswoven as interpretive clues) expresses the baptismal reality as a communication of light and life, grace and truth, fullness and the knowledge of God, by joining, in its rhythmic, circular language, the baptismal experience of the disciple with the event of Jesus' baptism.

> But to all who received him, who believed in his name, he gave power to become children of God; who were born, not of blood nor of the will of the flesh nor of the will of man, but of God. And the Word became flesh and dwelt among us, full of grace and truth; we have beheld his glory, glory as of the only Son from the Father. . . . And from his fullness have we all received, grace upon grace. For the law was given through Moses; grace and truth came through Jesus Christ. No one has ever seen God; the only Son, who is in the bosom of the Father, he has made him known. (John 1:12-14, 16-18)

John's Gospel opens up to us its unitive inner meaning when we read it in the light of this baptismal event with which it begins. To the prologue, understood in this way, are related many other elements in John: particularly the "I am" statements of Jesus and the conclusive unitive affirmations of the supper narrative in chaps. 13 to 17.[41]

It is here that we see the depth and power of Abhishiktananda's insight on the relation of the nonduality of the Vedanta—*advaita*—to the baptism of Jesus and to Christian baptism. Our new birth, the birth into our truest, deepest identity, is an awakening to the divine nonduality, to our being in God, our birth and life in the Only-begotten of God. It is at this point, also (though he rarely mentions baptism) that the nondual consciousness which shines out again and again in Meister Eckhart's writings finds its theological center.[42]

Asian spiritual teachers have recognized this nondual consciousness in Meister Eckhart.[43] Many centuries before Abhishiktananda's theological enlightenment, the German master realized that the primordial contemplative experience is the experience of our immersion in the one divine birth. Such is the radical importance of this point for Christian theology and spirituality that we may speak of a revolutionary *pivot of identity* which brings us to the center of a new Christian wisdom. While the new being of baptismal initiation is the basis of the New Testament and of the early patristic writings, it is hardly mentioned in most of our traditional spiritual literature.

It is important to remember that here we are concerned with the baptism of *adults*, not of infants. In the early church, people were baptized only when they were of an age to make a conscious and deliberate act of faith—to know what they were embracing—and able to have a personal experience of illumination. The sense of baptismal new birth gradually faded with the rise of a Platonist Christian theology, with the monastic insistence on progress through *praxis*, with the practice of infant baptism and, in the West, with the prevalence of an Augustinian anthropology in which the "new person" was hardly reflected.

The Centrality of Baptism in the New Testament

The Gospels and other New Testament texts were written in the light of the resurrection of Jesus, we are often told today. The light of the resurrection, however, is the light of the baptismal experience in which Jesus' resurrection was experienced personally by the believer. John's Gospel and first letter are flooded with the light of the baptismal experience: the one, unifying white light. The prologue of John's Gospel is a baptismal text, which occupies the place of the baptism of Jesus at the beginning of Mark's Gospel.

Paul presupposes the baptismal experience in those to whom he writes. The new being which they have received is the basis, again and again, of his instruction.

> For it is the God who said, "Let light shine out of darkness," who has shone in our hearts to give the light of the knowledge of the glory of God in the face of Christ. (2 Cor 4:6)

> Let me ask you only this: Did you receive the Spirit by works of the law, or by hearing with faith? Are you so foolish? Having begun with the Spirit, are you now ending with the flesh? (Gal 3:2-3)

> For as many of you as were baptized into Christ have put on Christ. There is neither Jew nor Greek, there is neither slave nor free, there is neither male nor female; for you are all one in Christ Jesus. (Gal 3:27-28)

If we find in the baptismal event our primary meeting point with the Asian spiritual traditions, we immediately discover at that point a divergence as well. This corresponds to the difference between the atemporal or transtemporal nonduality at the core of the Eastern wisdoms and the nondual or unitive *event* of Christ. In the Jesus of the New Testament we can imagine the intersection of two perpendicular axes[44] corresponding to the biblical and the Asian traditions: history and realization, relationship and identity, transcendence and immanence, or in Pauline terms, power and wisdom (1 Cor 1:22-25). The two dimensions become inseparably fused in Christ and in his continuing presence in the world. The one unitive event, after his resurrection, becomes a dynamism within the church and the world.

The two dimensions of the unitive event of Christ—vertical and horizontal, unity and history, identity and dynamism, beginning and unfolding, are reproduced everywhere in Christian life; indeed, human life has always been woven from them.[45] The two axes of the cross are implicit in Jesus' great double commandment of total love of God and equal love of neighbor (Mark 12:29-31)—a commandment that can only be fulfilled through that participation of divine life which is conferred in baptism.

The importance of this reality of our theological identity with Jesus cannot be exaggerated: this is the secret of the New Testament which is only understood when it is experienced—normally in baptismal initiation—after Jesus' death and resurrection and the gift of the Spirit. It is particularly in early Syrian Christianity that the "identity" between Jesus' baptism and the baptism of Christians is conserved,[46] but it has been almost completely forgotten in Western Christianity since patristic times. Our relationship with Jesus, like our relationship with God, is twofold: dualistic and intentional (i.e., "relational" as usually understood), on the one hand, but nondual and purely interior, on the other. Corresponding to this double relationship are the two great currents of mysticism which Evelyn Underhill identified in Christian tradition: "intimate-personal" and "transcendental-metaphysical."[47]

5. Theological Corollaries of the Principle of Nondual Baptismal identity

With the principle of nondual baptismal identity, we have arrived at the theological center, the essential connective focus and generative point of our Eastern turn. The further aspects and implications of Christian nonduality that we shall discuss flow from this baptismal identity—the pivotal "illumination"—as its corollaries. Each of them will be introduced briefly now and then unfolded more amply in the following sections.

I. The principle of unitive identity breaks through the dualistic theological container which had prevailed in both the Catholic and the Protestant traditions of Western Christianity. II. We awaken to a unitive interpretation of the *Christ-mystery* (an inclusive Christology) in which our theological vision is an expression of our own participation in the mystery. III. The *New Testament,* similarly opened to interpretation in the light of baptismal identity, takes on a new depth and immediacy. IV. From this understanding of the mystery in its New Testament expressions unfolds a *new sapiential theology* which is centered in the same unitive principle, now become explicit. V. Central to this sapiential theology is a *unitive anthropology,* a view of the human person which is grounded in our identification with Jesus, the incarnate Word of God. VI. It is implicit in this baptismal identity with the divine-human Jesus that the *fullness is present at the beginning.* This has revolutionary consequences for theology and spirituality. VII. The *shape of Christian life* is determined by this identity with Jesus, this initial fullness. We discover that the pattern of life is a movement from an original, seminal fullness to a mature fullness: from baptism to eucharist. VIII. Christian *contemplative experience* is similarly understood in terms of baptismal identity. IX. Finally, *history* itself—and in a special way the history of the "West" since the time of Christ—can be interpreted in terms of the unitive awakening and self-realization of the human person and of humanity as a whole.

Before continuing, we must face a major difficulty. The reader may find it difficult to accept this close relationship between the utterly convincing nonduality of the Asian traditions—as, for instance, an experience of the simple all-comprehending Absolute, in the unitive depths of the Self—and the Christian nonduality that I am proposing—often beyond personal experience and requiring faith, while too readily enclosed within forms and modalities and apparently submitting itself to theological articulation, perhaps even to domestication.

First of all, my assertion is qualified. I shall not propose that the two nondualities are identical but that they share a common element, even a common structure, which is based upon the common structure of the human person with its transcendent (unitive) core or ground.

Second, I shall continue to speak in the language of "as if": it is "as if" there were a continuum of nondual reality in the mystery and event of Christ, which differs from the Asian nonduality in assuming both form and movement (though in this way sometimes approaching an Asian nondual conception such as the Tao). My essential point is that the notion of nonduality opens Christianity to an inner continuum which is central to the New Testament and to a sapiential understanding of the event of Christ as it unfolds first in the New Testament and then in the lives of individuals, of the church and of humanity as a whole in the time that follows the event of Christ.

At the same time, the historical actuality of Christ brings about ("as if" once again) a transformation in the divine nonduality, so that it becomes manifest in the dimensions of form, of movement, and of matter. It is "as if" the divine nonduality has become incarnate, embodied in Christ, and continues to embody itself in those who live "in him." The body of Christ of which Paul writes is an embodiment of the divine nonduality in this world.

If we seem to emigrate from (the Asian) *experience* to (a Western and Christian) theological *conceptualization,* we do not leave nondual experience behind: it is to be found in the experience of baptismal initiation and then in the contemplative experiences of Christians. The central point for Christians is not experience, however—important as this may be, particularly as initiation to the mystery—but rather the new *reality,* the widening continuum of divine self-communication and of immanent divinity in the human person and in humanity. The reason for the conceptualization, for the theology, is this new *reality* which corresponds to the event of Christ and which continues in history as the unfolding and widening nondual event.

The experiential vividness and immediacy of the Asian nondual experience has often been present in the experience of baptismal initiation but with modalities of its own, as we see in the Acts of the Apostles and other early Christian texts. The experience must disappear, however—"the seed must fall into the ground"—so that the new reality can be appropriated by the individual in an active and truly personal (and unitive) way: that is, *by faith* (see John 20:29). In faith, the person continues to relate directly to the nondual reality not in the brilliant light of nondual consciousness but in a darkness and poverty that is the matrix of spiritual growth. The manifestations of this growth are precisely in the action of faith, hope, and love, or *fontality.* This, then, is how nonduality—imagined as the experience of *advaita, Atman,* of "the uncarved block," of *satori*—is manifest as it comes newly into this world in Christ.

6. (I) Breaking Through the Container of Dualistic Christianity

In our turn to the East, we arrive at a *pivot of identity,* which has revolutionary consequences for every dimension of our Christian life. The change in perspective is extreme for a Western Christianity that has moved very far from the all-comprehending unitive mystery of Christ, revealed in the New Testament, into a dualistic religious consciousness. In recent centuries Western Christians had come more and more to conceive of God as outside and above themselves; Catholics understood their relationship with God to be largely mediated by the authoritative institutional church. Under the influence of a one-sided interpretation of St. Augustine's doctrine, we had come to think of ourselves as relating to God over a great distance, with the church above us in the position of a divine and supernatural mediator, an extension of the divine incarnation, transmitting the grace of God to us. Divine union, if attained, was to be experienced as the fruit of a life of holiness, rather than as the initial gift of identity in Christ.

Now we discover, as did the first Christians, that God is within us, one with our very being, our self. Not only do we have a personal relationship with God in and through Christ but a union—even an identity—with Christ and thereby with God. Through baptism, we are originally one with God in Jesus Christ: here is the core of Christianity. Nothing stands between us and God but our own blindness and our own resistances. Though we are still in darkness much of the time, nevertheless we are light all of the time: at our core we have become one with the divine light shining in the darkness. At the point of meeting and fusion between West and East in the event of Christ, human existence and its history join identity, nonduality. The two—history and nonduality, or history and spirit—have become one in Jesus, and then they are one in ourselves: for we too are the divine incarnation, the body of Christ.

The Hebraic biblical tradition had always been centered in an emphatically dualistic relationship with God; this relationship and the covenant which solemnized it defined Jewish religious identity. In Jesus and in the New Testament, a vertical axis of unitive immediacy cuts across the horizontal axis of relationship (as well as the horizontal of a concrete historical journey) to produce the unique theological figure that we have discovered in our sapiential awakening.[48] In Jesus himself, in his church, and in each of his disciples, these two axes intersect. At every moment Christian life is the meeting place of divine immediacy and of history. Our being-with-God is at once relationship and identity, dual and nondual.

It can easily seem, however, that the unitive event of the New Testament was only a brief interruption in a consistently dualistic Judaeo-Christian religious tradition. Through the centuries, the unitive element in Christianity has regularly been suppressed by the dualistic element, embodied in the structures of institution, of worship, and of theology. It is our encounter with the Asian traditions today—in the decompressed atmosphere of Vatican II—that awakens us to the unitive core of the mystery of Christ—and consequently of Christian life and worship.

The balance in Christianity between duality and nonduality, between relationship and identity, though delicate, is at the same time maintained by the invincible coherent force of the person of Christ. It is not a theological subtlety but the essential inner structure of Christian life. It is of great importance that this inner structure be brought to light today and that this two-sided truth be expressed with courage and persistence. We cannot afford to allow the unitive light to be quenched once again and to return to the religious status of humanity—Jewish or Gentile—before the coming of Christ. The precious new freedom on which Paul insists with such vehemence in writing to the Christians of Galatia (Gal 4:1-9; 5:1-13) is the existential manifestation of nondual identity.

7. (II) Unitive Interpretation of the Christ-mystery

We awaken to a unitive interpretation of the Christ-mystery: an inclusive Christology which is an expression of our own participation in the mystery. In our first movement, we recovered a sapiential vision centered in the mystery of Christ. We can already sense a certain resonance or a tendency toward convergence with our second movement, the Eastern turn, as we see a simple, unified theological vision replacing the complex, compartmentalized structure of post-Reformation Catholic theology. As a partitioned rational structure gives way to a single theological organism—intrinsically one though mysteriously so—we sense the presence of a strong unitive force, a unitive principle. It is this unitive principle that, in Christ, draws together and holds together all reality.

> . . . for in him all things were created, in heaven and on earth, visible and invisible, whether thrones or dominions or principalities or authorities—all things were created through him and for him. He is before all things, and in him all things hold together. . . . For in him all the fullness of God was pleased to dwell, and through him to reconcile to himself all things, whether on earth or in heaven, making peace by the blood of his cross. (Col 1:16-17, 19-20)

Sapiential theology develops in the unitive light; its body is held together by the gravitational force of divine unity. Early in the sapiential awakening of the twentieth century, Emile Mersch, while still writing in the language of Thomistic scholasticism, insisted again and again on the essential unitive character of the mystery.

> The whole of Christianity is unity. And it has to be if the intellect is to point out what, in Christianity, is its essence. Christianity is the taking up of the universe of mankind into the unity of God through the unity of Christ. The science that explains Christianity, theology, must give expression to this tendency toward unity. It will be more truly itself, it

> will be more truly a science and the science of Christianity, in proportion as it resolves itself systematically, energetically, and exclusively into unity.[49]

The Second Vatican Council defines the church in terms of this unity:

> . . . the Church, in Christ, is in the nature of a sacrament—a sign and instrument, that is, of communion with God and of union among all [people]. . . .[50]

The unitive light, therefore, is the interpretive principle that opens the mystery of Christ to its deepest and fullest meaning. The unity which is the mystery of Christ lies beneath the surface of the four movements of our present journey. We shall find each dimension, each unfolding and manifestation of this mystery, to be characterized by a profound unity—but each differently.

8. (III) Unitive Interpretation of the New Testament

Since the New Testament is the immediate and primary literary expression of the mystery of Christ, it is pervaded by this unitive principle. The unitive principle is a primary interpretive key to its writings, though a key which has been ignored during the past two centuries of historical-critical biblical exegesis in the West. It is urgent that, along with the symbolic and literary interpretive approaches, the unitive hermeneutic principle be recovered today.

This principle is itself revealed in the New Testament. Unitive understanding is a gift to those who believe and are baptized. It is a fruit of the baptismal anointing with the Holy Spirit. Intrinsic to this understanding is the inner personal affirmation which is faith; it is not accessible to rational study alone. The Baptist had announced Jesus as the one who was to baptize not just with water but with the Holy Spirit. In his first letter, John reassures the baptized that they have within themselves a fullness of knowledge which is adequate to any need that may confront them. The "anointing"—the New Testament word carries baptismal resonances—is also "what you heard from the beginning." Gospel and initiation are experienced as a single reality within the believer. Here, as elsewhere, the Christian experience is a one-pointed experience, centered in the awakening of a new self.

> But you have been anointed by the Holy One, and you all know. I write to you, not because you do not know the truth, but because you know

> it, and know that no lie is of the truth. . . . Let what you heard from the beginning abide in you. If what you heard from the beginning abides in you, then you will abide in the Son and in the Father. And this is what he has promised us, eternal life . . . but the anointing which you received from him abides in you, and you have no need that any one should teach you; as his anointing teaches you about everything, and is true, and is no lie, just as it has taught you, abide in him. (1 John 2:20-21, 24-25, 27)

It is in baptism that the believer enters into the unity which is the mystery (or body) of Christ; the gift of unitive understanding is a participatory consciousness of the mystery.

> There is one body and one Spirit, just as you were called to the one hope that belongs to your call, one Lord, one faith, *one baptism,* one God and Father of us all, who is above all and through all and in all. (Eph 4:4-6)

In this baptismal gift of unity, as in the Christ-event, two axes can be distinguished: the vertical dimension of union with God and the horizontal dimension of communion with other human persons. Sometimes both of these dimensions are clearly evident in a single text.

> Now before faith came, we were confined under the law, kept under restraint until faith should be revealed. So that the law was our custodian until Christ came, that we might be justified by faith. But now that faith has come, we are no longer under a custodian; for in Christ Jesus *you are all [children] of God,* through faith. For as many of you as were baptized into Christ have put on Christ. There is neither Jew nor Greek, there is neither slave nor free, there is neither male nor female; for you are *all one in Christ Jesus.* (Gal 3:23-28)

The Pauline and Johannine writings are the great sapiential texts of the New Testament. John's Gospel and first letter continually invite unitive interpretation. The Pauline letters—most particularly those to the Colossians and to the Ephesians[51]—frequently begin with an exposition of the unitive mystery of Christ—a recalling of the gift that has been received—and then go on to unfold the moral and social implications of the gift of a new identity in Christ. Sometimes the unitive mystery will be proposed at the very beginning of a New Testament text, in a prologue, a kind of hermeneutic eye, through which the entire writing is to be read (see Heb 1:1-4; John 1:1-18; 1 John 1:1-3).

The unitive reality manifests itself in a variety of forms in the New Testament writings. Baptismal initiation, first of all, is an awakening to the unitive reality, and very often in the New Testament—especially where the unitive radiance is strong—baptismal experience is in the background, more or less consciously present to the writer even when it is not explicitly mentioned. Scholars have found that many New Testament texts have one or another functional relation to the baptismal event and context: as baptismal hymns, catecheses, and homilies. Baptism initiates, second, a new unitive participation in Christ, in the one body of Christ, from which derives Paul's preferred expressions for the new Christian reality: "in Christ," "in him." Third, a new communion between the disciples, the sacred *koinonia* and the *agape*, or spiritual love, in which this communion finds expression, is the immediate expression of the gift of Christ. This new *koinonia* is the heart of the church; one may even say that it *is* the church. Fourth, we find in the New Testament writings (particularly those ascribed to John and Paul) a new unitive knowledge (or *gnosis*) of God, of Christ, of the Christ-mystery. Finally, eucharistic participation is the moment of ritual actualization of the new *koinonia*.

As we read, we may find ourselves moving from a more or less objective seeking of unitive reality in the New Testament to a *personal* unitive experience. That is how the scriptural word functions. The New Testament is anything but an abstract textbook on unitive reality or knowledge; it is often, however, a *mystagogy*: an initiation into unitive experience. If we set out to find unitive reality in the New Testament, we must expect ultimately to know it less as an objective concept than as the very reality-density of our reading of these Scriptures. It will be manifest in our own resonance with the word, in our progressive union with the word, our personal unity realized in contact with the word: as our own assimilation to the One.

The unitive principle, ultimately, is God. Most immediately it is my self, the "first person." Mediately it is the Word, it is Christ, and it is the Holy Spirit. Historically and developmentally, it is the Christ-event, the Christ-mystery. Morally and spiritually, it is faith and hope and love, which can be understood as a single dynamism: *fontality*. We can apply the unitive principle to the New Testament from each of these perspectives.

It is sometimes appropriate to think of the entire New Testament (both Testaments, in fact) as a single, complex, and organic word. This is typical of the wisdom tradition of Christianity. In a typical passage from one of the church fathers, or from Bernard or William of St. Thierry, or even from John of the Cross, we find the writer taking biblical texts from everywhere rather than remaining within the confines of a single author, a single book. He seems to be giving rein to free association, sometimes digressing but usually pursuing a single point through widely different texts. This can be especially disconcerting when we find a writer invoking a Psalm verse to explain an affirmation of Paul or a Gospel passage.

The *Word* is *one:* the Old and New Testaments are one word, and the New Testament is one word. This principle must be applied with discretion, for the Scripture also says *many* things. But we can think of the New Testament as a single energy field, the global field of the Spirit. And we can imagine each text—sometimes even each word—as emanating its own little energy field around itself, as the aura or soul of the word. We can think of these little energy fields overlapping, interacting, joining and parting, resonating and engaging, fusing and multiplying. This is what we experience as we journey through the various New Testament texts: a continual series of interactions and permutations within the one great organism and energy field of the Word. Today this may be called not only an organic model but a systems model or a network model or a holographic model. While none of these metaphors perfectly renders the reality, each of them complements the others.

Unitive knowing is the *subjective* principle corresponding to the unitive objective principle of the divine Word or Wisdom which has become one with us in Jesus. This knowing is a personal participation, therefore, in the unitive principle not only of knowing but of being (see John 1:3; Col 1:15-17), which is the divine Wisdom. The unitive quality as well is both objective—all things together in this center which is Christ—and subjective—we know this by participation, that is, by union. And this is true because we are "in Christ," one with Christ by virtue of the baptismal event and the baptismal identity. The principle of *identity,* therefore—in both senses of this word—becomes the principle of interpretation.

As the sense of participation diminished in the course of history, this knowing disappeared as well. More precisely it was transformed into an almost entirely dualistic, objective knowing, in which we were only spectators and listeners rather than being—first of all—one with the principle of reality, of truth, of knowing, and of life.

9. (IV) A New Theology Centered in the Explicit Unitive Principle

We can distinguish several phases in the emergence of the unitive principle in the Christian sapiential traditions.

I. The early Christian sapiential theologians, such as Irenaeus, drew especially on the Pauline and Johannine writings and conceived the Christian mystery as the unification of all things in Christ.

> Thus there is one God, the Father, as we have shown, and one Christ Jesus our Lord, who comes in the entire Old Testament and recapitulates all things in himself. But in all things he is also man, a creature of God; therefore he recapitulates man in himself. The invisible is become visible, the incomprehensible is become comprehensible, and the impassible, passible; and the Word is become man, recapitulating all things in himself. Thus, just as he is the first among heavenly and spiritual and invisible things, so also is he first among visible and corporal things. He takes the primacy to himself, and by making himself the head of the Church, he will draw all things to himself at the appointed time.[52]

Here the unity is that of the Word, the *Logos* of John's prologue, while the concept of "recapitulation" in Christ comes from the Letter to the Ephesians (1:10). This is an objective unity.

II. In the early fourteenth century, Dominican theologian Meister Eckhart, under the influence of Neoplatonism, brought the unitive principle to a new level of explicitness. The perspective in which the unity appears has shifted from the objective mystery of Christ to a personal participation in the mystery.

> Man's highest and dearest leave-taking is if he takes leave of God for God. St. Paul left God for God: he left everything that he could get from God, he left everything that God could give him and everything he might receive from God. In leaving these he left God for God, and *then* God was left with him, as God is essentially in Himself, not by way of a reception or a gaining of Himself, but rather in an essentiality which is where God is. He never gave God anything, nor did he receive anything from God: it is a single oneness and a pure union.[53]

III. Today, in our new interaction with the Asian traditions, the unitive principle emerges once again, and with a new explicitness and clarity. This happens more often in the field of spirituality than in that of theology, and hence it is more frequently the subjective participation that is directly in focus. While few professional theologians show any interest in this approach, we have already noted some contemporary efforts to reinterpret Christian mysteries—particularly the Trinity—in the light of nonduality.

As the unitive principle becomes clearly differentiated—from the divine Word, from the Christ-mystery—we can begin to understand the relationship between Christianity and the Asian religious traditions. At the same time our understanding of the basic Christian doctrines of Trinity and incarnation attains a new level of simplicity and clarity. The essentially participatory character of Christian life and of sapiential understanding becomes more clearly evident, the unitive nature of the divine self-communication finds more adequate expression, and the principle of nondual Christian identity assumes its central place in our theological vision. Our theology, while continually in contact with the scriptural expressions of the mystery, is nevertheless freed both from a blind subordination to the biblical word and from captivity to the abstractions imported from the world of Greek philosophy.

Theology comes to life at its core with the simplicity, the immediacy, and the power that we have known in the New Testament. While we continue to develop our verbal interpretations, these continually dissolve and reconstitute in the simple central light of the mystery.

10. (V) Unitive Anthropology

Sapiential theology, as it is reborn today, returns from the impersonal objectivity and compartmentalization of the "theological science" of recent centuries to the participatory unity of the mystery, which is realized both objectively and subjectively. An essential part of the objective expression of the mystery is a unitive anthropology: an understanding of the human person deriving from the person's identification with Jesus, the incarnate Word of God.

Scholars write of a "turn to the subject" in the culture of the modern West, and of an anthropological turn both in modern philosophy and theology.[54] Similarly, we have proposed that the sapiential rebirth that takes place in the light of our contact with the Asian traditions involves a "pivot of identity." After an age of alienation, our attention returns to the human person, to ourselves. While the world becomes centered in the human person and consciousness becomes ever more individualized, however, there has never been less agreement about the nature of the human person. Every conceivable thesis can be heard, and the voices are divergent rather than convergent. Christian sapiential theology has always been both Christocentric and anthropocentric, and its vision of the human person has usually been a composite of biblical affirmations[55] and Greek philosophical structures.[56] In this age of the person, these old images of the person are more inadequate than ever; a new anthropology is needed.

If our sapiential theology is Christocentric and anthropocentric, perhaps our anthropology itself must be both Christocentric and theocentric—but theocentric in a new way, which is discovered in our Eastern turn. Let us consider further this possibility of a unitive, or nondual, anthropology. It would be grounded or centered in the unitive dimension of the human person which we have associated with baptismal initiation and the new identity. This corresponds, in a more universal context, to the True Self, or *Atman,* which we find at the center of Hindu Vedanta (and perhaps, in a paradoxical way—also at the center of Mahayana Buddhism). While the deepest human and Christian identity would be situated at the level of this unitive self, the deep unitive self would not constitute the totality of the human person—as it sometimes seems to do in the Asian traditions.

We shall, as we proceed through our Western turn and our global turn, discover further essential dimensions of the person which are related to bodily existence on Earth, to historical existence, to human relationship and communion, and to the unity of all of humanity.

Let us, at this point, establish more firmly two basic elements or levels of the human self, which correspond to our second and first movements, respectively:

1. The nondual or unitive or theocentric level, at which the person participates in the absolute oneness of God. The person, therefore, is one, and in this oneness is "capable of all reality." Here is the fundamental metaphysical principle of human knowledge, as developed in scholastic philosophy, but as a "transcendental" it pervades not only the life of the intellect but all human life, love, relationship, freedom, and activity. This principle is expressed (in terms of *Atman, advaita, satori, sunyata, nirvana,* etc.) both in Hindu Vedanta and in Buddhism, and also in the epistemology of Thomas Aquinas and, as we have seen, in the transcendental anthropology of Karl Rahner.[57]

2. The Christic level, at which the primal unity is differentiated and embodied, according to the pattern of the mystery of Christ. In chap. 2 (our first movement of sapiential awakening to that mystery, in section 7) and again in this chap. 3 (section 1, iii above), we have briefly observed the unfolding of the Christ-mystery in four dimensions (or two axes) corresponding to the figure—or "mystery"—of the cross.

The ultimate basis of Christian anthropology—as Karl Rahner has insisted again and again[58]—is Jesus Christ, who is the beginning (as divine creative Word) and the end (as the eschatological "whole Christ" or Mystical Body) of human existence. Both of the levels or basic dimensions that we have proposed for our anthropology relate immediately to the *identity with Christ* which originates in baptismal initiation. This identity is a primary expression of nonduality. In these two levels, therefore, we have the principle of unity and the principle of unfolding or differentiation of the mystery of the human person. From this basic mystery—at the level of oneness or nonduality—originate the more perceptible and rationally tractable elements of the person.

We have spoken already of the unitive identity which is realized in the baptismal event, and we have observed that the existence which expresses this identity has two principal dimensions. The vertical component is a fundamental unity with God in Christ; the horizontal component is a unity (communion) with other human beings—and particularly with other baptized persons—in Christ.[59] At this point the matter may appear to have become rather neatly systematized, and we must insist once again on the quality of *mystery* that belongs not only to God but to the human person as image of God. Olivier Clement distinguishes, in the human being, between *person* and *nature.* Person is transcendent, undefinable. We can ask of a nature, What is it?

> The person, however, goes beyond all questions. It cannot be defined, it cannot be captured by conceptual thought.
>
> The person, says Lossky, is "the irreducibility of the individual to his human nature," the person is irreducible. . . . The only approach to the mystery of the living God is by means of "negative" theology, which denies all possibility of limiting God to the capacity of our thoughts. And the only approach to the created person is through a "negative" anthropology. . . . To know something of the mystery of the person we must go right beyond its natural context, beyond its cosmic, collective, and individual environment, beyond all the ways in which it can be grasped by the mind. Whatever the mind can grasp can only be the nature, never the person. The mind can grasp only objects, whatever is open to inspection. But the person is not an object open to inspection, any more than God is. Like God it is incomparable, inextinguishable, fathomless.
>
> Individuals may be classified or grouped. But the person is always unique. It breaks groups apart, it is itself a breach in the universe. . . . The person, set by its very brilliance beyond the reach of rational analysis, is revealed in love. . . . knowing a person is unknowing, the darkness of night made luminous by love. [60]

Karl Rahner defines the human person as "the question to which there is no answer."[61]

The converse of this negative anthropology—as with a negative theology—is the *unitive* character of the human person. This nonduality of the human being finds its most absolute expression in the *Atman,* or Self, of the Upanishads. Clément has pointed out the "impersonality" of this Self which has been realized by a virtual withdrawal from terrestrial existence into the divine Absolute. We find something similar in Buddhism, despite its professed denial of the reality of such a self. Thomas Merton's True Self can be understood as a modern Western equivalent of this Asian absolute Self. It becomes clear from the body of Merton's writings, however, that the "person" at the center of his thought[62] is intensely alive in this present world.

Patristic and medieval Christian anthropology was constructed largely on the basis of the principle that the human person is created in the image and likeness of God (Gen 1:26-27). We cannot review here the various interpretations of this "image." Later in this book we will consider other aspects of the human person; at this point I suggest that we provisionally understand the person as the "image" of the One: of the transcendent God who is beyond conceptual definition and who is the ground and fullness of all created being.

I have mentioned the transcendental anthropology of Karl Rahner more than once.[63] Rahner has been a leader both in returning to Catholic theology its transcendent dimension (its continual, immediate encounter with God as "mystery") and in recentering theology in the human person (in anthropology).[64] Further, among contemporary theological views of the human person, it is Rahner's anthropology that seems most adequately to integrate this fundamental unitive level of the person which corresponds to our Eastern turn and to the specifically contemplative aspect of a sapiential theology. In this view, the transcendence or unitive openness of the human person is the ground and basis of every significant human experience and action.

> Man's power to know and love, assent and consent, grasps particular being against the background of being in general; thus all its particularized knowledge is implicitly based on the unthematic awareness it also has of Being *simpliciter,* which includes an awareness—however inarticulate—of God, spirit, and freedom and thus of the mystery above us and within us. Consequently the transcendentality of the human spirit is the essential foundation of the person, of responsibility, of religious experience (including mysticism), and of the possibility of God's self-communication in grace and revelation.[65]

In Rahner's bipolar view of the human person, this transcendent dimension is balanced by a "categorial" dimension of embodied, historical existence.[66] The human person lives in a concrete physical body, in the present moment of history.[67] The fact that God's word is heard historically is the basis of this historicity of the person. It is evident in the susceptibility of individuals to their environment, in their sexual and social nature, in the fundamental unity of the human race, in the nature of existence as a struggle, and in "the historical relativity and irretrievable unicity" of each person's situation.[68]

These two fundamental dimensions—transcendent and historical—of the human person and of personal existence may be imagined as two axes, vertical and horizontal, corresponding to the cruciform representation of the Christ-mystery that we have proposed. The two axes correspond as well to the "spirit and history" of patristic sapiential theology.[69]

11. (VI) Fullness at the Beginning

It is implicit in the Christian's baptismal identity with Jesus that the divine fullness is newly present in us from the moment of our initiation. The consequences for our understanding of Christian life are revolutionary.

In the Asian traditions, the spiritual journey often resembles a return to an original fullness. This pattern continues in the Christian West, in Neoplatonic currents of spiritual theology where the history of salvation is seen as a great *exitus-reditus.* Christians look back to a fullness in the time of the New Testament: the divine plenitude came into the world in Christ and was poured into humanity (see John 1:16; Col 2:9-10). When the early Christians received the Holy Spirit in baptism, the fullness of life and light that they experienced became for them the permanent measure of their new identity and the ideal to which they sought to conform their lives (Rom 8:1-17; Gal 3:2-5; 5:16-24).

In Christian life too, then, a fullness is present at the beginning. This is not the final fullness, and yet it is in organic continuity with it, already containing it as the seed contains the mature plant or the child contains the adult person. The gift is present, though not yet unfolded, not yet wedded to its world, not yet expanded to the other fullness that is realized freedom. If I insist on this point, it is because Western Christians have long been the victims of a subtle, disabling theft of identity, experienced as alienation and evacuation of self. It is this theft—or fall—to which our Eastern turn responds. Our argument hinges on this point: the fullness is yourself, what you are in Christ and in God. To know this in actuality is freedom. This is the gift of God, who is "not envious."

The history of Christian spirituality, as we distill it from the spiritual literature, can seem to resemble a series of mountain peaks, of ascending paths, of ladders. In most of this literature baptism is rarely mentioned, and the new creation which is the baptized person is practically forgotten. "Divinization" and the initial fullness have disappeared from view, and the spiritual journey is an upward climb from a fallen state of humanity toward union with God. This is the picture of the spiritual life that we have long been accustomed to in the Western (Catholic) tradition, but it is also common in Eastern Christianity strongly influenced by Platonism.

In the revolution that Jesus initiated, the towers and the ladders of the old order have been demolished—only to be rebuilt, again and again in the course of the centuries, by his disciples. This regression usually takes place when the structures of a contemporary—and often a prevalent—culture replace the intrinsic structure of Christian life. An aristocratic anthropology creates a hierarchical order of spirit or intellect, and of a life of contemplation or *gnosis,* above body and psyche and ordinary human existence. The earliest and most notorious occurrence of this distortion was in Christian Gnosticism. Subsequent verticalizing movements took place under the influence of Platonism and Neoplatonism. We can see this distortion emerging in the writings of Origen, the great Alexandrian Platonist, as Christian life begins to be interpreted as an ascending movement from body to psyche to *nous,* or contemplative intellect. At the same time, invariably, the individual spiritual life begins to be conceived in isolation from community and from history.

This whole tendency will be carried further in the writings of the monastic theologians of the medieval West. The image of Jacob's ladder (Gen 28:10-22) comes to preside over the tradition of spiritual theology. Examples of these ascending ladders have appeared earlier in this book: the scheme of the four senses of Scripture and Guigo's "ladder of contemplatives."[70] While this ascending paradigm may seem to conform—at least for awhile—to personal experience, and while it has some pedagogical value, it invites the unwary to replace the dynamism of the Christ-event—both simple and subtle in its immediacy and fullness—with a flat and linear arithmetical formula, and to replace the divine agency of grace with a program of human efforts.

It is a typical implication of the revolutionary unitive principle—of Jesus' revolution, in short—that in the light of the initial fullness of baptismal illumination, we discover a reversal of the two parallel schemes: the four senses of Scripture and the ladder of contemplatives. In the mysteries of Christian initiation, the spiritual life begins with a great illumination, which corresponds both to the mystical (or anagogical) sense of Scripture and to *contemplatio,* the fourth rung of Guigo's ladder. It is in the light of this initiatory experience, then, that the spectrum of scriptural meanings opens up and that one descends the ladder from interior experience to an illuminated reading of the scriptural text and to concrete action in the world.

Scholars have noted that the traditional order of the senses of Scripture is reflected to some degree in the history of theology and spirituality.[71] In a first phase, Christian theologians occupy themselves with the objective allegorical or doctrinal elucidation of the mystery of Christ in the Scriptures, and when this work has been completed, spiritual theologians proceed to elaborate the subjective tropological or moral overtones of the biblical mystery. We can imagine this succession of phases continuing, in the thirteenth and fourteenth centuries, when the work of the great twelfth-century Cistercian spiritual theologians has concluded and a new realization of anagogy bursts forth with the unitive consciousness that appears incipiently in Thomas Aquinas and then more fully and explicitly in the Beguine mystics[72] and in Meister Eckhart. At this moment, once again, a graduated pedagogy gives way to the fullness and immediacy of the baptismal mystery. The lamp is placed once again on its lampstand. Our Western history since the attainment of that metaphysical summit can be imagined as a long incarnational descent into the human world. Between the lingering influence of ascending theological constructions and the spiritual darkening of the modern West, however, it has become very difficult to recover an understanding of the place of this unitive divine light in our Christian life. Inevitably, from time to time we find ourselves lost in the obscurity of our modern lowland or under the returning shadow of the towers of the old order, and we lose touch with our innermost identity. The undivided light can be found once again turning to the Gospels or to the letters of Paul, who never tires of preaching the freedom that is the obverse of this simple, all-comprehending unity of the baptismal gift.

> But you are not to be called rabbi, for you have one teacher, and you are all [brothers and sisters]. And call no man your father on earth, for you have one Father, who is in heaven. Neither be called masters, for you have one master, the Christ. (Matt 23:8-10)

> See to it that no one makes a prey of you by philosophy and empty deceit, according to human tradition, according to the elemental spirits of the universe, and not according to Christ. For in him the whole fullness of deity dwells bodily, and you have come to fullness of life in him, who is the head of all rule and authority. (Col 2:8-10)

12. (VII) The Trajectory of Life: From Baptism to Eucharist

The presence of the fullness at the beginning deconstructs the human paradigms of ascent, as we have seen, and from this initial fullness Christian life emerges, gradually manifesting an intrinsic form of its own. This pattern can be deduced from the life of Jesus, which began formally when he heard the voice from heaven declaring, "You are my beloved son," and the Holy Spirit descended upon him at his baptism in the Jordan. Jesus' public life unfolds from this starting point until his death on the cross and the sacramental expression of that death. To Jesus' death on the cross correspond the last supper and his institution of the eucharist. We can understand his life sacramentally, then, as proceeding from baptism to eucharist.

What is the existential significance of these two sacramental events? At his baptism, Jesus received (not only symbolically) the plenitude of the Spirit, the anointing that he needed for his mission, which was about to begin. Symbolically, he received at this moment, his sonship, his divinity. His life of ministry was an embodiment of this divine light, as he communicated light and life to those who came to him. As his life was coming to its end, on the night that he was arrested, he instituted the eucharist, in which his body and blood were ritually shared with his disciples. This sacramental action is the ritual equivalent of his death and resurrection, I believe: cross and eucharist—tree of life and bread of life—are two expressions of the same event, the same transmission of life to humanity.

The life of a Christian can be understood theologically as following the same pattern from baptismal sunrise to eucharistic sunset; from the receiving of the divine gift of Self in baptismal initiation through a life of service to the final gift of self in death. In the martyrs of the early church, the pattern is clearly manifest. Often the martyr's death was understood eucharistically.[73]

The continuity between the baptismal beginning and the eucharistic end of such a life can itself be interpreted in unitive terms. Corresponding to the totality of the gift of divine-human identity in baptism is the totality of the gift of self that is constituted by a eucharistic life and eucharistic death according to Jesus' words, "the Son of Man also came not to be served but to serve, and to give his life . . . for many" (Mark 10:45). Through the witness of such a life and/or death, the spark of faith and of the awakening divine life is enkindled in other persons. So the vitalizing wave of the gospel travels outward from its source until it has touched all human beings.

This form of life—the journey from baptism to eucharist—can be observed in Paul's letters, and is especially clear in his second letter to the Corinthians. Paul writes of his new creation in Christ, in the dawning of the divine light within his heart.

> For it is the God who said, "Let light shine out of darkness," who has shone in our hearts to give the light of the knowledge of the glory of God in the face of Christ.

Then he continues immediately with the "other side" of this gift.

> But we have this treasure in earthen vessels, to show that the transcendent power belongs to God and not to us. We are afflicted in every way, but not crushed; perplexed, but not driven to despair; persecuted, but not forsaken; struck down, but not destroyed; always carrying in the body the death of Jesus, so that the life of Jesus may also be manifested in our bodies. For while we live we are always being given up to death for Jesus' sake, so that the life of Jesus may be manifested in our mortal flesh. So death is at work in us, but life in you. (2 Cor 4:6-12)

Paul conveys the image of a continual welling forth of new life within him which is counterbalanced by a continual dying on the outside. This dying itself, in the pattern of the death of Jesus, somehow involves a communication of the new life to others. "So death is at work in us, but life in you" (2 Cor 4:12).

The new life in Christ is a "fontal" life; the human person discovers himself or herself as a wellspring of life, flowing from unseen depths into the person (John 4:13-14; 7:37-39) and then flowing forth from the person to others in a movement which is incarnation and eucharist. The God who said, "let light shine out of darkness" (2 Cor 4:6), has shone in the heart of this person; now this person continues to bring forth light from the interior darkness and becomes light for others in the midst of the world's darkness. This is the paradigm of Christian life. The movement is from the baptismal receiving of self in the Spirit to a eucharistic giving of self to others in the same Spirit. The person becomes wellspring and sun in this new incarnational life which moves between the dawn of baptism and the sunset of eucharist.

In the central section of Mark's Gospel (8:27–10:45), we find Jesus teaching the same way, in the face of the persistent incomprehension of his disciples. The "way of the cross," which Jesus teaches his disciples in the course of his final journey to Jerusalem, cannot be understood until after his resurrection: that is, until both Easter and Pentecost have transpired, and the disciples are filled with the new life. Jesus' instruction is equivalent to an operating manual for the plenary baptismal gift, the new self. The clash of views which we observe at the beginning of this central section of Mark (8:27-38), in the interaction of Peter with Jesus, appears again at the end of the section (10:32-45) when the crass ambition of the two brothers, James and John, is gently reproved by their Master.

Peter, filled with the joy of his divine illumination in which he has been given to recognize and confess Jesus as the Anointed One (Messiah) of God (Mark 8:29), can see nothing but this light; hidden from his eyes is the dark obverse of Jesus' mission in this world. When Jesus begins to describe this other side, the way of the cross, Peter balks and receives a crushing rebuke from his master. The gift is inseparable from the way; the Spirit and the glory are inseparable from the cross, as the divinity of Jesus is inseparable from his humanity. Later, as the disciples ascend toward Jerusalem with their Master, still full of expectations of imminent glory, Jesus' continuing teaching of the way of descent remains unheard. James and John, who together with Peter were Jesus' most intimate disciples, disclose their complete deafness to this teaching of Jesus; in their raw ambition they surpass Peter's obtuseness. Jesus is more gentle in his response to these two, however. He replies in sacramental language—cup and baptism—which point toward a participation in Jesus' destiny (and in a new humanity to be born from that death) which is very different from the seats of honor that they had coveted. It is significant that Jesus chooses to speak of his death in this language of baptism and eucharist.

The way of Jesus is a way not of ascent but of descent; only in the fullness and power of the Spirit, which the disciples will receive after Jesus has risen and disappeared from among them, will they be able to hear—and to live—this teaching. Then their life is to assume the same shape as his life, for they have received the gift of his life within them. The same lesson is found in John's narrative before Jesus' last supper and his passion.

> Now among those who went up to worship at the feast were some Greeks. So these came to Philip, who was from Bethsaida in Galilee, and said to him, "Sir, we wish to see Jesus." Philip went and told Andrew; Andrew went with Philip and they told Jesus. And Jesus answered them, "The hour has come for the Son of man to be glorified. Truly, truly, I say to you, unless a grain of wheat falls into the earth and dies, it remains alone; but if it dies, it bears much fruit. He who loves his life loses it, and he who hates his life in this world will keep it for eternal life. If any one serves me, he must follow me; and where I am, there shall my servant be also; if any one serves me, the Father will honor him. (John 12:20-26)

Jesus has been invited to transgress the boundary that had been fixed for him—the boundary between Israel and the Gentiles—and, implicitly, to anticipate the divine plan by ascending to the position that is to be his after his resurrection. Once again, he turns decisively from this proposed way of ascent to the way of *descent*, taking up the image of the seed falling into the ground with which he had begun his parables of the kingdom. Once again, the symbolism is eucharistic. This is the movement toward eucharist which the disciples, too, will be called upon to follow.

In the sixth chapter of John's Gospel, as Jesus begins his long discourse on the "bread of life," we are apparently to understand Jesus himself in the symbol of this bread, partaken of as the divine Wisdom, as the light of life. But toward the end of his discourse, Jesus begins to unfold the same metaphor of the bread of life in explictly eucharistic terms: his flesh will be bread and his blood will be drink. Wisdom becomes eucharist. This is the movement of incarnation that will also determine the pattern of the disciple's life:

> unless you eat the flesh of the Son of man and drink his blood, you have no life in you; he who eats my flesh and drinks my blood has eternal life, and I will raise him up at the last day. For my flesh is food indeed, and my blood is drink indeed. . . . (John 6:53-55)

In the Synoptic Gospels, the brief accounts of Jesus' last supper are centered on the institution of the eucharist. Here is the sacramental eucharist which has become, in John's supper account (chaps. 13–17), a *sapiential* eucharist: the final banquet of the divine Wisdom become incarnate. The movement of Jesus' life, however, is ultimately the same in all four Gospels: from self-revelation to a total incarnational gift of himself, from teaching to eucharistic death. Jesus' teaching on the way of descent appears, in John's Gospel, in the implicitly eucharistic context of the last supper. Instead of the eucharistic ritual, John presents us with Jesus' ritual action of washing his disciples' feet. Beatrice Bruteau writes of the two phases of Jesus' "Holy Thursday revolution." First, he symbolically deconstructs the old "domination paradigm," which has prevailed in human society since the beginning, by this inversion: the master washes his disciples' feet.[74] Then he sacramentally inaugurates his new order of communion in the world by his institution of the eucharist.[75]

In the middle of the Johannine supper narrative, Jesus develops his eucharistic symbolism further with the image of the vine and the branches. The one principle of life for his disciples will be to *abide* in him as the branch abides in the vine. This abiding in him is achieved in the keeping of his commandments; his commandments, however, reduce themselves to the single law of love: "even as I have loved you, . . . you also love one another" (John 13:34). John very simply resumes the twofold principle of Christian life in his first letter, "And this is his (God's) commandment, that we should believe in the name of his Son Jesus Christ and love one another, just as he has commanded us" (1 John 3:23). To this faith in Jesus Christ corresponds the beginning, the new life of baptism, flowing into the person from the invisible Ground which is the Father. To this love of one another corresponds the end, the eucharistic gift of self in which one "bears much fruit."

The journey of Christian wisdom, according to the New Testament, begins in the wilderness, in the waters of baptismal initiation. The spiritual fullness that is received in this beginning which is initiation contains within itself the principle of its progressive incarnation in one's personal life and finally in one's death—which corresponds at once to Jesus' death and to his gift of the eucharist. The Wisdom which is Christ continually moves in this descending direction of incarnation; the light of life received in faith becomes flesh and blood, given in love.

13. (VIII) Contemplation as Conscious Experience of Baptismal Identity

I have already noted the new understanding of contemplative experience that has been developing in the West as a consequence of our contact with the Asian traditions during the past fifty years. A typical earlier Catholic definition of contemplation, derived from the writings of Thomas Aquinas, was that of Adolphe Tanquerey: "a simple, intuitive gaze on God and divine things proceeding from love and tending thereto."[76] St. Francis de Sales defined contemplation as "a loving, simple, and permanent attentiveness of the mind to divine things."[77]

Thomas Merton, influenced particularly by his study of Buddhism, gradually developed a different conception of the contemplative experience, which we find in the writings that appeared at the end of his life. *In Zen and the Birds of Appetite,* for example, after describing the dualistic, modern Cartesian consciousness of the West, he continues:

> Meanwhile, let us remind ourselves that another, metaphysical, consciousness is still available to modern man. It starts not from the thinking and self-aware subject but from Being, ontologically seen to be beyond and prior to the subject-object division. Underlying the sub-

> jective experience of the individual self there is an immediate experience of Being. This is totally different from an experience of self-consciousness. It is completely nonobjective. It has in it none of the split and alienation that occurs when the subject becomes aware of itself as a quasi-object. The consciousness of Being (whether considered positively or negatively and apophatically as in Buddhism) is an immediate experience that goes beyond reflexive awareness. It is not "consciousness of" but pure consciousness, in which the subject as such "disappears."[78]

From the Christian perspective, an experience of nonduality is both an experience of God and an experience of one's deepest identity: an experience of our identity at its nondual or divine-human level. This can be understood as an experience of our baptismal identity. But there remains also the properly relational aspect, a personal encounter with God in faith and love. We continue to relate to God, and to Jesus, also as Other. In the same way, Jesus himself related to the Father both as the Ground and Source of his being, one with himself, and as the Other to whom he turned in prayer.

It is not immediately obvious how the unitive baptismal illumination of a Christian relates to the nondual realization of a Vedantist or of a Zen Buddhist, but there is doubtless a deep correspondence between the two experiences because of the universal spiritual structure of the human person.[79] At the same time, each experience takes place within a totality from which it cannot be isolated, and from which modalities of the experience itself may be inseparable.[80] Because of the initial fullness recognized by both the Asian and the Christian traditions, and because of this universal structure of the person, there are many similarities between Asian and Christian forms of asceticism and contemplative discipline.

14. (IX) History Understood in the Light of Unitive Self-realization

The human person is a unity, and, as we have seen, the ground of human experience is a unitive consciousness. This consciousness may be conceived as a unitive light that irradiates the mind and shines on all the objects of human perception and thought. The development of a human individual takes place in this unitive light of consciousness, and the self-awareness of the person is an awakening to this light itself at one's center. The history of human consciousness—at least since the Axial period—may be considered in terms of the awakening of unitive awareness, but only if this unitive consciousness is recognized also in its objectifications and its descents into the material world. This is particularly true as we move from East to West. In the Asian cultures—at least those that have developed under the influence of Hinduism, Buddhism, and Taoism—nondual consciousness is explicitly recognized and frequently a subject of scholarly reflection. In the West, however, an explicit recognition of unitive consciousness or unitive reality is rare, and unitive consciousness expresses itself—almost always without explicit self-awareness—in a large variety of *objective* forms. We shall examine some of these expressions in the next part of our study.

We have already considered some of these objectifications of the unitive light of baptismal identity: in the interpretation of Scripture, in the development of a sapiential theology, and particularly of an anthropology. Unitive consciousness, as we have seen, is not restricted to those who have been baptized into Christ; this is abundantly evident in our encounter with the Asian traditions. In the development of the Christian and post-Christian secular West, we observe a continuity, a progression that often resembles the development of an individual person. The evolution is punctuated by certain moments of awakening—individual discoveries and creative breakthroughs which are, at the same time, self-realizations. These individual awakenings flow into a progressively developing general self-awareness of the human person in the West.[81]

Our Eastern turn allows us to interpret these successive discoveries, illuminations, or self-realizations from the viewpoint of unitive consciousness—as if we were following the progressive awakening of a single human person to his/her divine-human or spiritual identity. We shall return, from time to time, to this continuum, or baseline, of nondual consciousness, which we have posited as a fundamental and essential element of the human person. The nondual light is objectified at one moment in a metaphysical intuition, at another moment in a revolutionary musical innovation, in a third moment in a movement toward social justice and human rights. It will appear in the form of a synthetic philosophical or scientific idea or formula, in the creative fusion that we sense in poetic metaphor, in the exultant cry that expresses one's experience of the radical truth of personal freedom. Our study of the modern West will put the credibility of this theory to an extreme test, as human community, human thought and culture, religion and spirituality splinter into innumerable fragments. Yet each far-flung sliver glitters in its place with the same sovereign light. Postmodernity, finally, will seem to stretch this credibility beyond the breaking point as it mercilessly deconstructs every metanarrative, every synthetic assertion, every hopeful generalization in the same one, quiet, living light.

In this unitive light is the ultimate spiritual identity of the person, and from this light, or this ground, is born every human thought, action, creation, and experience. History itself, therefore, with all its complexity and obscurity, its ascents and its descents, unfolds in the unitive light.

4

Movement III

The Western (Modern) Turn

1. Modernity

i. The Return

EACH OF OUR FOUR MOVEMENTS IS EXPERIENCED AS A HOMECOMING, BUT in a different way, and sometimes in more than one way. The sapiential awakening is a return to the integrity of the Christ-mystery, to the homeland of our faith, and can be experienced as a self-discovery. Our second movement, the Eastern turn, may be experienced as an awakening to one's own center, to a "still point" beyond time and change which is both beginning and end. As citizens of the modern West, our third movement—the Western or modern turn—is a return to our own time and historical situation: a return to our own existential context after a spiritual and sapiential initiation.

The Two-step Journey

In the Western world of today, many people become alienated from their Christian and Catholic background early in life. Then, awakened to a transcendent reality and experiencing no vitality in their own religious tradition, they feel compelled to undertake a pilgrimage in search of that spiritual fullness that has touched them. Some of them eventually return: their journey unfolds in two stages. The first step resembles a seeking for *initiation*, for the experience of God in baptism, for the great awakening, the rebirth that is so powerfully expressed in the New Testament—especially in Paul's letters. Baptized probably as infants, they have never experienced anything like this. But instinctively they know that they need it, that life is meaningless without it. First they go East, to attain an experience of *spirit*, of a reality beyond the ordinary reality they are used to—and the ordinary religious climate in which they were raised. Some actually go to Asia—to India or Burma—and live in an ashram, a Zen monastery, find a guru, a *roshi,* submit to an austere and demanding contemplative discipline. Such a pilgrim will very likely experience, in the course of that life of meditation, a further encounter with transcendent spirit.

Then, after some years, many of these seekers find that their hunger is not being fully satisfied. They begin to look westward once again, and into Christianity—tentatively, cautiously, stepping carefully over the sleeping bodies. They may be attracted to the eucharist or to Francis of Assisi, certainly to Jesus. Eventually they begin the journey back, looking for an acceptable point of contact with the church. The first movement is away from the past, the ordinary, dead religion, and toward life, toward God, toward spirit. The second movement is back from the experience of spirit, the awakening, the illumination, toward incarnation, toward a faith and a spirituality that is not only spirit but heart—one that can embrace all of humanity and all of life. We can see something like this in the lives of Thomas Merton and Bede Griffiths. Many of us have to make the same journey if the church is to be alive in our time and in the future. But we do not necessarily have to go to India to do it.

ii. Modernity

During the past five hundred years, the West has taken a very long step in a certain direction, which has brought it far out in front of the other cultures of the world.[1] And this progress has involved an impoverishment in other dimensions of human life. But I would like to think of modernity as beginning much earlier—before the eighteenth-century Enlightenment or the Industrial Revolution, before the discovery of the new world, before the Italian Renaissance—in the twelfth and thirteenth centuries. Let us think of modernity as the emergence of the autonomous individual person in the West, beginning already in the time of Abelard and Francis of Assisi and Thomas Aquinas and Dante. At that time the collective mold is beginning to break.

Modernity, understood in this way, has many other aspects. Modernity has confronted the church in successive waves. It has been called new thought, liberalism, humanism, secularity or secularism, and sometimes modernism (nineteenth and twentieth centuries). In confronting the church it has often taken the part of the person against the institution or of the secular world against religion. After centuries of defensive rejection, the Roman Catholic Church addressed modernity in the Second Vatican Council in a refreshingly new spirit, attempting to respond to the situations and the mentalities of people in the modern West with understanding and compassion.[2] We shall return to look more carefully at this revolutionary change.

Profile of Modernity

Let us, then, briefly characterize modernity,[3] as we shall understand it here. I will point out several principal factors, which we shall consider more carefully as we proceed.

1. Central was the emergence of the *individual person* from the collective matrix of religion, society, and culture. One began to realize oneself with a new autonomy, differentiating oneself from religious and cultural traditions and institutions. Hence, we may refer to this modern era—especially in its beginnings—as the *Western Axial period.*
2. Fundamental to this emergence of the autonomous individual was the new *intellectual autonomy* of the person: the liberation of individual human reason. Stepping away from the obligatory consensus of traditional Catholicism, the individual began to think for himself or herself and to arrive at independent conclusions. A space opened up for critical thought and free discussion; gradually everything was subjected to questioning. Scientific method—involving reproducible experiments and empirical observation—prevailed over traditional wisdom. Knowledge became more and more rationally verified and organized, more and more publicly available. As a new scientific mind emerged, rational thought prevailed over the old intuitive wisdom.
3. Together with this new autonomy of reason, however, came a new sense of personal freedom and *creativity*. The individual, stepping out in different directions from collective rule, tradition, and institution, began to actualize a capacity for innovation, for bringing newness into the world.
4. As the human person emerged from the collective mentality of tradition and as the fields of human thought and action became autonomous and differentiated, a new, autonomous sphere of human existence came into being. We refer to it as the *secular world.*
5. As the static crust of tradition and institution began to give way, a new Western person, as if stepping out of an invisible cloister, began to see the world and life differently. As repetition gave way to innovation, a new *progressive dynamism* appeared within history. Static structures—especially the ancient structures of social privilege—were questioned, and people began to realize their power to bring about changes not only in their material environment but in the structures of society itself. The general social and cultural movement assumed a descending course; in many areas a process of equalization could be observed. Inequalities persisted, however, and the continuing unequal position of women in modern societies indicates a deeper imbalance in the culture.

6. Finally, it is in the modern West that we find the birth of a *historical sense*—that is, a growing ability to interpret reality in terms of a process of development. This is exemplified most obviously by the biological theory of evolution, which arose in the nineteenth century, but the new perspective is evident in all areas of scientific thought, indeed everywhere in contemporary Western culture.

It is evident that all these factors are closely related. Indeed, they are expressions of a single, massive historical process.

The Challenge

What, exactly, is the challenge of modernity to a wisdom Christianity? We have seen that it was to this modernity that sapiential Christianity succumbed at the end of the Middle Ages. Both sapiential consciousness and theology, and the monastic life that had been their matrix during the Middle Ages, went into eclipse at about the same time, at the beginning of the modern era. If a wisdom Christianity—indeed, if Christianity itself—is to have vitality in the future, it must somehow confront and come to terms with these factors and with the one great movement that they express. Within this challenge—however we may come to understand it—lies a positive potential, toward which some contemporary theological prophets direct us:[4] if the unfolding mystery of Christ is at the core of this Western development as a whole, and if the understanding proper to this mystery of Christ is a sapiential theology, then Western modernity represents the invitation—indeed the imperative—to Christian wisdom to awaken and expand into the larger dimensions—and personal vitality—of this new world. The path of this development will lead us through new and, at first, disconcerting places.

iii. Self and Person

I have proposed that the heart of modernity is the emerging person. It will be helpful to distinguish Eastern "self" from Western "person." We have seen that the *self* in the Asian traditions is realized through detachment from this world and from the ego, and ultimately by absorption of the individual into the beginning, the Absolute, the One. *Atman* is *brahman;* one's individual self is lost in *nirvana,* in a return to the One, to the uncarved block. The Western *person,* on the other hand, is relational, active, projected into this world and making a home here. The person is creative, participating in a significant story and a progressive history.

Our Western spiritual traditions, woven in a tension between the spiritualizing influence of Neoplatonist philosophy and the incarnational dynamism of the gospel, have led us along a historical path wavering between Eastern contemplative withdrawal and Western existence—between self and person, as it were, with little theological understanding of the territory. Jesus, in whom God is manifest as a human person, reveals the unity and continuity of the Eastern and Western, or spiritual and bodily/historical hemispheres of the human being.[5] In our time both aspects of the person become visible and therefore accessible to us, and we become skeptical of reducing the human person to one of the two archetypal extremes.

A Christian wisdom, to be adequate today, must open itself both eastward and westward: to the nondual self and its uncontained consciousness (or simple light) and to the emergent conscious, free, and creative person in the world—as well as to the dynamism of history, understood as centered in the Christ-event. These westward elements, I believe, are fruits of the Christ-event. The church must open itself in the same two opposing directions. From the Eastern perspective, the church of today has grown too far out from its roots into the world, and Christian consciousness has followed in the same westward direction. While the emergence of the individual person from the collective religious and cultural matrix has characterized the modern West, the emergence of woman, of the feminine, has proceeded more slowly.

2. The Vocation of the West

It is very difficult to understand the history in which we are still participating—the history of this modern Western world—and futile to attempt an overall understanding as long as we can only guess how long this period of history will continue. Today, however, we find ourselves on a kind of threshold, which is often called *postmodernity.* This provides a tentative punctuation: we can try to read the history of the West backward from this terminus. The picture becomes much clearer when we translate postmodernity into *globalization*—globalization not only on the most obvious level of economics and politics but as the deeper process of the realization of *one humanity.*

This approach to Western history was suggested by Karl Rahner's schematization of the history of the church in an essay on the Second Vatican Council[6] which we have already cited.[7] Recall the three stages of this scheme: (1) the short period of Judaeo-Christianity; (2) the period of the church in a particular cultural group, that of Hellenism and European culture and civilization (from the first century until Vatican II); (3) the period in which the church's living space is from the very outset the whole world. (This period begins with Vatican II.)[8] Rahner proposes, accordingly, that the council marks the beginning of the third phase of the history of the church: the inception of a "world church." In this perspective, the second or middle phase of church history—the age of European Christianity—takes on a unique theological importance. This age (which comprehends the patristic, medieval, and modern periods) corresponds roughly to the era of what I have been calling "the West." We can infer, in fact, not only that the church of this second, intermediate phase has a particular theological importance but that the particular *cultural group* of Europe has a distinctive importance as well. We can begin to speak of the theological role of the West between the Christ-event and the achievement of a global Christianity—or the appearance of a global human unity.

The West—compounded of Greek, Latin, and Germanic elements—is distinguished by a peculiar conjunction of two characteristics: (1) it is the largest human group that has been constellated by the Christian revelation, or Christ-event; (2) it is the one cultural group that has, without close parallel,[9] mediated the unification of humanity, the movement toward one world. The West is in the singular position of standing between the Christ-event (in which it is rooted and from which it derives its central character, its peculiar gifts, and its integrity) and the one world or one humanity which is emerging in our time. The West, then, has apparently been endowed with a mediatory role between (1) the Christ-event, or incarnation, and (2) one humanity, one world, planetary unity.

The genesis and development of the European (and now North American) West have unfolded under the influence of Christianity, in contrast to the many preexisting cultures that have undergone Christian influence: for example, Greek and Roman classical cultures, or African and Asian cultures. The West was gathered into a unity by the Roman Empire and then by the Latin church.[10] While the Roman Catholic Church had aspired to gather the whole world into that unity by converting it not only to Christianity but to a Latin, European Christianity, instead the vessel broke and the wine spilled forth.

It is the West, however, which has been the central agent in bringing humanity together. The process has been going on for more than five hundred years. It began with the explorations and discoveries, the improvements in navigation and transportation, the colonial conquests, the concurrent expansive military, commercial, and missionary movements in the new worlds. It continues today with the Western achievements in technology that are facilitating transportation and communication to an astonishing degree. A convergent Europeanization of world cultures has been brought about by the Western political and economic and military powers that have dominated the world for centuries. Even the European world wars of the twentieth century have (paradoxically) resulted in a further unification of humanity.[11] Common nuclear and ecological dangers have made the need for international collaboration on a global scale incontrovertible. All of these unifying forces—with their continual ambiguity—have originated in the West.

While an *exterior* unification of the world, of all humanity, is rapidly taking place through science and technology (as well as political and economic associations which proceed along with the growth of the technological fabric), the world is riven with increasingly dangerous conflicts. The achievement of a corresponding *interior* unification of humanity[12] becomes more and more urgent.

The continuity between the Christ-event, Western civilization, and one humanity is developed by Karl Rahner in another essay.

> this fusion of the history of every nation into one had its real starting point in the very birth of Christianity and in the place where Christianity first took roots in the world and in history, viz. in the Western world.[13]

The transition from Christendom to a secular Western world, therefore, is a further unfolding of the event of Christ, a process of cultural universalization which makes it possible for humanity to become one. The liberation of the human person into a new universality "in Christ" (Gal 3:27-28) recurs on the the level of cultural history as humanity awakens to its unity through the universal rationality—the common language of modern international relations, of scholarship, science and technology—which has come into being through the modern West. Freedom, that fundamental gift of Christ which has flourished uniquely in the West, emerges after two thousand years on a global scale, as this one humanity awakens to itself. With mad synthetic abandon, one might imagine Eastern nonduality, metamorphosed through the Christ-event into Western rationality and freedom, moving toward its final embodiment as global unity.

3. The Shape of Western History

i. Three Historical Schemes

If the project of discerning a meaningful overall pattern in history is a notoriously difficult and uncertain one, this must be particularly true of the history of the West, with its dynamic complexity. Nevertheless, many orientations, forms, and inflections in this history can be described with clarity. In the course of the centuries numerous attempts have been made to schematize the history of the church, of the Western world, or of humanity as a whole.[14] I will briefly review three such schemes, each of which envisions history as unfolding in three stages.

1. Joachim of Fiore

Joachim of Fiore (ca. 1132–1202) saw the whole of human history as divided into three periods, corresponding to the three persons of the Trinity. The age of the Father, and of the *ordo conjugatorum,* is the first period, when humanity lived under the Jewish law; it concluded with the coming of Christ. It is followed by the age of the Son, and of the *ordo clericorum,* the time of the New Testament and the following centuries, which is lived under grace. Finally the age of the Spirit, that of the *ordo monachorum,* or *ordo contemplantium,* will be lived in the freedom of the *spiritualis intellectus.* Joachim expected this third age to begin in about 1260 C.E.[15]

Here we have an *ascending* view of history, corresponding in its verticality to the spiritualizing tendency of its era, and typical also (particularly of a monastic author) in its hierarchical ordering of monks, clergy, and ordinary people. What is unusual for the time is the *progressive* vision of history. Trinity, history, and a peculiar hierarchical ecclesiology have been conflated to produce this scheme, which remains enclosed within the preconceptions of the church and spirituality of its age—except for that progressive dynamism. History since the time of Joachim has indeed taken an increasingly progressive course, but in a direction nearly opposite to that which he projected.

2. Auguste Comte

Auguste Comte (1789–1857), representing the mind of the European Enlightenment, offers a schematic view of history—specifically, the history of thought—which appears to run almost exactly contrary to the scheme of Joachim. Comte sees each field of knowledge and each society passing through three phases: a theological, a metaphysical, and finally a positive scientific stage. In the theological stage, everything is understood in terms of the gods; in the metaphysical stage, understanding is achieved through the most general abstractions of thought; in the final, scientific stage, knowledge is obtained by the correlation of observed facts. It is this empirical scientific knowledge that, for Comte, is finally valid.

The two systems contrast in their direction of movement—ascending or descending; in their general context—Catholic and religious or secular; and in their preferred mode of knowledge—contemplation or empirical observation.

The orientation of consciousness itself appears to have changed radically between the former and the latter scheme: from upward and inward to downward and outward. The two schemes represent orientations characteristic of their two ages: the Christian age of faith, centered in a patristic-monastic theological vision, and the secular age of reason, dominated by empirical rationality.

3. Pitirim Sorokin

A third three-phase scheme, proposed by Russian sociologist Pitirim Sorokin (1889–1968), embraces within itself opposed visions corresponding to those of Joachim and of Auguste Comte. According to Sorokin, each society has a particular view of reality. If reality is perceived as "nonsensate and nonmaterial, everlasting Being (*Sein*)," the culture is "ideational" (equivalent to our more usual term *spiritual*). In this culture, "the needs and ends are mainly spiritual," and their fulfillment is sought through the reduction of physical needs. If, on the other hand, reality is understood as only that which is perceived through the senses, the culture is "sensate":

> [The sensate mentality] does not believe in any supersensory reality; at the most, in its diluted form, it assumes an agnostic attitude toward the entire world beyond the senses. The sensate reality is thought of as a Becoming, Process, Change, Flux, Evolution, Progress, Transformation. Its needs and aims are mostly physical, and maximum satisfaction is sought of these needs. The method of realizing them is not that of a modification within the human individuals composing the culture, but of a modification or exploitation of the external world.[16]

According to Sorokin, these two types of culture are diametrically opposite to each other in their views of reality and corresponding patterns of thought and life. Between the two he sees a third, idealistic type of culture which joins the ideational and sensate views, but with a predominance of ideational traits.

> For it [the idealistic culture mentality] reality is many-sided, with the aspects of everlasting Being and ever-changing Becoming, of the spiritual and the material. Its needs and ends are both spiritual and material, with the material, however, subordinated to the spiritual. The methods of their realization involve both the modification of self and the transformation of the external sensate world: in other words, it gives *suum cuique* to the ideational and the sensate.[17]

Sorokin demonstrates at great length the consistency of the religion, philosophy, science, art, and law of each of these three distinct historical ages. A typical order of progression through the three ages is (1) the ideational culture; (2) as the sensory principle begins to replace the spiritual principle, the idealistic phase of culture; and (3) the sensate age, when the sensory principle has become dominant. Then the sensate age itself begins to decay and, in favorable circumstances, gives way to a new ideational or idealistic cultural age. The three cultural phases are exemplified by the evolution of European culture from its ideational medieval stage through the idealistic culture of the fourteenth and fifteenth centuries to the sensate culture of the modern West, beginning in the sixteenth century. "In this way the modern form of our culture emerged—the sensory, empirical, secular, and 'this-worldly' culture."[18]

Sorokin's picture of the succession of ages can seem somewhat rigid and mechanical. A rhythm of alternation between the two great principles—spiritual and sensory—does not offer a very satisfying ultimate basis for historical changes of this magnitude.[19] Nevertheless, I think that his overall empirical picture of the cultural history of the West is valid. Within this picture, Joachim of Fiore's vision of history—culminating in "contemplation"—is representative of the ideational or spiritual phase of culture, and Auguste Comte's scheme—arriving at a final factual knowledge as the truest knowledge—is clearly representative of the sensate cultural phase.

ii. The Arch of Western Culture

On the basis of Sorokin's three historical ages, I will propose a simple visual scheme of the evolution of Western culture as a framework for our own investigation.

	II integrating (idealistic) 1000–1500	
I ascending (ideational) 500–1000		III descending (sensate) 1500–2000

We need not retain Sorokin's three terms for the three phases. We shall find that a number of different sets of terms apply to the three phases on our diagram. Let us adopt, for the time being, these three: I. ascending; II. integrating; III. descending. Sorokin sees the intermediate idealistic phase of Western culture beginning about 1200 and ending about 1500. Retaining his divisions approximately, let us begin our intermediate period a little earlier, about 1000 (or 1100).

Historians might see our second, intermediate phase as a peak in several different senses: politically (the period of a unified Europe), ecclesiastically (the period of greatest development of a unified Catholic Church), culturally (the time of a protracted "renaissance," which was the birth of a distinctly Western art and literature), philosophically (when the Platonic and Aristotelian systems coexisted and interacted, when the epistemological spectrum could comprehend at once contemplative, rational, and empirical ways of knowing), theologically (when faith and reason lived in a fruitful dialogue). Speaking generally, this is the period when a unity has been realized and a new differentiation has begun, and unity and differentiation coexist without a decisive rupture, the moment of maximal tension before the breaking of the vessel. From the point of view of our own study, this is the time when the old sapiential consciousness is still present and active, while the new, more rational and dialectical, mode of theological thought has emerged to interact with it. The intermediate second phase of Western history, from 1000 to 1500, can be seen as a crest of Western development, therefore, both on the collective and on the individual level. But it was necessarily a passing phase—a brief united kingdom—intrinsically limited and imperfect. To canonize that period and its institutions or attitudes as if they could continue perennially in the same forms would be a terrible mistake.

4. Renaissance

i. Emergence

Let us look more carefully at the second of our three periods of Western history, the crest that extends from about 1000 to about 1500. At the inception of this period, a European civilization is just beginning to emerge out of the chaos of the preceding centuries. Church, emperor, and monastery have taken on the role of agents of reform. As yet, there is little opportunity for the emergence of the individual person; life's options are almost completely confined within the structures of feudal society and the limitations imposed by one's birth. The word *renaissance*[20] is not intended to be understood in the sense of a renewal of ancient or classical cultural values, but rather as a comprehensive awakening of the human person: primarily, a personal birth, and, secondarily, a cultural rebirth. The new, free appropriation of classical thought and style is itself an expression of something deeper: the human person coming into a new self-possession and simultaneously beginning to generate a human world.

The word "renaissance"[21] itself is suggestive of rebirth in the Christian theological sense, and this has a further appropriateness, as will become apparent. I shall propose that the human and humanistic renaissance that is evident during this whole period is a historical expression of the Christ-event. We seem to observe at this time a recurrence of the human rebirth that appears in the New Testament, but in a new Western context and with a distinctly worldward orientation. The twelfth-century rebirth is at once Christian and secular; this is one of the dualities, held in a shifting equilibrium, in which the new vitality of this time can be seen.

Colin Morris has described the widespread emergence of the individual—a renaissance—in the European world of the eleventh and twelfth centuries:

> Its essential features can be found in many different circles: a concern with self-discovery; an interest in the relations between people, and in the role of the individual within society; an assessment of people by their inner intentions rather than by external acts. These concerns were, moreover, conscious and deliberate. "Know yourself" was one of the most frequently quoted injunctions.[22]

The eleventh-century reformers established the autonomy of the church from secular power, and the liberation of the spiritual realm was a crucial—if paradoxical—first step toward a more widespread, personal autonomy. Like a second Baptist introducing the new era, Gregory VII purified the clergy from servitude to the world through his struggles against simony, against clerical marriage, and against lay investiture. The papal claim to supreme secular power initiated a struggle between pope and emperor in which the two powers gradually came to be clearly distinguished. Meanwhile, in the midst of this conflict, a new space of personal autonomy began to appear.[23]

ii. The Twelfth-century Shift: Rediscovery of the Gospel and the Liberation of the Person

M.-D. Chenu has studied in depth the twelfth-century renaissance and its dynamic polarities: grace and nature, sacred and secular, faith and reason, wisdom and science.[24] At the source of this movement of new birth was a rediscovery of the gospel, of evangelism, and of the preaching of the word of God. The context of this rebirth was the growth of a new social order as feudal society, dominated by a landed aristocracy, gave way to a society centered in towns and cities, as a new merchant class gained power, and the mobility of people and of money increased. As the power of the German empire dissipated, the new national states were consolidated.

The evangelical movement that was initiated in the eleventh century entered a new and more vigorous phase. New religious movements came forth; the dominance of monastic life receded with the growth of groups of canons regular and religious "poor men." As the gospel was rediscovered and the new classes of people were evangelized, religious poverty assumed a central importance, both as witness and as the "salt" which maintained the purity of this new religious life within the world. Theology and literature began to appear in the vernacular languages; twelfth-century theologians began to express a sense of contemporary newness, of renaissance. As minds awakened to an active interest in history, history began to be written with a new realism; Christendom became aware of its historical evolution.[25]

A central principle emerges from Chenu's studies of the twelfth century. That is, in this new social, economic, and political situation, the *recovery of the gospel brought about a liberation and animation of human creative activity in the world.* The recovery of the gospel in the twelfth century was the critical factor in the access of new and creative life in the church, in theology, and in the other realms of human endeavor at that time.

> . . . history shows that it was the Christian's return to the gospel which guaranteed his presence in the world and that it was this presence in the world which secured the efficacy of the gospel. . . .
>
> When St. Thomas Aquinas defined the transcendence of grace by invoking the Aristotelian idea of nature, he was not merely making a reasoned option in favor of the Philosopher. Rather, he was giving supreme expression to that Christianity in which a return to the gospel had secured for the believer a presence in the world, for the theologian a mature awareness of nature, and for the apostle an effective appreciation of man.[26]

The personal awakening that characterizes our renaissance is evident in a new self-awareness of the human person as a rational agent. In the new rational theology of the twelfth and thirteenth centuries, however, we can also discern an *incarnational* movement: a descent from the earlier epistemology. Faith, writes Chenu, is an incarnation of divine truth which finds its complement, on the level of human existence, in *reason.*

> Henceforth men wished, in the light of faith and by using the heritage of revelation, to intellectualize and systematize their beliefs and to explain the word of God in a human way. As the incarnation of divine truth in the human mind, faith was not some extraordinary charisma whose transcendence would keep it above human modes of thought.

> Faith put to work the various resources of reason, thus introducing them into the mystery of God. By engendering a theology, faith was achieving its logical perfection.[27]

This logic can be pursued further. Faith and theology are not yet a full incarnation of divine truth, for they are not quite physical, not yet bodily, though they live in a bodily context, a bodily situation. Rather, the full embodiment of divine truth is a human existence according to the gospel (see Jas 2:14-26), and this is what we see, for example, in Francis of Assisi. But the new theology is on the way toward embodiment, toward incarnation, for it is bringing faith and gospel into the real world; it is a mediating halfway house to incarnation. And it goes further in this direction than the earlier monastic theology had done.

Now we can bring our arch figure of Western history to a further level of interpretation. We can think of the crest or renaissance from ca. 1000 to ca. 1500 as a time of relative equilibrium between two forces in tension. In the simplest possible terms, these forces—spiritual and mental orientations, intentionalities—can be called simply God and world, or spirit and matter.[28] On the one hand, there is a consciousness of spirit or God, and, on the other hand, a consciousness of world and matter; and these two minds pull in opposite directions throughout the whole course of Western history. The crest of our renaissance represents a certain equilibrium between these two orientations or forces. While both forces remain actively in play—while the interaction continues with a relative balance of forces along the crest of the figure—the metaphysical tension within the human person and the culture is greatest, and human synthetic and creative potential is manifest in its greatest depth and fullness. In this phase the vertical axis of our diagram indicates the degree of actualization of the human person (not only as externally manifest or quantitatively measurable, however, but also in terms of metaphysical or spiritual depth). This will be a central guiding principle as we continue our study: the human person (though perhaps the traditional "man" is a more accurate word within the limits of this history[29]) exists in its greatest creative vitality in the tension and interaction between the two sides: spirit and body, God and world, faith and reason, grace and nature. We speak of "renaissance man" as having a kind of universal potency. We think often of the renaissance as being the time of greatest cultural vitality and fertility in Western history. It is such a human amplitude—though with a greater spiritual depth—that is to be attributed to the period of renaissance at the crest of our figure.

In this understanding of the figure, we can still speak of the initial phase as "awakening." It is an awakening to God, but at the apex it becomes an awakening to the transcendent or nondual dimension of the human person, the self.

This is precisely the meaning of a nondual experience of God: the simultaneous and indivisible awareness of God and self. This realization will be objectified in Aquinas's idea of God as pure *esse, actus purus,* etc. It will be expressed participatively in Eckhart's unitive language.

The new autonomy of "the natural," which has appeared with the recovery of the gospel, finds expression in many different ways: (1) in the new "gospel liberty," manifested in a general way by the new disciples of the *vita apostolica*; (2) in freedom from the sacred enclosure of monasticism, a system of rules and customs that had confined human life; (3) in a renewed valuation of the literal sense of the Scriptures; (4) in the autonomy of human reason—a liberation from confinement within the biblical world of thought, to generate a "human" system of theology (this was expressed in the new *quaestiones,* in the free space of disputation that succeeded the traditional silent assent to authority); (5) in the freedom to preach the gospel where it was needed; (6) in a new freedom of the divine word itself from the sacred structures which had fettered its dynamism and muted it; (7) in a new freedom of historical movement, from the static structures of church and of traditional consciousness; (8) in a freedom from the sacred distinctions that had separated clergy from laity; (9) in freedom from sacred traditions of biblical interpretation and theological construction; (10) in a growing confidence in the autonomy of secondary causes; (11) in a new autonomy and differentiation of the secular political order, as exemplified by the desacralizing of empire and civil authority, as well as by the cessation of the traditional oath of vassalage.[30]

This simultaneous recovery of the gospel and liberation of nature in the twelfth century joins for us the two points that fix the central axis of our present study: the event of Christ and the emergent human/secular autonomy of the modern West. Further, we observe here the existential emergence of a "metaphysics of grace and nature," in which the transcendence of grace is recognized in such a way that nature can participate positively in divine grace rather than competing with grace in a quasi-adversarial way, as often seems to be the case in the Augustinian theological tradition.[31]

iii. Twilight of Wisdom, Dawn of the Person

In the twelfth century, we observe the rise of a new, more rational and analytic theology in the city schools, which gradually began to supplant the sapiential theology of the monasteries. The new thought, soon to be developed with the help of Aristotelian methods, was abstract, conceptual thought, proceeding through analysis and definition, following the methodology of the *quaestio* and, in the thirteenth century, giving birth to the great *summas,* rational constructions which rose to stand alongside the Scriptures.[32] This new theology did not hesitate to incorporate philosophical concepts, especially from the Greek tradition. The contrast with the old sapiential theology of the fathers and of the monks was clear. First, the structural and operative primacy—the organic integrity and vital power—of the biblical word gave way to rational philosophical structures and rational methods. Second, the participatory and experiential quality of the old wisdom yielded to an objectivity in which participation was nearly eliminated for the sake of clarity. Third, the symbolic and metaphoric flow of the old theology was supplanted by the quasi-mechanical efficiency of rational abstraction and analysis.

While the new theology encountered much resistance from traditionalists, it soon prevailed in the new social and cultural milieu of city and university, and the old sapiential theology retreated into the monastic cloisters; even there it was already losing its vitality.[33] From the viewpoint of the sapiential tradition, the change appears to be a nearly unmitigated disaster; the exchange of wisdom for science seemed a very poor bargain. The transaction, once concluded, however, has never been reversed. It is essential for us to grasp the inevitability and the positive side of this historical change. We have already glimpsed the "evangelical awakening" that prepared and accompanied the advent of this new thought. This reactualization of the gospel suggests an analogy between the historical transition we are observing and the beginning of the New Testament event: coming forth from the (now highly institutionalized) "wilderness" of monastic tradition, the gospel of the kingdom of God begins to be heard once again. "Wisdom" enters a new phase of life in this world: a phase shaped by the gospel impulse of *incarnation.* We can think of this long period of renaissance as a Western Axial time, in which the potentialities of the human person will unfold with a new fullness.

Francis of Assisi (1182–1226) is a symbolic figure in the history of the West, who can be interpreted from many different perspectives. From the viewpoint of our study, Francis appears as a quasi incarnation of divine Wisdom. At once Mary and Martha, hermit and evangelist, he brings Christian faith down from its high Eastern elaborations in the preceding patristic and monastic ages; the ladder of the senses of Scripture collapses into a literal gospel. The word is lived in poverty and simplicity and preached in its direct, native power.

iv. Coincidence of Opposites and Incarnation: Bonaventure

St. Bonaventure (1217–1274), following the new way of Francis of Assisi, moved forward also in the theological direction of the new scholasticism, with its conceptual and analytical rationality. Bonaventure, however (in contrast to Thomas

Aquinas), retained in his thought and writing much of the character of the older sapiential tradition. He combined the new Aristotelian rationality with the older Neoplatonic philosophical principles and spirit—especially the unitive principle, which is always present and often central in sapiential thought.

Bonaventure, close to the beginnings of the Franciscan movement, brought into theology the strong incarnational dimension[34] of that movement, counterbalancing both the ascending Neoplatonic orientation of earlier tradition and the abstract, analytical tendency of the new Aristotelian scholastic thought. I believe that Bonaventure's synthetic vision has a unique significance because of its fusion of two principles. First, he grasps in his own way the unitive principle, thus participating in the metaphysical breakthrough which we have seen in Aquinas and in Eckhart. Second, this unitive principle—we can, with due caution, call it nonduality—is identified by Bonaventure not only with God, absolute Spirit, but with *Jesus Christ.* The nondual Absolute, in other words, has become incarnate in Christ.

The unitive principle, evidently a powerful force in Bonaventure's psyche, finds various expressions in the rich symbolic garden of his thought. His symbolic intuition often expresses itself in the language of geometry and number. Unity, or the center, is represented by the *axis mundi,* or tree of life, by the figures of circle and cross, and particularly by the mandala.[35] Bonaventure frequently uses the number four in his theological writings, and, often enough, this suggests both an implicit mandala[36] and the multiple "coincidence of opposites" that the mandala represents:

> the mandala, as a symbol of total integration, reflects the distinctive quality of Bonaventure's synthesis. . . . For he integrates Aristotelianism and Platonism, mysticism and scholasticism, affectivity and abstraction, the simplicity of Francis and the subtlety of the schools.[37]

The figure of the mandala, representing the reconciliation or integration of polar elements, is the natural expression of that which, according to Ewert Cousins, constitutes the center of Bonaventure's thought: the *coincidentia oppositorum.*[38]

Bonaventure has rediscovered, in the course of his life and thought, the "Christian mandala", as we found it in Paul and in Irenaeus—which proved to be a basic expression of the Christ-mystery in our first movement, the sapiential awakening.[39] His arrival at this quaternary expression is a manifestation of the incarnational descent, which we have observed in Francis of Assisi. In the synthetic thought of Bonaventure, however, this incarnational descent is simultaneous with the ascending metaphysical breakthrough to unity or nonduality. In this expansive movement we glimpse something like the multidimensional flash of unity and diversity, of divine light and human autonomy, which Chenu had pointed out in the evangelical awakening of the twelfth century.[40]

Bonaventure's unitive intuition and mandalic symbolism, as well as the centrality of the coincidence of opposites in his thought, relate him to our Eastern turn (that is, to the principle of nonduality). At this point we can see from a new and direct perspective the relationship between our first and second movements: that is, the essential equivalence between the Christ-mystery or Christian mandala, on the one hand, and nonduality, or the unitive principle, on the other hand. The Christ-event is the *incarnation of nonduality.* In Bonaventure's synthetic vision there begins to emerge, as well, a relation between our third movement, the Western or modern turn—at a crucial early moment of its emergence in this thirteenth-century metaphysical breakthrough—and the first two movements.

Ewert Cousins proposes that, in receiving the stigmata in his own body, Francis of Assisi became an "incorporated mandala" and, further, that his vision of the six-winged Seraph at the same time functioned as an integrating mandala in his life.[41] Bonaventure's explicit introduction of the symbol of the mandala into his theology corresponds to the peculiar Franciscan "incarnational" quality of his thought. It is as if a completion is attained at this moment, as if the expression of the mystery of Christ has, after many centuries of a detached trinitarian theology, recovered its fullness through "incorporation," through a theological recognition of the incarnation. This same gestalt, the same arrival at a full expression of the event of Christ, can be perceived in the singular person who is Francis of Assisi. He can seem a "second incarnation," in which divine Wisdom and the divine Spirit have once again come to dwell in a human body with nothing further—no cultural superstructure—needed. Francis himself is the eloquent visible sign of a larger movement, in which the Christian West realizes its own identity and finds its freedom. The human person begins to come forth in this world in the full magnitude of its dimensions, and Francis, in his universality, expresses this actualization in the simplest and most demanding of languages—that of the body, of physical human existence.

v. Supreme Idea and Secular Autonomy: Thomas Aquinas

Thomas Aquinas is widely recognized as a culminating figure in the history of Christian thought in the West. The new scholastic philosophy and theology achieved in Aquinas its definitive maturity and crystallized into a theological system that has remained dominant in Roman Catholicism until our own time. From the perspective on Western history which we have adopted,[42] it will be consistent to expect in his vision a new "coincidence of opposites" or a new equilibrium of opposing forces. Aquinas heralds a new autonomy of human reason, of philosophy, of secondary causes—and, ultimately, of the secular[43]—which can be understood in relation to the evangelical awakening in the century preceding him. In the twelfth and thirteenth centuries we behold the gospel light breaking through the crust of tradition and the smoky tumult of human struggle to illumine the human person from within, opening the person to her/his magnitude and destined role in the new creation of the world.

If in the scholastic movement as a whole we observe a transition from wisdom to science, this science attains in Aquinas an intuitive apex from which the traditional wisdom itself is newly illumined. This is the metaphysical moment at which the supreme abstraction—the idea of being, the Western expression of the unitive—is attained.[44] We must try to grasp the significance of this achievement, which goes far beyond its explicit philosophical value. The attainment of the idea of being—participable *esse, actus purus*—at this time marks not only a supreme theological conception of the Godhead but, implicitly and virtually, *a new self-realization of the human person.* An intellectual event of this magnitude must be read not only literally (objectively) but also, so to speak, on the levels of Christology, tropology, and anagogy. The lamp is lifted on its lampstand; unitive being, reflexively known, shines forth as the unconditioned core of the person. The great Copernican revolution of the modern West is initiated.

In this metaphysical liberation of God from created metaphors and symbols, the human person—and the creation itself, as humanly known—is released from the old servitude to images and simulacra of the Divinity, to participate in the limitless divine life (Galatians 3; Romans 8). The old Christian wisdom had remained within the cloister of biblical symbolism, reverently backing away from the liberating baptismal illumination, from the I AM at the heart of the gospel. Now the light flashes through by analogy, in a philosophical theology that is the product of creative human reason. The good news begins to shine through human activity itself—through the secular activity of thought—in a fresh wave of incarnational energy. All of this remains implicit in the austere technical rationality of Aquinas. The theological process is taking place deep beneath the explicit surface of theology itself.

In this metaphysical breakthrough of Aquinas we find a double realization of transcendence: first, the transcendence of God, through explicit metaphysical articulation; second, the transcendence of human spirit, which, participating in the divine Being, is able to know being and in its light to know all other things. As participating image of God, the human person emerges into freedom and sovereignty with respect to all other created things[45]—freedom from the container of a static ecclesiology, from the old order, whether physical or cultural, from the collective consciousness of antiquity, from tradition and convention. The most radical freedom, however—and the most precarious point on which one may stand—is the *freedom from God,* which belongs to the human person as an autonomous, spiritual secondary cause.[46] Here begins the fissure that will divide the modern West between a Christian and a post-Christian or secular world. But here as well are rooted faith and love and the emergent creativity of the human person.

After St. Augustine, the West inherited a version of the mystery of Christ which was doubly constricted. First, the order of grace—God, Christ, the church, what would later be known as the supernatural order—was so sharply distinguished from the world and nature (conceived as under the dominion of sin) that the divine order could seem to be opposed to the natural order. Second, the human person, radically infected by original sin, was conceived as evacuated and depotentiated, and human activity as vitiated to such an extent that human history as a whole remained futile and hopeless even after the Christ-event.[47] If Augustine, at the time when the Roman Empire was collapsing around him, led Western Christianity into the shadowland of a theological pessimism ruled by his doctrine of original sin, Thomas Aquinas, in the springtime of a new Christian Europe, played a leading role in liberating Christian consciousness into an expansive new vision of self and world as participating in the divine Being. Karl Rahner, as he writes of the significance of Thomas Aquinas for today, points out that what is most characteristic of our modern West, rather than representing a rebellion against Christianity, derives from the spirit of Christianity. It is Aquinas who recognized and integrated into theology this central principle of the modern world which we have called *autonomy*.

If Bonaventure's vision was centered in an explicitly conceived "coincidence of opposites," we find in Thomas Aquinas as well a joining and interaction of opposite poles: faith and reason, revelation and philosophy, wisdom and science, nature and grace, universal and particular. Implicit in these dualities is the awakening of the human person both as the medium between God and the natural world, and as an indeterminate fullness in which all things come together.

vi. Identity Unveiled: Meister Eckhart

To the supreme idea of Thomas Aquinas—unitive reality objectively known as "being" (*esse*)—corresponded the "coincidence of opposites," which Bonaventure expressed both conceptually and symbolically, and which he found embodied in Jesus Christ. The same metaphysical awakening appeared dramatically in the preaching and writing of Meister Eckhart (1260–1327), who developed it in the direction of contemplative experience and of identity. While Aquinas constructed a systematic synthesis in which this concept of pure being is center and capstone, Eckhart's theology remained closer to the spiritual theology of the sapiential tradition, more often homiletic than systematic, moving in the direction of interiority, direct experience, a personal realization of the One. If, among the theologians and spiritual writers of the Christian tradition, Meister Eckhart stands out as the one who is most widely recognized by Asian scholars as resonating with their own spiritual traditions,[48] this is because Eckhart's vision is centered in nondual reality and experience. Eckhart's unitive vision, developed in contact with the Neoplatonic current of Christian tradition,[49] anticipates the twentieth-century views of Abhishiktananda and others who have been influenced by Asian spiritualities. Eckhart finds nonduality and the nondual self (though not, of course, in these terms) at the center of Christian revelation, and reflected everywhere in the Gospels.

The overall structure of Eckhart's thought[50] corresponds to the Neoplatonic pattern of *exitus-reditus*. The *exitus*, or flowing out, takes place in two successive stages: *bullitio* within God and *ebullitio*, the outpouring of created things from God. The return of all things to God also occurs in two stages: the birth of the Word in the soul, and the "breaking-through" of the soul into the divine ground, "God beyond God."[51] The divine birth in the soul roots this vision deeply within the mystery of Christ as we find it in the New Testament—and, implicitly, in baptismal initiation.

> Why did God become man? So that I might be born God Himself. God died that I might die to the whole world and all created things. It is in this sense that we should understand the saying of our Lord: "All that I have heard from my Father, I have revealed to you." *What* does the Son hear from his Father? The Father can only give birth, the Son can only be born. All that the Father has and is, the profundity of the divine being and the divine nature, He brings forth all at once in His only-begotten Son. That is what the Son "hears" from the Father, that is what he has revealed, that we may be the same Son. All that the Son has he has from his Father: essence and nature, that we may be the same only-begotten Son. . . .[52]

Geometrical symbolism, coincidence of opposites (Bonaventure), a metaphysical conception of unitive absolute Being (Aquinas), and a nondual interpretation of the New Testament Christ-mystery centered in personal mystical experience (Eckhart): these are alternative expressions of a single realization—manifold in its simplicity—that rose to its noonday during our long period of renaissance and that illuminates the whole period. This is the emergence of the nondual ground into consciousness; it corresponds to the baptismal illumination of the New Testament.[53] It is in this divine birth, this self-communication of divinity in the Christ-event, that our historical renaissance is rooted.

vii. From Sacred to Secular World: Dante

Before moving on from this renaissance, let us recall one other figure, Dante Alighieri (1265–1321), who brings us to the Italian Renaissance. Hans Urs von Balthasar, presenting Dante as a theologian, underlines the dramatic *newness* that marks his work. This newness appears in Dante's triple "conversion" (1) to the *vernacular*; (2) to *history* (and to the particular, the personal and existential); and (3) to the *laity* (giving central place to his own personality, his destiny, his eros) or ordinary human life.[54] Dante, therefore—while continuing to generate theology—breaks out of the high sacred, uniform—clerical and elitist—language of Latin, the static philosophical and theological world of essences, and the celibate clerical theological world. Von Balthasar credits him with originating a new theology in response to the new world that is being born in his time.[55]

Once again, it is opportune to recall Chenu's interpretation of the new twelfth-century thought as deriving from the contemporary evangelical awakening—and hence from the intrinsic liberating power of the gospel—in such a way that nature, society, and self are opened to a new autonomy. It is this incarnational liberation that appears in Dante's long step toward a new world. As the human spirit, mind, and imagination shed their age-old fetters, the human person begins to bring forth a new world from hitherto unplumbed interior depths. This movement has continued through the centuries, though obviously not without arrests and regressions. It is striking to recall that we have experienced in the church of Vatican II the same threefold expansive movement: from a monolithic, or monotropic, church enclosed within late Thomistic modes of scholastic thought and dominated by a celibate clerical mentality, toward a pluralistic, dynamic, and basically nonhierarchical ecclesiology of communion. The overall movement is a movement of incarnation. The divine disappears into the human, transforming the human and the earthly into something new. And the something new itself, insofar as it is a new humanity, has the power of generating and communicating newness.

viii. Renaissance Humanism

We have looked at a few typical figures and events within this long renaissance which extends from approximately 1000-1500 C.E., and observed dramatic new developments in several directions—all within the Christian tradition and the theological world. At this time there begins an external manifestation and unfolding of human potential which is hardly commensurable with anything that had previously happened in the history of the world. History itself will take on a new dynamism from this moment. It is as if the human person—individually and collectively—was awakening and beginning to move, newly conscious of his/her potential and destined role in the world.

The new awakening of the human person will find expression in the humanism of the Italian Renaissance. While the common understanding of the word "humanism" has shifted from age to age, the Renaissance movement certainly marks an anthropocentric turn both from the earlier scholastic philosophical tradition and from the Augustinian tradition.

> The early Italian Humanists were primarily concerned not with philosophical speculation but rather with the development of a cultural and educational ideal that was based on the study and imitation of classical antiquity. Yet when they were driven to justify that ideal and the significance of their classical studies, they claimed that these studies contribute to the formation of a desirable human being and are hence of particular concern for man as man. This argument is reflected in such expressions as *studia Humanitatis,* the "Humanities," and the "Humanists." This emphasis on man is one of the few ideas—perhaps the only philosophical idea—contained in the program of the early Humanists. When Pico [della Mirandola], and Ficino before him, worked out a philosophical theory of the dignity of man in the universe, they were merely giving a more systematic and speculative development to a vague idea that had dominated the thought and aspirations of their Humanist predecessors for several generations.[56]

In these early modern humanists we see, under the combined influence of Christian tradition, Platonism, and the expansive human spirit of the Renaissance, a maximal unfolding of the metaphysical amplitude of the person. While the centrality of the person will persist in the Western culture of the following centuries, this range of consciousness will not often be evident.

ix. The Scientific Enlightenment

As we have given the word "renaissance" a broader meaning here, so I will do with the term "enlightenment," which is usually employed to denote the European rationalist movement of the eighteenth century. In the modern period of Western civilization there begins a powerful movement of human rationality which is something new in the world's history. It is most evident in the external realms of discovery and conquest.[57] This Western enlightenment is an awakening to human potencies within this world, powers that rationally comprehend and then transform the natural environment of humanity. This active movement into the world is diametrically opposite to the direction of Asian forms of enlightenment (*samadhi, satori, sunyata*),[58] in which the self is actualized through absorption into the unitive Absolute.[59]

Let us focus for a moment on the *scientific* realization of this new human awakening. We have become so accustomed to living within the world that has been created by science and technology that we are seldom aware of the novelty of this phenomenon. The very universe that is known to us has been immeasurably extended and rationally penetrated by the scientific mind. The new awakening of the human person within the world is realized both symbolically and actually in the Copernican revolution—the astronomical breakthrough pioneered by Copernicus and Kepler, in which humanity begins to awaken to its actual position within the solar system and the universe. For these natural philosophers, the great discovery had not only a cosmological meaning but a metaphysical and theological significance. As "man" awoke from his mythical slumber, he not only beheld the physical sun blazing in its sovereignty as the gravitational center and luminous source of his world, but realized the sun of divine intellect suddenly shining forth at his own center, and so found himself the radiant center of the universe around him.[60] This moment in human history calls to mind Michelangelo's Sistine Chapel fresco of the awakening of Adam by what appears to be the transmission of a divine energy through the extended hand of God.

Again and again, at these pivotal moments of scientific discovery—as in our earlier epiphanic moments of philosophical and theological renaissance—the image returns of a single human person awakening and standing erect for the first time at the center of a waiting universe. The awakening flashes over and over again down through the ages, from the first ignition of the nuclear fire of intelligence in the universe—like the sudden birth of a star from the great cloud of dust and vapors which is its matrix. The recurring lightning flash of this awakening in the history of Western humanity follows, I believe, from the same historical Christ-event that illuminated the human spirit two thousand years ago.

> *For it is the God who said, "Let light shine out of darkness," who has shone in our hearts. . . .* (2 Cor 4:6)

x. The Double Movement

I believe that the central characteristic of *personal autonomy* which we have identified in this renaissance corresponds theologically both to creation and to re-creation in Christ. In the act of creation, God places the creature outside the divinity, in a distinctness which is identical with freedom. In the new creation which takes place comprehensively in the Christ-event and then individually in baptism, this distinctness of the individual human person is actualized in a new depth and fullness of autonomy. To be reborn as a child of God is to be born as "God outside God," in a radical freedom (Gal 3:23–4:11)—which is yet a participation in God. This emerging personal autonomy is the first principle or inner "form" of Western history. We have found it springing forth in different directions and with different modalities in each of our renaissance figures.

A second principle of Western history is the *descending* movement, which we have noted in the figures of Francis of Assisi, Bonaventure, and Dante—and then in the new anthropocentric turn of renaissance thought and in the turn toward empirical scientific study of the world. This is an expression of the incarnational revolution of the New Testament. We shall continue to observe this descent as we follow the history of the Western world into modern times.

5. The Modern Individual

i. Differentiation: Four Dimensions

As we move forward into the modern age, I shall focus on one central characteristic of this period of Western history: the differentiation of the human person. "Differentiation" is intended to include these two related meanings: (1) the emergence of the autonomous individual; (2) the differentiation and autonomous development of the various dimensions, faculties, or powers of the person. We have found the autonomy of the human person to be at the center of the long renaissance that preceded the modern age. We might see the next step, into what we commonly understand as modernity, as the step from autonomous person to *disengaged individual.* At the center of our renaissance we observed something like the expansion of the human person to the fullness of its dimensions, and the transcendent ground of this expansion found expression in the metaphysical breakthrough that appeared in Bonaventure, Aquinas, and Eckhart. During that age the emerging person seemed to remain in contact with its transcendent or metaphysical ground; the universals had not yet gone into eclipse. The new dialectic still lived almost entirely within a matrix of consensus within a common Christian faith and a common worldview.

Borrowing the language of Owen Barfield,[61] we can say that the renaissance individual lived still within a context of *participation,* both conscious and subconscious. Toward the end of that period—with the advent of nominalism—this participatory consciousness begins to give way to an isolated or atomic individual consciousness. With the loss of a conscious sense of relation to a metaphysical ground, to an all-comprehending mystery, with the loss of metaphysical memory, there comes also an eclipse of a sense of participation in a preexisting human or ecclesial body, and a new sense of detachment from nature. The epistemological change that has taken place from the medieval to the modern West has been depicted dramatically by Bede Griffiths as a collapsing of the triplex world of spirit, psyche, and matter—corresponding to the vision of the perennial philosophy—into a single flat, material world. This, for Griffiths, is the tragic victory of materialist reductionism in the modern world.[62] Charles Taylor, a Canadian philosopher, in his essay "Overcoming Epistemology," has traced the contraction of the modern Western philosophical consciousness in more detail, from its decisive inauguration in the thought of René Descartes.[63]

If we have begun our study with a sapiential awakening followed by an Eastern turn, it is because our starting point lay within the contracted epistemology of the modern West. The two great principles which have been left behind in the swift forward movement of the modern Western mind are the event of Christ (or simply Christian faith) and, the unitive or participatory principle. While there may have been some kind of historical necessity in this momentous forgetting, the progress of the modern West has since been haunted by a deepening shadow, an ironic echo.

Let us look at the further development of the modern West in the light of the two principles which emerged from our study of the renaissance period: (1) a new awakening, self-awareness, a new personal sense of identity; (2) a new orientation toward the world, a descending incarnational movement. We had seen both of these movements, which exist in a dialectic relationship, as grounded in the double (ascending and descending) movement of the Christ-event: an awakening to identity and then an engagement in the process of incarnation.[64] The ironic one-sidedness of the modern Western development of the person appears when we note that the awakening to individual identity has involved a forgetting of the transcendent ground, while often the incarnational descent has actually become the materialist reduction lamented by Bede Griffiths. That the divinity of the modern person may become other than ironic, that these two dialectical movements may ultimately be true and fruitful, they must regain contact with their double transcendent root: in the One and in the Christ-event. Charles Taylor's major work, *Sources of the Self*,[65] traces the development of the modern self: "what it is to be a human agent: the senses of inwardness, freedom, individuality, and being embedded in nature which are at home in the modern West."[66] He selects three major characteristics of this modern self for his extended study: (1) "modern inwardness: the sense of ourselves as beings with inner depths, and the connected notion that we are 'selves'"; (2) "affirmation of ordinary life, which develops from the early modern period"; (3) "the expressivist notion of nature as an inner moral source." He traces the first "through Augustine to Descartes and Montaigne, and on to our own day"; the second, "from the Reformation through the Enlightenment to its contemporary forms"; and the third, "from its origin in the late eighteenth century through the transformations of the nineteenth century, and on to its manifestations in twentieth-century literature."[67]

A fourth dimension appears in the course of Taylor's treatment of modern "inwardness." It is referred to first as Descartes' "disengaged reason."[68] I would like to add this to the three primary characteristics of the modern age already mentioned, and to take these four dimensions as a starting point for our brief exploration of the modern person. The reader will have noticed the sly introduction of another quaternity. I shall accent the parallels by adopting the same Roman numerals for these four dimensions of the person that we have used for the corresponding poles of our earlier quaternary figure.[69]

ii. The Historical Evolution

The central line of development that runs through Taylor's history consists of three major phases, a prelude, and a postlude. The three major phases correspond to the three successive factors of modern identity which make up the core of Taylor's book: (1) *Inwardness* (centered in the Cartesian internalization of moral sources); (2) *affirmation of ordinary life* (as expressed in the Deism of Calvinist Puritanism); and (3) *expressivism* (manifest most clearly in the Romantic movement). The prelude is St. Augustine's initiation of Western inwardness, and the postlude is the further modernist development of the expressivist "epiphany."[70] Two further elements are also essential to the development: (4) *disengaged reason,* which is the key to the new interiorized sense of identity introduced by Descartes; and (5) *nature,* to which the self relates differently in each phase of the progression. A critical factor in the birth of expressivism is the notion of "nature as internal source": that is, an apparent internalization of nature. The evolution of modern identity proceeds, according to Taylor's account, from an Augustinian inwardness of the private space of "self-reflection" to a Cartesian inwardness of disengaged reason which leads to the "punctual self" of John Locke. At this point we are already in the era of a Puritan Protestant Deism, and the "affirmation of ordinary life" has begun to influence the story. Quietly also, the transcendent horizon or openness to the unbounded, which had almost vanished from the inner world of Descartes,[71] has now been completely excluded as Locke seals a rationalist container around the disengaged self. Here, in Locke, we seem to have reached a point of maximal isolation from God, short of the atheism which is to come. At the same time, the self is isolated from body and world. The pendulum has swung far enough to provoke the counterstroke, which appears in a re-engagement with nature that goes beyond the classical natural order by *interiorizing* nature. Nature becomes an internal source. The rationalist line of development continues into its post-Christian phase of radical Enlightenment, while the school of moral sentiment and internalized nature leads to expressivism and to Romanticism.

Western consciousness, as Taylor follows this particular current of its development, has moved from the opening of an inward sense of identity through the nonparticipatory rationalizing of this identity to a return to participation through inner feelings in which the individual is one with nature, which has become an inner voice. At the same time, the person has descended from an original—let us call it *passive*—participation in which he or she was joined with divinity to a new *active* participation in which one is joined with nature in his or her own expressive activity. "Participation," therefore, emerges here as a key hermeneutic concept. We shall return to it.[72]

In the course of this history we have moved from a climate of Christian faith (first in its Catholic and then in its radical Protestant Deist mode) into the secular or nontheistic climate of radical Enlightenment and of Romanticism. Already in the Augustinian prelude, a change had taken place from the Christian consciousness of the New Testament and of Eastern Christianity. The opening of the Augustinian "private space" was accompanied by a receding of the sense of divine immanence and an eclipse of the original baptismal sense of self which had been expressed in the term "divinization," or *theōsis.* The solar center, the inner light, of the New Testament sapiential theological vision was yielding to the surrounding shadows. Augustine's radical version of the biblical story of the Fall, which has had so much influence on the history of the West even in its post-Christian phase, can seem a theological parable of the loss of this original plenary identity, which precedes the story of the Western self. Essential to our understanding of the modern development of the self, which Taylor narrates for us, then, is an awareness of the eclipse both of this baptismal identity and of the sapiential vision and consciousness that it had illuminated. Perhaps the double eclipse was necessary so that a new personal depth might be developed and so that the human person might be constrained to develop from within, from the central spark of its own freedom and creativity. Perhaps we had to pass through the desert of nonparticipation, our own historical "land of unlikeness," in order to encounter the divine fullness as mature human persons. This journey through naked individuality is a precarious and frightening passage, however. In the twentieth century we have witnessed the demonic potentialities that it holds when the light of faith has been extinguished.

In our renaissance segment of history, we moved from an Augustinian tutelage, a diminished humanity and diminished world, seen from the viewpoint of an authoritarian parental church, to a Thomistic world of integration and positive participation in which a liberated person, world, and nature begin to stand erect in their mature autonomy. As we have followed Taylor into the world of the modern self, however, the unitive ground of our renaissance, the intellectual sun of unitive Being, and the matrix of participation have disappeared, and we seem to find ourselves once again naked and isolated, in a dualistic half-light. Taylor traces the inwardness of the modern self from Augustine directly to Descartes and onward, as if Augustine had fathered the whole development. The modern Western person seems imprisoned in an ambiguous inwardness, in an acute subjectivity, in a self that is isolated from God and from the natural world.[73]

But if the modern theological world from the Reformation until the 1960s had been dominated by an Augustinian dualism which depressed self and nature, the *secular* world which grew to autonomous adulthood during this time could be described as (in one sense at least) anti-Augustinian. This was a new world of secular humanism, of self-assertion, in which sin, original sin, and even God became identified with the old order against which one reacted. But the Augustinian premises still determined the agenda. Augustine had personally set the pattern for the story of the Western self—isolated by and within its own bright consciousness, its own vigorous rationality, its own intensely reflective subjectivity. The ghost of Augustine ever haunts the Hamlet-like modern Western mind, with its ambivalence: ambivalent in its very strength, its brilliant clarity and certainty, tossed and torn in its own internal dialectic,[74] but far from the simple, ultimate clarity of Augustine's faith.

6. Freedom

i. Radical Autonomy

Freedom, or autonomy, and the related sense of a distinct identity, of a personal self, has emerged as a pivotal transitional point on the way from Christianity to the modern secular West. It can appear that this emergence of the autonomous individual contains, compressed within itself, the whole subsequent development of theWest. Christianity has given birth to the modern Western world by conferring upon the human person a new autonomy, a distinct personal identity. The gift of personhood, once conferred, is absolute, so that it can set person and culture free from Christianity itself. And it is also swiftly contagious, passing laterally outside the world of Christian faith.

Nicolas Berdyaev perceived with brilliant clarity the origin of Western freedom in the event of Christ.

> The exceptionally dynamic and historical character of Christianity is the result of the fact that it conclusively revealed for the first time the existence of the principle of freedom, which was ignored by both the ancient and Hebrew worlds. Christian freedom postulates the fulfilment of history through the agency of a free subject and spirit. And such a fulfilment constitutes the essential nature of both Christianity and history, because the structure of the latter is impossible without the postulate of a freely-acting subject determining the historical destinies of mankind.[75]
>
> Christianity affirms man's primordial nature, independence, and, above all, his freedom from the baser elemental processes. This made possible the apprehension for the first time of both the human personality and its high inherent dignity. Thus the development of the human personality constitutes the peculiar achievement of the Christian period of history.[76]

The root of this liberation—and its first outbreak—is, then, within the New Testament itself. It appears most explicitly and emphatically in Paul's Letter to the Galatians.[77] If this new autonomy characterizes Christ's basic gift to humanity (new birth as a child of God), it can be traced back through the center of the Christ-mystery to the one birth within God, the generation of the Son by the Father. This is the generation, within God, of a "second and equal God."[78] If on the one hand this birth is the total self-communication of divine life, on the other hand it is the distinctness or divine autonomy of the Word, this "second God," equal to the Father. Here the Christian view of God is distinctive. This first, divine, autonomy is reproduced in the autonomy of the created order as it exists outside of God. This autonomy of creation finds expression in Aquinas's teaching on the autonomy of secondary causes—not competing with God through their own powers but participating in God precisely through actualizing their own potentialities.

Equivalent to the nonduality that is experienced as contemplation, as enlightenment, as *moksha* (liberation) in the Asian traditions, is a new freedom-in-this-world experienced in the Judaeo-Christian tradition. Between the Eastern and the Western realizations of nonduality, however, is a divine movement *into the world*, a movement toward incarnation. Israel is born in the divine liberation which is the exodus from Egypt, and the Christian is reborn in the liberating exodus of baptismal experience, initiating a new identity as a child of God. In both cases—that of Israel and that of Christian initiation—the liberation is not, ultimately, from this world but in this world. And it is a beginning of the liberation of the world itself (see Rom 8:19-23).

ii. The Anthropology of Freedom: Aquinas and Rahner

If Western modernity is defined by rationality and freedom, what is this freedom? Freedom corresponds to the actualization of the person, but both rationality and freedom elude precise definition. Freedom is not easily defined except in negative terms: freedom *from*. . . . In the progressively expanding world of freedom, the person discovers itself and simultaneously discovers the content of freedom. In the course of Western history, we can observe this taking place along different lines, and these different developments are interdependent. Political freedom opens a space for intellectual freedom, which in turn enlarges the space of social and political freedom. History has been written from each of the various perspectives.

I will suggest an understanding of freedom, then, which is clearly related to nondual consciousness and, hence, to our Eastern turn. In the epistemology of Thomas Aquinas—as interpreted by Karl Rahner—the unitive (or nondual) light[79] is that in which every object is known, and in which free choice takes place. This is the basis of Rahner's own epistemology, and it can be found in innumerable places in his writings. I will draw from Rahner's essay "True Freedom."[80] From this perspective freedom is not, essentially, the possibility of choosing between different objects, among which would be God. Rather, freedom is the undetermined spaciousness of transcendent spirit open to God: "this infinite transcendence exists only insofar as it envisages the original unity of being in every act that is concerned with a finite object and insofar as it is constantly open to its 'Whither,' which we call God."[81]

True freedom, deriving from the transcendence of the human person, is always "before and toward God," whether or not we are explicitly conscious of God.

> wherever freedom is really exercised, this happens in stretching beyond all individual data into the ineffable, quiet, incomprehensible infinity of the primeval unity of all thinkable reality, in an anticipation

> of God. Thus we experience precisely in freedom what is meant by God. . . . God is not one of the many realities with which we are concerned in the freedom of our affirmation or rejection, but originally he is the infinite horizon which alone makes the free choice of individual things possible. As such a horizon God is always encountered in the free act and is present in it.[82]

Freedom, conceived in this way, is oriented toward the future with openness and so becomes a font of creativity. Freedom, writes Rahner, is "the will to the unlimited, . . . the freedom of creative hope that accepts itself, anticipating what has never yet been realized."

> Hence freedom is never only the free repetition of what is already there, it is no endless copying of the same models in a neutral space and time. Nor is it the obedient respect for the law as for that which commands always the same. Finite freedom, too, is creative freedom in authentic history, prepared for new things which are both one's own and unexpected and unplanned and only experienced in the hopeful journey into an open future.[83]

This theological understanding of freedom is not confined to the orthodox Roman Catholic tradition. Twentieth-century philosopher Simone Weil understood her personal experience in this way.

> God is above all determinations, since he does not limit himself to a single idea; he is thus free; better expressed, he is freedom itself. . . . I can agree to call God my own freedom. This convention has the advantage of freeing me from every God object. . . . If God is my freedom, he is and exists every time that my freedom manifests itself in my ideas and movements, which is to say every time that I think.[84]

Another twentieth-century thinker, Eugen Rosenstock-Huessy, distilled from his own life experience another version of the same principle.

> We should recognize as God's specific quality in us the power to break away from the established order of mind and body and create a new future.[85]

The recurrent springtime of the West, the age of the Spirit that is always beginning and never quite realized, flows forth from this intrinsic charism of historical origination, of newness. The words of Rahner, Weil, and Rosenstock-

Huessy convey the peculiarly Western experience of the gift of Christ, and at the same time recall the principles through which we have been attempting to interpret Western history. At this point, there comes into view a continuity between the principles of our first, second, and third movements: between the event of Christ, Asian nonduality, and the awakening personal freedom from which has come forth the modern Western world.

iii. The Descent of Political Freedom

Eugen Rosenstock-Huessy[86] (1888–1973) interpreted the last thousand years of Western history in terms of a series of political revolutions, each of which was accompanied by broad cultural changes. His external history offers a useful complement to Taylor's narrative of the development of the Western self in terms of inwardness. Like Taylor, Rosenstock-Huessy is able to embrace both the Christian and the secular phases of Western history positively, bringing out the emergent values in both periods. Both authors can be understood as interpreting Western history as a progressive unfolding of human freedom. Alternatively, we can understand their history of freedom as a history of the emergence of the human person. Freedom and the individual person—here we have the spirit of the modern West.

Rosenstock-Huessy rejects the division of Western history into three periods. The Middle Ages, he writes, are a projection of certain German Protestant scholars, and he sees the past two thousand years roughly divided into two millennia. It is the second thousand-year period which is his concern. He sees Western humanity emerging from under the despotic local powers of earlier times with the aid of the Holy Roman Emperor acting as protector of the individual.[87] The series of emergences or revolutions, then, begins with a "papal revolution" in two distinct phases. In the first, the "Gregorian" phase (1075–1200), the pope extricates himself and the church from the power of the emperor, and the papacy becomes a center of universal power.[88] For the author, this is a pivotal step in the liberation of humanity in Europe. In the second, the "Guelphian" phase of the papal revolution (1200–1269), the free Italian city-states emerge under the protection of the papacy. In the space of freedom thus opened, the Italian Renaissance is born.

The third great revolution is the German revolution (Reformation), initiated by Luther in 1517 with the support of the German princes.[89] Autonomous monarchy emerges from under papal power. In the fourth revolution, the English Revolution (1649), the aristocracy seizes power from the monarchy. The fifth great revolution is the French Revolution (1789), in which the center of power descends—at first—a further step, to democracy.[90] Finally, in the Russian Revolution (1917), freedom and power descend—in principle—to the working class.[91] While it is obvious that the actual historical outcomes of these political revolutions, particularly of the last two, diverged widely from their professed goals, each of these steps marked a further descent that would have enduring consequences. Each of these political revolutions stands out as one dominant and conspicuous feature in a broad wave of social and cultural changes.

The historical narrative of this cascading series of revolutions, then, parallels in a general way the evolution of the Western self as described by Charles Taylor. The history of freedom (or personal autonomy) takes on an embodied form in the visible world of society and politics. This narrative too corresponds to the descending incarnational movement of Western history, which we have attributed to the intrinsic dynamism of the Christ-event.

iv. The Structure of Modern Freedom

It is paradoxical to speak of the structure of freedom. The autonomy in question, however, is an autonomy of the whole person, grounded in the transcendent personal core. The whole person is set free, released into the openness of the world. This autonomy therefore embraces—or releases—all of the potencies of the person. These potencies or faculties have a certain internal relationship, which we have attempted to express with our anthropological mandala.[92] Taylor begins, in the course of developing his portrait of the modern self, to suggest something like an internal structure of freedom.

> Another major idea we have been developing is that of the free, self-determining subject. This is a freedom defined negatively by the decline or erosion of all those pictures of cosmic order which could claim to define substantively our paradigm purposes as rational beings. But it is also defined positively by the reflexive powers which are central to our modern subject, those which confer the different kinds of inwardness on him or her, the powers of disengaged reason, and the creative imagination.[93]

The lateral axis of this freedom stretches between the disengaged reason of Descartes, on the one hand, and modern Western expressivism (or creative imagination), on the other hand. Enlightenment and Romanticism confront one another and interact across this axis. On one side stands the "punctual self" with its power of distinction and negation: an irreducible, dimensionless center of consciousness, distinct from every other reality, objectifying every other reality. At the opposite pole, the self, still unobjectifiable, knows itself as one with all reality, as embodied and expressive, as an indistinguishable flux and vortex of unitive energy.

The longitudinal or vertical axis of modern freedom stretches between inwardness as the "pure reflection" of self with self, which Taylor finds in Augustine and then in Descartes and his successors,[94] and the "affirmation of ordinary life," which emerges dramatically in the Protestant Reformation. These are the dialectical poles of a historical process of incarnation.

From a theological viewpoint, the one gift—immanent divinity—unfolds into four dimensions in its human embodiment. We can depict this unfolding in terms derived from both Taylor and Rosenstock-Huessy with another mandalic figure.

I. Inwardness, self-possession, awareness

II. Disengaged reason + III. Unitive expressiveness

IV. Political-social freedom

These four modalities may be understood as *forms* of freedom. Poles I and IV can also be imagined as spaces: the inner, private space of Taylor's account and the outer or public space of freedom which is described by Rosenstock-Huessy. Poles II and III, as well, are diametrically contrasting forms of freedom. A common metaphor for both might be *relationship*. The rational person realizes herself/himself—actualizes her/his freedom—in distinct duality, in a relationship of clear separation, in the distance of externality which allows it objective perspective and a knowledge of distinct things in relation to one another. In unitive expressiveness, on the other hand, one actualizes oneself—realizes one's freedom—in participatory relationship with the other, in a unity of being, and in the stirring of the common matrix within oneself. If the vertical duality resembles that of soul and body, the horizontal duality recalls that of particle and wave.

7. Jesus' Revolution and the History of the West

Our first movement brought us to the central Christ-event, and our second movement, the Eastern turn, brought us to a point in time before the Christ-event—the time of the Axial awakening in the first millennium B.C.E.; but it also pointed further, to an undifferentiated beginning in the absolute Source. In our third movement, the Western turn, we leaped far forward in time, to an era in which the Christ-event is unfolding within a particular culture: that of the West. We crudely imagined this unfolding in the form of a line ascending and then gradually descending through the centuries to our present moment in history. This long historical descent corresponds to the overall movement of incarnation, which is the descent of God into this world. In the event of Christ, the transcendent God enters newly into the world and, specifically, into the human person and human community, and the same descending movement prevails and continues in the life of the person and in that of the community, the church, the culture.[95]

At this point it may be useful to summarize the central elements that we have encountered in our Western turn (chap. 4) and relate them to our earlier discoveries. I have proposed that the new entry of God into this world, in Christ, has two components or vectors, an ascending phase and a descending phase: (1) the emergence of the autonomous person in this world, and the emergence of an autonomous (i.e., secular) world; (2) a descent into embodiment and universality. By now the successive pattern—an ascending movement followed by a descending movement—will evoke some echoes. We have already found this sequence more than once. It appeared in the "shape of life," which began to emerge in chap. 2 (the sapiential awakening), section 12, and became explicit in chap. 3 (the Eastern turn, section 12), as the movement from baptism to eucharist: that is, from awakening to embodiment.[96] The same form emerged as the "shape of Western history" in the present chap. 4 (section 3), as we examined this history externally—more or less empirically—rather than theologically. The parabola of Western consciousness and culture rose to its crest and then began its descent. This figure that confronts us again and again as we survey the course of history corresponds to the shape of a creaturely life, whether that of a plant, an animal, a human person, or a social organism.[97] God, in coming into this world in human form, has assumed as well the form and trajectory of human existence. In doing so, however, he has transformed both human existence and human history. I have proposed that this transformation is particularly evident in the history of the West.

Now it is time to look once more into the event of Christ and to determine, if possible, the inner form of the theological event that underlies the Western history that we have been studying. When seen against the background of world history, this Western development stands out as unique. I would like to develop further an approach that was introduced in chap. 2[98] by examining the Christ-event as *revolution*. There are very good reasons for taking this perspective. Against the background either of Western pagan antiquity or of Judaism—or of the religious traditions of Asia—the event of Christ represents a radical change. This one great transformational event will look quite different from the viewpoint of each of these older traditions.

Let us recall the revolution of Jesus in three phases, which can be summarized (resuming the numbering of the phases used in chap. 2, section 8) as III. new birth and identity, IV. reversal, and V. embodiment.

Recurrences of the Revolution

The three phases of Jesus' revolution are reproduced, I believe, in the history of the West. There is an obvious correspondence between the parabolic or arched shape of Western history as I have sketched it and the sequence of ascent, reversal, and descent that appears in the three stages of the revolution. The emergence of the autonomous person corresponds to the new divine birth (III), and the descending evolution of consciousness since the late Middle Ages corresponds to the incarnational descent into the body of humanity (V). At the crest of our Western history we observed a full awakening and differentiation of the human person, in which dependence gave way to autonomy and conformity gave way to creativity. At this point the human person awakens to his/her presence and potencies in this world, so that an outward flow of creative energies begins.[99] This transition corresponds to the "reversal of flow" that I proposed as the center of Jesus' revolution (IV).

We can contemplate this figure from the perspective of the life of an individual Christian, or in terms of the history of the Western church, or the history of Western civilization.

(1) After a preliminary phase of partial and gradual illumination, one awakens to the divine-human identity, realizes the vital reversal brought about by the Holy Spirit, newly dwelling within oneself, and begins to follow Jesus along the descending way of incarnation, that is of eucharistic life. (2) On the plane of the history of the Western church, we observe an ascending movement of self-realization followed by a short crest period of unity and dominance, and then by a long descent into division and alienation; the trajectory recalls that of the biblical history of Israel until the time of Christ. (3) From a more general perspective of Western history during the past fifteen hundred years, we have sketched a parallel figure of ascent, momentary balance, and descent which represents the widening and subsequent contraction both of the cultural spectrum of consciousness and of the amplitude, range, or potential of the person. This parabolic figure, it must be remembered, is only one of a number of possible models of the historical process and captures only part of the massive and complex reality.

To conclude this section, I will recall once again the two principal lines of historical influence, which are related to the central phases of Jesus' revolution: first, the new autonomy or creative freedom, and second, the new participation, through which one is incorporated into the body of Christ that is finally to assume the dimensions of all humanity.

1. *Freedom, creativity, and historical progress.* Since the time of Jesus we can observe an *ascending* course of human history, a historical progress which is particularly evident in the modern West. With the collective growth of rationality and the broadening space of personal freedom comes a new historical momentum and, during the last two centuries, a new consciousness of historical progress. Humanity seems to awaken from a kind of cyclical, dreaming existence into a progressive history. Now something is being constructed; a cumulative process begins; nature becomes humanized. History takes on a new dynamism and directionality. In our time this ascent, to the postmodern eye especially, often appears very negative. The shadow of the dominant West, visible in its world wars and ecological disasters, sometimes appears to eclipse completely the benefits that it has brought to the world.

2. *Incorporation, incarnation.* At the same time, we observe a *descending* historical movement. We can discern an incarnational dynamism at work in the history of the West and in the changing relation of the West to the rest of the world. This too, from a narrow perspective, often looks negative: for example, as a loss of the high old values—the contemplative wisdom or the aristocratic culture or the clear ecclesiastical and theological structures—of an earlier age. We can understand the movement theologically, however, as a progressive unfolding of the revolution—the event of Christ—in which the gifts infused into a limited part of humanity, chiefly the Christian West and then the post-Christian secular West, are diffused through the whole body of humanity.

In this chap. 4, we have been chiefly concerned with the *ascending* movement of personal realization; in our fourth, global movement (in chap. 5), we shall look forward along the *descending* line of incarnation toward its destination in the greater body of Christ. This descent is a recovery of participation on the scale of humanity and world.

8. Participation and History

i. Barfield's Theory of Participation

The revolution of Jesus may be understood in terms of *participation;* we have already encountered Owen Barfield's participatory vision.[100] Here I will briefly summarize Barfield's theory. He sees the evolution of human consciousness as a movement from "original participation" to "final participation." Original participation is tribal, mythical, preconscious, pre-personal, unfree. The flow of influence is from outside inward, as the human person remains a pupil of the universe, of an external cosmic order. Final participation, on the other hand, is free and creative; the person assumes a new "directionally creator relation"[101] to nature and the world. The movement is now from within outward.

The revolution from original participation to final participation, in Barfield's view, is initiated by Jesus Christ. The New Testament is the written account of this revolution. The transition from original participation to final participation passes through a phase of (virtually) *no* participation: we experience this in the literalism, the flat rational-empirical epistemology of the modern West. This reductionist epistemology is called "idolatry" by Barfield.

The two Western traditions of Israel and Greece have led to a suppression of participatory consciousness. Our modern Western idolatry has arisen from the fusion and interaction of these two traditions. The Greek tradition after Plato extinguished participation by the use of increasingly objective—that is, dualistic and nonparticipatory—thought: through conceptual and analytical reason. Jewish revelation and tradition, on the other hand, extinguished participation (as it had existed in the natural or cosmic or primal religions) by divine authority, prohibiting the use of images and of all forms of implicitly participatory representation.[102]

Jewish revelation, however, had developed one new and profound mode of participation through the revelation of the Name of God: "I AM," in which not only is divine identity revealed but, incipiently, human identity as well. According to John's Gospel, this human participation in the divine identity has been brought to its perfection in Jesus and then communicated to his followers.[103]

Barfield sees the maximal historical expression of final participation in the creative outburst of the Romantic movement,[104] in reaction to the radical elimination of participation from Western consciousness by the reductionist rationalism of the scientific revolution and the European Enlightenment.

ii. The Participatory Revolution

The interpretive principle of participation brings a powerful light to the three central phases of Jesus' revolution, which we have examined in the last section. Phase III of the revolution, a new birth into divine identity, is precisely a new participation in God. Equivalent to the nonduality of the Asian traditions, this is the apex or ground of all participation. This new absolute identity, received in baptismal initiation (1 Pet 1:3; 2 Pet 1:3-4),[105] becomes the basis and source of a new life, which, ideally, freed from the old egoistic gravitational force and the corresponding self-centered modes of participation in the world (Gal 5:19-21), flows outward and downward (the reversal of flow that we have called phase IV) in the direction of incarnation. This new embodiment—a new *eucharistic* mode of participation in human community and in nature itself—is phase V of the revolution of Jesus.

The human person, created as the medium between God and the material universe, participates from the beginning in the three worlds of the divine, of the human community, and of the material world. The divine incarnation in Jesus Christ joins these three worlds in a new way; on each of the three levels, the mode of human participation is transformed. This is evident in many New Testament texts (e.g., Rom 8:9-23; Col 1:15-22; Eph 1:7-10). The mystery, at its center, is one and simple, but it is complex in its ramifications and its historical unfolding. Here we can touch only on a few of the principal aspects of the participatory revolution on these three levels. God is no longer only the transcendent Other but has become the divine ground of one's identity; even, we might say, the transcendent/immanent Subject, whose light and energies are participated in our own consciousness, our relationships and activities, so that these take on a divine quality. We have given the name "fontality" to this new mode of divine participation, which expresses itself in faith, hope, love, and creativity. It is because of this new transcendent source that our modes of participation in human society and in nature are also transformed, taking on the character of gratuitousness, spontaneity, love, and creativity (Gal 5:22-23).

iii. Disengagement and Re-engagement in Western History

A central strand of Charles Taylor's account of the evolution of the modern Western self is a two-phase movement of disengagement from and re-engagement with the world, or nature. The disengagement is seen most clearly in the Cartesian step to a new epistemology of disengaged reason. The re-engagement appears in the later movement of expressivism, in reaction to that rationalistic withdrawal from participation. These two phases can be seen clearly in their relation to each other in the eighteenth-century Enlightenment and in the Romantic movement, respectively. Barfield has written of the same two phases of Western mind and culture—disengagement followed by a re-engagement—in terms of participation and in the context of a larger overall scheme of the evolution of consciousness.[106]

The expressive re-engagement, which is identified by Taylor and described by Barfield as a creative "final participation," is relevant to our quest for a new wisdom. The return to participation is, potentially, a return to a *sapiential consciousness*. We do, in fact, find a re-emerging sapiential consciousness expressed in the writings of the Romantic poets and the philosophers who shared their inclinations.[107] A sapiential consciousness had always been present somewhere in the culture of Europe, even after the near-total eclipse of sapiential Christian theology. It can be seen, for example, in the work of Dante and of the Renaissance Platonists, and in that of the English metaphysical poets. Usually the influence of the Neoplatonic tradition can be traced in these modern sapiential literary expressions.[108]

What is *new* in this new participation that Barfield discovers? What is peculiarly modern in the sapiential consciousness and work of the great Romantics and their successors? (1) A new *autonomy* with respect to traditions. This is a secular wisdom which, in most instances, jealously maintains its independence from the religious traditions of Christianity; (2) *individuality* and a sense of the emergent person, a taste of freedom and of uniquely personal experience; (3) *creative agency:* this wisdom, in its new autonomy, is no longer something passively received, nor even something embroidered upon a pre-existing template. It is brought forth as something new, as if the poem or other work were a living symbol of the newness of the emergent person who simultaneously discovers himself/herself in this discovery of his or her free creative powers; (4) *post-rational holism:* The unity and wholeness of the person and the unity of the person with the natural world are asserted in conscious opposition to the dualistic and analytical rationality of science; (5) *universality:* the new consciousness refuses to grant more than provisory validity to traditional boundaries of race, nation, class, and religion. Humanity is seen as one in itself and as one with the natural world; (6) *unbounded affirmation:* this new expressiveness flows forth as a deep, unqualified affirmation of being which overflows those same traditional boundaries.

The human person vibrates freely like a violin string suddenly released from the pressures that had held it mute, the whole of it now singing, and knowing itself as song. Our metaphysics, our nonduality, returns, as an embodied affirmation ringing out into the world. To discover within oneself this music is to discover the music hidden within the whole world. The treasure hidden within the apparent chaos of modern poetry is the knowledge of this inner freedom of the person.

The kingdom, present, is known in the certainty of feeling.[109] In the language of Joyce and Taylor,[110] this realization is an "epiphany." Unlike the epiphanies of the old Christian wisdom tradition, however, this experience wells forth in a desert of secularity, where the divine word no longer sounds, where nature is bereft, and revelation awaits our own word. "As the reason destroys, the poet must create."[111] Is the space cleared by the destruction which disengaged reason brings, the very space of the liberated self, in which the poet is able to create? Enlightenment and Romanticism are co-conspirators, secret collaborators in this sense. "Destroy . . . create": much of the drama of modernity takes place in the interaction between these two opposite forces. Critical mind deconstructs the limited and limiting complexes that have been assembled; creative imagination, drawing from the inner ground, brings forth unities, primal and new: a supreme fiction and an original oneness.[112] The epiphanic unity is known through personal participation.

9. Wisdom and the West

i. The Challenge: Wisdom and the History of the West

In our third movement toward the rediscovery (and rebirth) of a Christian wisdom, we have encountered the modern West. Our approach has been through a selective review of the thousand-year period which is terminating in our own time, the time of the Second Vatican Council. Following Karl Rahner, we have proposed that a new era is beginning at this moment. In our fourth and final movement we shall attempt to look ahead into that new historical period.

The quest for a new Christian wisdom proceeds, first, through the understanding of a historical process—of the transmutations of consciousness through which a sapiential tradition came to birth, flourished, and gave way to a more ordinary rationality, and, second, by a further penetration through the visible surface of culture and thought to the basic theological process at the core of this history. At this depth we come into contact with the substantive root of Christian wisdom in the chemistry of the Christ-event as it unfolds in time, actualizing itself at each moment in the life around us. In attempting to understand the relationship between the mystery of Christ and our human history, we are already attempting a new sapiential theology.

We have distinguished, perhaps a little artificially, two components in this new movement. First, there was the awakening, the new self-awareness, the illumination of consciousness. In the light of the metaphysical noonday that shone forth in Bonaventure, Aquinas, and Eckhart, the preceding monastic theology, in its biblical docility, can seem an ancient servitude, a regression to some intellectual Old Testament (see John 16:25). But the new immediacy and fullness—too precious to renounce—itself went quickly into eclipse. The nondual realization, that veritable *lumen orientale,* was submerged once again, "as if" to emerge in the West in a new form: as *freedom.*

Second, there appeared—both in the experience of individuals and in the visible course of history—a new orientation toward the world, a descending movement that represented a change of direction from the religious cultures of the East and of the earlier West. In actual fact, the common experience was probably more like a single awakening to self in the world, with a corresponding orientation toward that world. I have suggested that this comprehensive awakening corresponds to the event of Christ; it is a re-emergence of that event in the new context of the developing West.

Our first phase, the ascent to personal self-realization, seems to have reached a maximum amplitude about 1300 C.E., in the middle of the period that we have called "renaissance." The second phase, a descending movement that we have called "embodiment," is evident from about 1300. The descent from spirit and sacred hierarchy to matter, ordinary life, and secularity is evident in every area of social and cultural life. It is as if the central light of personal identity, first realized within a few individuals, was then buried as seed or leaven within a widening mass of humanity, to gradually awaken the whole to personal consciousness, to freedom, and creativity. The widening, descending movement continues as we cross the threshold of postmodernity.

Both of these movements, I believe, are rooted in the event of Christ. The historically unique movement of personal self-realization (in this present world—contrasting with the Asian realization of absolute spirit) which is visible in the modern West corresponds to the singular historical event of Christ. The historical descent from spirit into matter and world corresponds to the descending incarnational movement that characterizes the Christ-event and the New Testament (Phil 2:5–8; 2 Cor 4:6–15).[113]

While theological interpretation of world history—or of the history of the Western world—is a notoriously uncertain and hazardous undertaking,[114] correlations with the Christ-event can be found. As Giambattista Vico wrote, if we can understand anything we should be able to understand *history*—because *we have made it*. We must, however, try to discern the limits of the possibility of a theological understanding of history and to remain within them rather than weaving another theological fantasy. At the same time, we must understand that interpretation is a participatory and creative act rather than a purely scientific induction. We may need to hazard some bold hypotheses if we are to describe the bold act of divine self-communication which is unfolding in the history of the world since the coming of Christ. How does this history of the West relate to our second movement, the Asian turn? The great Asian traditions of nonduality—Hindu Vedanta, Buddhism, Taoism—originated in the Axial period, near the midpoint of the first millennium B.C.E. We have called our renaissance at the end of the Western Middle Ages a *Western Axial time*, and have observed at its apex the metaphysical illumination in which the nondual identity of the person is revealed. Here—in Aquinas, in Eckhart—shone forth the Western equivalent of the Asian Axial enlightenment, but the illumination soon disappeared as Western consciousness pursued its characteristic movement downward and outward into the world. In this incarnational movement, nonduality, or absolute being, retreated from consciousness to become the sunlit *sky* of consciousness under which the world is deciphered by human reason. Absolute being also became the space into which the human person expanded, as it awakened to its potentialities; indeed, as we remarked, nonduality (or transcendence) has emerged in the West as freedom.

The order of discovery in which our four movements follow one another has apparently conflicted with the historical order of events: the second movement, the Eastern turn, seemed to interrupt the chronological order of our three other movements as we looked back to the Asian traditions originating centuries before Christ, in the Axial time. When we recognize a Western Axial time at the end of the medieval period, however, this turn to nonduality, or a metaphysical realization of absolute Being, falls into place in the historical progression of the emergence of the human person in the West.

Let me repeat once more this basic affirmation, upon which our interpretation of Western history will rest: *the singular historical phenomenon which is the modern West corresponds to the unique event of Christ.* The rationality, freedom, and progress that are often seen as defining the modern West[115] derive negatively from that basic gift of autonomy which we have ascribed to the Christ-event. Further, I believe that the Western flowering is largely a positive fruit of the continuing creative energy of that event.

In the course of this study it has become apparent that wisdom—Christian theological wisdom—is not itself the primary issue. What is of central importance is the process itself, the working out of the Christ-event, which takes place at an incarnational depth beneath the level of our consciousness and thought. Yet, in the course of this history in which wisdom has been eclipsed by human rationality, we are awakening to a conscious participation in this historical process of incarnation. Scientific reason is not adequate to the challenge of this participation; only a new sapiential conscousness—a consciously *incarnational* wisdom—can enable us to respond to the opportunity.

ii. The Noonday of East and West

> *The Church . . . believes that the key, the center and the purpose of the whole of human history is to be found in its Lord and Master.*[116]

Suppose that we live in the evening of Western civilization and on the eve of a global humanity. Suppose that one of the gifts that belong to our late hour is a depth of historical vision—like the ability that we acquire through our contemporary radio telescopes and particle accelerators to look back nearly to the beginning of the universe—a heightened vision with which we can trace the unfolding of the mystery of Christ from its beginning in the New Testament through the centuries to our own time. Our time is distinguished by an oversupply of knowledge, an inundation of historical information and critical evaluations and theories, that makes it difficult to find one's bearings, to make sense of the story. If we look carefully and long, however, and if we allow the New Testament to be our compass, gradually some great and simple shapes emerge from the swirling fog that surrounds us. It may be that we have to move forward toward these truths, go to meet them with a strong affirmation, a supposition made of the same bold stuff as the gospel, as the incredible good news that is the substance of our belief.

In that spirit, let us suppose that Jesus is the noonday of history, between the morning light of the East and the afternoon or evening light of the West. Theologians have distinguished "morning knowledge" *(cognitio matutina)* from "evening knowledge" *(cognitio vespertina)*, as, for instance, the angels' knowledge of created things in God or in the divine Word, in contrast to their knowledge of the creatures in themselves.[117] This powerful metaphor fits well the contrasting modes of consciousness that characterize the venerable Asian religious traditions and the swiftly evolving modern West: wisdom and science, contemplation and rationality, the experience of unitive spirit and the experimental, empirical knowledge of material nature.

The same duality, in fact, can be found between the earlier Christian tradition, both in the East and then in the West (say until 1200), on the one hand, and the later secular Western tradition on the other. Let us recall Pitirim Sorokin's distinction between *ideational* (equivalent to *spiritual*) consciousness and *sensate* consciousness. He found each producing its own form of culture, and the two alternating in the course of history, with a third *idealistic* culture—like that of the early renaissance—between them, combining the traits of both.[118] The movement from ideational to idealistic to sensate culture is quite evident in Western history during the past thousand years.

This cycle of history can be represented by a parabolic figure. The image recalls a similar figure that can sometimes be glimpsed through the shifting mists of biblical history—not only the mountains of Sinai and Tabor but the dramatic rise and fall of narratives: the story of Saul and David and Solomon, the narrative of Jesus' own life in the Gospels. On the crest of the mountain, the *axis mundi*, flashes forth a double revelation of *identity*—simultaneously that of God and of the human person—anticipated by the revelation of the divine name to Moses at the foot of "Horeb, the mountain of God" (Exodus 3).

In Jesus, the morning light which is the divine Word has "become flesh" (John 1:1-5, 9, 14), so that the divine Wisdom is newly present within bodily human beings in history. Further, this descending dynamic of incarnation becomes the form of a new history and brings forth a new evening light: the enhanced light of human rationality that gradually creates a human world. We can see this humanizing process in the evolution of the Western sense of the person, of justice, of human rights, and human potential in this world as well as in the still more material flourishing of science and technology in the West.

Noonday in the Gospels

The same parabolic form appears in the life of Jesus himself as he grows from childhood to the epiphany of his baptism by John in the Jordan river to the noonday of the Galilean ministry (the miraculous feeding of great crowds of people, the transfiguration on Mount Tabor); then begins the descent toward his passion and death. Jesus' first lesson to his disciples is an *ascending* enlightenment: the revelation of his divine identity; his second and more difficult teaching is the way of the cross, of *descent*, which follows with an intrinsic necessity from this identity. The same path of ascent and descent—from baptismal birth to eucharistic death—is to be walked by the disciples.[119]

Noonday in Western History

We have seen that the peoples and the church of the West have a strange and unique role to fulfill in the historical progression from the Christ-event to the advent of a world church (which Karl Rahner saw appearing in the Second Vatican Council[120]) and a global humanity. It is not surprising, therefore, that the same drama of morning, noon, and evening be visible in our Western history. In the late Middle Ages, for a century or two, Europe was unified within the matrix of Catholic faith, and at the same time there began a swift unfolding of the full potential of the human person, before the fragile equilibrium was broken and the process of differentiation and division prevailed, leading to the fragmentation of our modern Western culture. That brief medieval/early modern noonday was not the attainment of a perfect church or society, nor was it something that we can return to. Yet, reflecting the original moment of incarnation, it was a revelation of human fullness that continues to shed its manifold light on us. We continue to look back to the unsurpassed cultural achievements of that long renaissance as to a range of towering mountains.

Looking back over the past two thousand years of Western history once again in the most simplistic way, one can imagine the first millennium—the age of unity—as the Eastern slope of the mountain, ruled by the morning light of monastic contemplation. The second millennium—the age of autonomy—is the Western slope, presided over by the afternoon and evening light of human rationality. During the brief noonday between those two slopes, contemplation and conceptual reason were held together in a fertile interaction. It was the metaphysical moment of the West in which the divine light shone forth clearly at the center of the human person and, simultaneously, the person awakened to its freedom and to the autonomy and unlimited scope of its reasoning power.

In the interior morning light that shone brightly before that noontime, the monastic theologians can be imagined climbing a spiritual ladder toward the contemplative realization of divine union. One expression of this mode of consciousness is Guigo II's "ladder of contemplatives," by which the spiritual person ascends from *lectio* to *meditatio* and then to *oratio* and finally to *contemplatio*—that is, from reading the Scriptures to reflection on the word of revelation, then to the ascent of the heart toward God, and finally to the repose of divine union. Parallel to this is the scheme of the four senses of Scripture, ascending from the literal, or historical, meaning of the word through an allegorical (theological or christological) level of meaning and a personalizing, tropological sense to arrive finally at the anagogical sense, which is to be understood either as the final kingdom of God or as the experience of unitive contemplation. The ascent and its sequel are played out in the historical evolution of Western consciousness.

The divine union or contemplative experience, which culminates both of these ascending ladders, marks the metaphysical crest of our figure, which is the profound awakening of the human person. It is equivalent to the discovery of the [true] self *(Atman)*, which we have found at the heart of the Hindu Vedanta. From the perspective of the morning, this is the unitive experience of God, or of the divine self, beyond the phenomenal world. From the perspective of the New Testament, this is simply the bursting forth of baptismal illumination and the new divine identity which is given in Christ. From the perspective of the evening, this illumination and this transcendent identity have been eclipsed by the sovereign light of human rationality, and the contemplative realizations of an earlier age are rationally deconstructed to become examples of primitive consciousness. This is doubly illustrated by Auguste Comte's scheme[121] of the evolution of consciousness from theological to metaphysical to positive (i.e., scientific, rational-empirical). Comte, theorizing in the evening light, proposes an epistemological scheme of development that culminates in that same evening light of empirical reason.

After noonday, then, we have watched Western philosophy begin its swift descent into the earthly knowledge that is our modern empirical science. While secular scholars are inclined to write off the earlier period as a time of sterility, monastic thinkers, shocked by the apparent eclipse of wisdom in the modern

West, have often been led to dismiss the modern developments as the sinister—or at best ambiguous and largely futile—fruits of an abandonment of sacred Truth.[122] The stakes in this controversy are very high, and these heavy-handed judgments are too costly.

The challenge to a new Christian theology is to bring forth the continuity, meaning, and direction of this history, and so to save both the morning light and the evening light of our Western tradition. When we have expressed the problem in these terms, perhaps we have come halfway toward a solution. At least we know where it is to be found—in Jesus Christ, who is the perennial noonday between the Eastern morning light and the late Western light. He is the Word or Wisdom of God—itself divine and the source of the created world, according to the New Testament—who has become an embodied human being: *The Word became flesh. . . .* In this event of incarnation, he becomes the noonday sun of human history.

The Incarnational Descent

Let us recall once again Joachim of Fiore's three-phase scheme of history: an age of the Father (or of the law), an age of the Son (or of the gospel), and an age of the Holy Spirit, which was to begin, he calculated, in the year 1260—at the center of our "crest" of Western history. While history has not borne out Joachim's prediction of a dawning age of contemplatives (his third age, of the Spirit), the trinitarian scheme is not completely unconvincing. After all, it is not difficult to see it unfolding within the New Testament itself. We can imagine John the Baptist or Jesus' baptism marking the conclusion of the age of the Father, and John the Beloved Disciple or Pentecost initiating the age of the Spirit.

Can, then, the three phases of our present scheme be interpreted in terms of these three ages? I believe that they can. We can think of the age of the Father as an era in which the divine Absolute, source of the universe, while dwelling on a metaphysical level completely transcending world and humanity, can be experienced at the apex of the human spirit—even to the extent, in the ancient Asian traditions, that the human person realizes the Absolute as its own ultimate identity *(Atman)*, and the human personality disappears into the undifferentiated Source. We can think of the age of the Son as the era in which the divinity comes forth into world and humanity in such a way that the human person attains the perfection of its form in this world, in a *single* human person, that is, in Jesus Christ. Finally, we can imagine the age of the Spirit as the time in which this singular presence of the fullness of divine-human union (or incarnation) gives way to a *multiple* realization in an ever-increasing number of human persons, and in which human persons awaken to the divine freedom (or spirit) as their own autonomy. Through the first toward the second age, humanity (in its advanced representatives) follows an *ascending* path toward divinity. From the second through the third age, the divine gift *descends* from its one perfect and archetypical realization into multiple realizations to continue its widening incarnational descent into all of humanity.

The arch or parabola which is described by these three ages is like the parabola of organic life, rising from birth to maturity and then declining to death. Following the event of Christ, this figure takes on a new magnitude: this augmentation is what we see particularly in the development of the West, with its worldwide consequences during the past five hundred years. While Joachim would certainly not have recognized this history as corresponding to his age of the Spirit—nor would Roman Catholic ecclesiastical authorities—the captivity and exile of Israel and the rejection, passion, and death of Christ were similarly shocking to the theological minds of their times. Our human rationality does not understand *descent* and its transformations; slowly and with great difficulty do we learn the lesson of incarnation. Perhaps the dawn of the age of the Spirit is the sunset of our ordinary reasoning, as Jesus seems to imply in his words to Nicodemus, the "teacher in Israel": "The wind blows where it wills, and you hear the sound of it, but you do not know whence it comes or whither it goes; so it is with every one who is born of the Spirit" (John 3:8). Perhaps, as we might infer from Bede Griffiths's suggestions,[123] the Holy Spirit as "divine feminine" presides over this incarnational descent and our understanding of it.

We have already seen, however, that the history of our Western world confronts us not only with theological darkness but with the growth of a new, secular light. In the noonday light of embodied divinity, there is a chemistry, an energy of transmutation. The light itself, taking on flesh, becomes something new; human reason takes on something of the reach and power of the *Logos*. The intellectual history of the West has been woven almost entirely from two traditions that emerged in the Axial period: the Jewish biblical tradition and the Greek philosophical tradition. Both are traditions of the word: the biblical Word of God and the rational *logos* of philosophy, in contrast to the three Asian traditions of Hinduism, Buddhism, and Taoism, which are centered in a nondual metaphysical Absolute that can be thought of as preverbal.

Between the two slopes of this Western history stands the watershed that corresponds to the pivot of Jesus' revolution. Around this center a process of incarnation can be observed that governs the course of history and governs particularly the evolution of human consciousness which takes place in this world of *logos*. To oversimplify it once again, the unitive divine *Logos*—the sun of the Eastern, morning slope—becomes incarnated in the rational human *logos* that has dominated the development of the Western world during the second millennium of our era.[124] Wonders surpassing the miracles of divine power that accompanied Israel in its beginnings come about through the human mind and human efforts, now that the divine mind has entered into humanity and into the human mind. But the mental level that is most accessible to us is only the upper surface of this incarnational process which exceeds the range of our consciousness and our thought.

Incarnation is a *transcendental* principle of Christian theology, which permeates it at every level and every point. The principle goes beyond visible Christianity, however, to generate the secular world of the modern West. As we have seen, the birth of this secular world out of its Christian matrix involves a second principle as well, that of autonomy. This principle too bursts forth at the late medieval crest of our Western intellectual history, as exemplified in the liberating insight of Thomas Aquinas. The metaphysical liberation of God from the great chain of being[125]—from the mesh of concepts and images—is simultaneously the liberation of the human person from its umbilical cord of passive dependency,[126] as the person awakens to her/his own inner potential and generativity. Such is the explosive noonday of our Western story, reproducing the noonday of Easter and Pentecost.

The New Creation

Silent, in unchallenged majesty, the sun blazes in its sky, free and unsupported, life-giving source and gravitational center of our world. This lord of physical reality is the image of a metaphysical sun—the nondual Absolute discovered by the ancient sages of the East: *brahman-atman-purusha*. Between these two kingdoms appears a third, the human world, out of which a new, supreme center emerges. Between the metaphysical sun and the physical sun arises a third: the embodied divine sun which is Jesus Christ—in whom the metaphysical and the physical have become one—not in a heavenly body but in an earthly, human body. This is the event that becomes the luminous center of history, giving place and meaning both to human events and to the evolution of the universe.

Irenaeus saw that in the Christ-event God had entered into the natural form of earthly reality, which he imagined as quaternary: in the midst of the four elements of ancient science, the four winds, and the four directions of the earth, emerged the four Gospels and the mystery of the cross.[127] Our Christocentric interpretation involves a parallel assertion about historical process, borrowing Sorokin's empirical scheme of three phases. Each living thing—plant, animal, and human—evolves from birth through a process of growth to a stage of flowering and fruit bearing, then to decline, and finally return to the earth from which it came. In the event of Christ, God enters into this natural course of organic life. With the appearance of Jesus at the center of history, however, the descending path takes on a new significance as the embodiment of divinity and as a cascading flow of divine light and energies into the world to create a new, human world and a single humanity. This eucharistic destiny is, I believe, the inner meaning of the disconcerting history of the modern West, where God is to be found nowhere and everywhere, anonymous and disguised within the ordinary, bringing the human person to life from within himself/herself and awakening us to our common humanity.

The missing link in contemporary attempts to bridge the gap between nondual Asian wisdom (or the ancient sapiential traditions more generally) and Western science[128] may well be an understanding of Western history in the light of the event of Christ. It is likely that the marriage of East and West is to be found, ultimately, in the event of incarnation through which the human person gradually awakens to the nondual divine light as his/her ultimate identity, and awakens to the divine power within itself as its own generative freedom, the capability of creating a human world.

10. The Shadow and the Destiny of the West

In underlining the positive relationship between Western historical attainments and the event of Christ, I have ignored the strong revulsion that most of us feel today toward further manifestations of Christian triumphalism and of a Western sense of superiority. This double diffidence—toward the claims of Christianity and the claims of Western civilization—is so prevalent in our postmodern age that it has become difficult to see what should be most obvious: the unique fruitfulness of the Western culture and the relation of this fact to the unique historical event which is the incarnation. There are very good reasons for the ambivalance: first, the massive infection of historical Christianity by attachment to worldly power and its abuse, by institutional inertia and complacency, by collective self-exaltation and exclusiveness; and, second, the chronic self-seeking, arrogance, and violence of the Western powers in their relations with other peoples and their resources, with the un-privileged of the West, and with the Earth itself.

It is time for us to look at this shadow of the West, and it will be best understood in the light of the "vocation" of the West,[129] if we can dare to speak of such a thing. I have asserted that the West occupies the unique position of being the one great civilization that has been united and formed by the Christ-event and that has mediated the unification of humanity. It is largely through the peoples and civilization of the West that the gifts of the incarnation have been distributed to the world. These gifts include not only Christian faith but—touching many more people—the human and social values, the rationality and freedom, the science and technology that gradually humanize the world and bring it together as one world.

In this light, the shadow of the West derives from the self-serving appropriation of that which had been given to the West for all of humanity. While the analogy to biblical Israel and its mission is obvious, the gifts entrusted to the West have been not only religious and spiritual goods—faith, love, interiority, a personal relationship with God—but cultural and material riches as well. I have suggested that the West has been entrusted with the revelation and liberation of the *person*—the human person in this world. To the extent that this light and this spirit have been passed on to the other peoples of the world, the West has fulfilled its vocation. We are well aware, however, that the message transmitted to the world—more in deeds than in words—has often been the anti-gospel of raw power and exploitation, of blind collective narcissism, and irresponsible self-indulgence. As we stand on the threshold between a declining colonial age and a new global age, these infidelities are mirrored back to us on every side. The voices of the biblical prophets echo back from the world around us.

The prophetic voices sound also from among us, and particularly from those who have remained marginal while dwelling in our midst. Perhaps the most deeply penetrating of these voices is that of *woman*, and this voice speaks from a situation of inequality and oppression that has been nearly universal throughout the world and throughout history. We become aware that something of ourselves has been suppressed, has been unable to express itself; this is the internal, psychosocial side of the great shadow of which I have spoken.[130] To the feminine hemisphere of the human person[131] belongs a privileged capability for participatory relationship and knowledge. The liberation of woman is a central thread of the positive historical process, and the quality of our future will depend largely on the attainment of a new relationship between masculine and feminine, between identity and relationship, between knowledge and participation, power and love.

I have presented the pattern of maturation of *a human life* as a progression from initiation to surrender, from baptism to eucharist, from illumination to embodiment. The same pattern manifests itself in the collective life which is *history.* In our survey of the second millennium of our era, we have followed the civilization of the West from a moment of *initiation* in what we have called the early renaissance of the twelfth and thirteenth centuries, through a long descending movement which has continued until our own time: a movement downward and outward, of popularization and diffusion of the goods of the West. We behold a genuine *embodiment*—an incarnation of the light, as it were—in the recognition and spread of human values as universally applicable, as common property. We observe the development of a new valuation of ordinary human life, of the dignity and rights of every human person, of the significance of personal experience.

On the other hand, we are surrounded by the artifacts of false embodiment, of various illegitimate incarnations, from an overinstitutionalized church to the corporate (the word is significant) domination of government, society, and the common mind, to the litter of a materialist consumer culture. These false embodiments—and our internalization of them and the idols they beget—stand in the way of that great, ever-widening, process of incarnation which is the core and inner meaning of our Western history and of the history of humanity.

5

Movement IV

The Global (Postmodern) Turn

1. Postmodernity

i. The Phenomenon

THE PRESENT MOMENT OF WESTERN HISTORY, OFTEN REFERRED TO AS THE *postmodern* era,[1] is characterized by a religious, intellectual, and cultural fragmentation which has become an ironic wilderness, by an extreme individualism, and by a critical self-consumption of Western rationality or *logos*. The beginnings of this era can be discerned at least as early as the first quarter of the twentieth century, with its revolutionary springtime. The decades before and after the epochal catastrophe of the First World War were marked by the startling breakthroughs that we know as the new art and poetry of modernism and the new science of relativity and quantum physics. In these fresh stirrings, the human spirit is breaking out of some invisible mental container into an unbounded field of possibility that is, once again, hospitable to sapiential consciousness.

This chaotic time of transition cannot be easily characterized. It has been said, for example, that four currents coexist within our generation: modernism, postmodernism, antimodernism, and premodernism.[2] The most characteristic postmodern intellectual stance may be described, however, either as an absolutized *critical rationality* or as a radical *historical consciousness*. With the totalizing of human intellectual freedom, every other totalization, every universal statement, is rejected. Postmodern criticism, in effect, arrives at a point of convergence with the epistemology of Buddhism.[3] Both would dissolve the reality of the subject and the reality of any intellectual structure, any general or universal statement, any proposed order. Two great structural principles of Christian theology are subjected to this radical questioning: the validity of universal assertions and the consistent nature of the human subject.

Corresponding to the postmodern age within the church is the astounding event of the Second Vatican Council, with its promise of a rebirth of Catholic Christianity. Among the other characteristic events of the time, as we have seen, are the initiating of interreligious dialogue, opening a new relationship between Christians and the Asian religions,[4] and a new opening of the church toward the modern—and postmodern—"secular" world.[5]

Postmodernity, like the modern and secular era that preceded it, is a child of the Judaeo-Christian tradition. Even when all the obvious elements of this tradition have been excised—deconstructed—by a blind and ruthless criticism, there remain beneath ground level the roots of *personal* consciousness: values of human dignity, equality, and transcendent freedom—as well as, ultimately, the immanent divine light itself.

The time of postmodernity has witnessed an unchaining of the human spirit in two directions: (1) toward an absolutizing of critical rationality: everything is subjected to deconstructive criticism; (2) toward the realization of a personal creativity completely freed from rule and convention. It is ironic that both of these liberations are radically indebted to the Judeo-Christian tradition and that both hold promise for a rebirth of Christian wisdom. A further component of postmodern thought that bears promise for our project is the enactive or creative nature of human knowledge: involved in our knowing and in our vision of reality are not only observation and rationality but freedom, empathy, hope, and creative imagination.[6] Further, as Richard Tarnas notes, the flat literalism that had prevailed in the modern West has been more and more questioned and is beginning to give way to an appreciation of "the multidimensional nature of reality, the many-sidedness of the human spirit, and the multivalent, symbolically mediated nature of human knowledge and experience."[7] In this new climate we observe a resurgence of "wisdoms" everywhere around us.

The horizons of a Christian wisdom today include—besides postmodernist criticism—contemporary philosophies, especially existentialism and personalism, the great Asian religious traditions, transpersonal and other advanced psychologies, the various liberation movements and their philosophical reflection, contemporary science (including the new physics, biology, cosmology, and ecology), feminist studies, and sapiential currents of Judaism and Islam.

The postmodern world (like the modern world that preceded it) is divided by a great boundary—often not immediately visible to the eye—between the personal and the antipersonal, the personal and the postpersonal, the human and the dehumanizing. Theologically, one might speak of a "front" between the world of the true image of God, which is the human person, and the world of idols and of the "cosmic powers." One can imagine these archaic powers returning in modern times to imprison humans once again in the works of their own hands.

ii. The Horizon

It may be helpful, before going on, to look for a moment at some of the movements and currents that make up the broad front called postmodernism. It is difficult to define the beginning of a postmodern age, since it could be said to be present wherever the experience of modernity is subjected to critical reflection. Charles Dickens, Karl Marx, and Friedrich Nietzsche, in this sense, can be called postmodernists.

An emphatic boundary line does appear around the time of the First World War, when there arose among Europeans a widespread sense that the end of a civilization had arrived. The "modernism" in art and literature of that time can best be seen as an early expression of postmodernism. Here we find a new and acute sense of subjectivity and a new dissociation of the individual person from institutional structures of society and even from society itself. As the shell of conventional forms is broken, a new immediacy of personal experience and freedom of creative expression bursts forth.[8] At the same time a new "post-Newtonian" science is appearing: physics and cosmology are revolutionized by relativity and quantum theory. Science achieves a "nuclear" penetration in the twentieth century not only in physics but also in biology (genetics, molecular biology). With the development of a "transpersonal psychology" at the boundary of psyche and spirit, a similar depth penetration is attempted in the world of psyche and consciousness.

The culture of postmodernity, ruled by an indiscriminate eclecticism, can seem a kind of compost heap.[9] An intense criticism—historicist and deconstructionist—arises on every side; every principle and theory—philosophical, sociological, political, psychological, theological, even biological—has been re-evaluated from the perspective of ideological criticism, of a hermeneutic of suspicion.

The postmodern spirit—if such there is—lives intensely in the social, economic, and political worlds. It finds expression in the various liberation movements—feminine, racial, political, economic, in critiques of "the system" and in theories that propose alternative structures of society. Western capitalism continues to spread its tentacles over the globe while it is subjected to wave after wave of criticism and protest. Globalization takes place at an accelerating pace in economics, in communications and transportation, in the development of a worldwide technological infrastructure; at the same time, we observe a growth of international organizations and cooperative efforts, and the beginning of a global consciousness. Central to this is a new ecological consciousness: the sense of a single humanity living on the one planet Earth. As the known universe expands dramatically through scientific advances, a new cosmological awareness dawns at the edges of consciousness. Late in the twentieth century several of these postmodern tendencies—as well as "systems theory"—began to converge into what came to be called the "new paradigm," a holistic, post-Newtonian vision of reality.[10]

In this new age, historical scholarship, philosophy, and theology attempt to take a perspective outside the modern West and from that viewpoint to subject modernity to critical evaluation. Philosophy becomes more and more engaged with the problem of epistemology but remains largely enmeshed within the epistemological presuppositions of modernity. Some philosophers attempt to dig beneath and get beyond the whole Western philosophical perspective.[11] The Second Vatican Council expresses a dramatic change of phase within the Roman Catholic Church which corresponds to this horizon of postmodernity and, as we shall see, suggests a theological interpretation of the postmodern age. To put it most succinctly, the church turns toward *the other:* that is, toward the world, toward humanity as a whole, toward the other Christian churches and the other religions. The transition is from monologue to dialogue: dialogue within the church, with the other churches, with the other religions, and with the modern world. Here begins, in the language of Karl Rahner, a *world church.*[12] We shall look further at this epochal change.

Can we identify any continuity, any common features among this great diversity of postmodern phenomena? Here are a few suggestions, subject to further verification: (1) a penetration or removal of separating *boundaries* and definitive *limits;* (2) a new context of *totality;* (3) the *deconstruction* of every strong assertion, every distinct positive principle, and the leveling of every particular eminence—especially assertions and hierarchical structures associated with patriarchy and exploitation; (4) a breakthough that is simultaneously *inward and outward:* for example, the scientific penetration of atomic nucleus and of space; the theological recovery of the simple mystery of Christ and of the multicultural universality of Christianity.

iii. The Challenge and the Promise

What does this complex situation imply for a new sapiential theology? In this world of multiple postmodernisms, our first task is no doubt that of an attentive and sympathetic listening to the voice of the other in the spirit of dialogue that we have learned from the church of the Second Vatican Council. Then follows the huge task of discernment in a new world of unlimited variety and ungoverned contradiction. Here a Christian wisdom—Christianity itself, indeed—needs to be able to hear and understand, to reflect and to speak in the language of *incarnation,* the common language, *lingua franca,* which is simply the human person. The person is also the criterion of discernment. Christianity and Christian wisdom must preserve the wisdom of the person in a world that becomes postpersonal both in the blind nihilism of a critical rationalism which destroys its subject and in the domination of a technological culture which flattens the person into its own image, as machine, as copy, as mere surface.

A postmodern attitude may be postpersonal, then, or it may be intensely personal—as are liberation theologies when they have not become narrow and dogmatic. On the global scale, we can discern a single dividing line running through everything, between (1) the nonpersonal and postpersonal collective and (2) the personal collective, one humanity. A Christian wisdom must discern between these two potentials and currents of postmodernism in the light of an in-depth understanding of *the person.* Christianity offers to help the modern and postmodern West to understand itself—to interpret its own story—by bringing out the emergence of the person as the center of Western history. But little reflection is required to reveal what a turnabout it will require on the part of a highly institutionalized and centralized church to accept a vision of history centered in the human person awakening as a self-creating being in an essentially open world. The incarnation of divine Wisdom is expressed in the person and life of Jesus, in his infallible sense of the person and its primacy. A Christian wisdom today needs to be animated by the same spontaneous sense of the person.

In our "explicate" time,[13] a Christian wisdom is called upon to bring forth a depth-anthropology which will integrate the postmodern attainments of radical critical rationality and unconditioned creativity—together with the Enlightenment values of universal human dignity and rights—into a view of the human person grounded beneath human consciousness in the nondual divine mystery. In response to the radical postmodern questioning of the existence of a free subject, however, our Christian wisdom will emphatically affirm the reality of the *person,* which exists not in isolation, however, but precisely in virtue of its own self-transcendence, that is, its divine ground. In the empty space of postmodern doubt and negativity, a Christian sapiential voice can speak from its deep root the great, inclusive word of *affirmation,* an affirmation of divine fullness embodied in the human person: in every individual and in the one emergent "person" which is humanity as a whole. We must resist the negative dogmatism of some postmodern deconstructionists, which is often uncritically accepted today as if it were based on irrefutable scientific evidence. In such an intellectual climate it has become impossible to make any affirmation of meaning. Christianity rests on a huge affirmation of meaning, an infinite claim of truth, precisely upon a *metanarrative* of universal comprehension. The healthy skepticism that is at home within the world of Christian faith does not attack the basic affirmation by which we participate in the mystery nor deny the light itself in which we question; rather, it questions every construction, every secondary proposal that makes far-reaching claims. This robust skepticism lives in the light of the One. And, as we shall see, it knows the descent, the embodiment, the humanity of the One.

If, as I have proposed, these developments—which we call modernity and postmodernity—derive from the historical energy of the Christ-event, it will be possible in the light of Christian faith to understand them not only from outside, objectively, but also from within, as our participation in them becomes transparent to consciousness. The inner dynamic principle of this history may be discovered to be intrinsic to our sense of self.[14]

Our postmodern era is a time of cultural decomposition. This is evident both on the critical side (deconstruction) and on the creative side (ironic art and literature) of contemporary culture. The season is late autumn.[15] Among the positive gifts of postmodernity, however, we noted both a freeing of human creativity from its confinement within conventional forms and rules and a new awareness of the enactive, creative nature of knowledge itself. These two movements toward the liberation and realization of the human person are strongly suggestive for our project. We are invited to examine carefully the presuppositions and limitations accepted, often without question or reflection, by our earlier sapiential tradition and then to exercise boldly and even playfully the imagination of faith.

iv. The Process: Globalization

The phenomenon of *globalization* may prove to be the defining characteristic of the postmodern world. Let us focus on this complex movement. Within the Roman Catholic Church, this is experienced most immediately in the shift from institutional differentiation and containment toward totality. This shift is evident on different levels: (1) the shift from primacy of the institution to primacy of the person and of the communion of persons, and (2) the shift from primacy of the institution to a global perspective in which everything is understood in terms of the whole of humanity or (ecologically) in terms of the whole world. Both movements begin to be evident in the documents of Vatican II, especially in *Gaudium et Spes* and *Nostra Aetate.*

We have already noted a parallel to this shift—a partial one at least—in our present change in perspective from a Eurocentric to a global view. This is happening in the various sectors of economics, politics, the arts and sciences, and finally in theology and spirituality. Perhaps we can view the twentieth century (or the end of the second millennium) as the historical moment of the *breaking of the European cultural container.* The two world wars were the violent convulsions that shattered the shell of the egg. Vatican II represents, among other things, this breaking of the container within the Roman Catholic Church[16] and within Western Christianity in general.

The movement toward globality is accompanied on the personal level by a breaking out of inherited cultural containers—let us say, first of all, the European cultural container—toward the fullness of the human person. "Person" and "all humanity" are analogous, then, and this analogy is ultimately rooted in a unity and solidarity of humanity both "in Adam" and "in Christ" which is such that the whole of humanity is present and active in the individual person.

2. Interpretations of Globalization

i. Planetization: Pierre Teilhard de Chardin

Pierre Teilhard de Chardin has situated the current phenomenon of globalization within a great evolutionary vision through his concept of human *planetization.* At the critical moment of transition in which we live today, he sees this evolutionary movement becoming visible on the scale of human history.[17]

1. Signs in the Present World

The forces of collectivization, Teilhard observes, are manifested at the present time in multiple and obvious ways: in the overall rising of "the masses," in the tightening fabric of the world economy, in the appearance of totalitarian political regimes, and in the impossibility of isolation as "the other" presses on us from every side.[18] The troubles of our time—including particularly the two world wars—are related to this accelerating movement of collectivization. These great wars, "two successive turns of the screw," rather than fracturing and dispersing humanity, have forced it more tightly together.

Teilhard identifies three basic axes of growth in this process of human convergence: (1) " the continuous rise of social unification (rise of masses and races)"; (2) "the growth of generalised technology and mechanization"; and (3) "the heightening of vision"—in a few words, "unification, technification, growing rationalization of the human Earth."[19]

The mutation in human consciousness that is called forth by this change of phase is comparable, writes Teilhard, to the cosmological revolution four hundred years earlier from a static universe to a universe in motion. Now we must make the passage to a universe in evolution and, in terms of human development, "from the concept of a static and dispersed humanity to one of humanity biologically impelled toward the mysterious destiny of a global anthropogenesis."[20]

2. Interpretation of the Evidence

In the broad evolutionary context of Teilhard's thought, the various phenomena signify a major transition in the evolutionary journey—a shift which, resulting from forces of cosmic magnitude, is ultimately irresistible. The single great event that defines our present moment of history is "the rise of the masses, with its natural corollary, the socialization of mankind." This process moves irresistibly toward its end, when human consciousness will develop to the point of total "reflexion (or planetization) of itself upon itself"[21]

Our fearful resistance of this convergent movement is futile and wrong; futile "because no power in the world can enable us to escape from what is itself the power of the world." Again and again, Teilhard underlines the cosmic dimensions and the irresistible force of this movement. Under the pressure of great forces, "there is only one way in which the tide can flow: the way of ever-increasing unification. . . . The last day of Man will coincide for Mankind with the maximum of its tightening and in-folding upon itself." "It is as impossible for Mankind not to unite upon itself as it is for the human intelligence not to go on indefinitely deepening its thought! . . ."[22]

The present shift is a consequence of the interaction of two factors: the limited space of Earth's surface and the development of a humanity with more and more effective means of communication and interaction, both tending toward an overall internal concentration of humanity.[23]

This evolutionary vision of human history implies revolutionary consequences for a Christian consciousness and theological vision. Of first importance is a new understanding of the relationship between matter and spirit: "spirit being no longer independent of matter, or in opposition to it, but laboriously emerging from it under the attraction of God by way of synthesis and centration." This reconception of the nature of spirit affirms and underlines the double doctrinal foundation of Christianity: "the physical primacy of Christ and the moral primacy of charity."[24] Teilhard's new and thoroughly incarnational Christology comes through clearly in this insistence on the central importance of Christ's *physicality*.

The Long View: A Cosmic Process

The evolutionary moment of human planetization is another critical step in the progressive development of the single process of human "reflection."

Reflection, or "consciousness *in the second degree,*" which is the basic characteristic and distinctive power of the human person, can be developed only in interaction with other persons.

> It is essentially a *social* phenomenon. What can this mean except that its eventual completion and wholeness must exactly coincide (in full accord with the Law of complexity) with what we have called the planetization of Mankind?[25]

Recapitulating the evolutionary story, Teilhard employs technical terms that he has used elsewhere, writing of this new phase of reflection as "super-complexification" and "super-interiorization." He believes that the scientific evidence is already sufficient to prove that the present "social infolding" is simply an extension of the "process of cosmic in-folding which gave birth to the first cell and the first thought on earth."[26]

3. The Choices

"The Grand Option," in the light of this contemporary movement of human convergence, is the choice between resistance, on the one hand, and commitment to the ongoing process, on the other. The final choice—and this is true with regard to human progress in general—is between an attitude of self-sufficiency and a disposition of faith, "between arrogant autonomy and loving excentration."[27]

4. A New Humanity

It is natural for us, with our highly developed individualistic instincts, to fear that the accelerating force of compression operating upon "the human mass" will deprive us of our hard-won personal identity. The fear is illusory "because the real nature of this impulse that is sweeping us toward a state of super-organization is such as to make us more completely personalized and human."[28] The new union can take place only through the attainment of a new degree of *love,* a shift from the emergent "global brain" to a still undiscovered "global heart." Only in this way can the collectivization pass from an enforced stage to a stage of freedom. . . . "It is not harshness or hatred but a new kind of love, not yet experienced by man, which we must learn to look for as it is borne to us on the rising tide of planetization."[29]

Teilhard looks to the emergence of a force of attraction between human beings—comparable to nuclear energy in the physical universe—which is strong enough to overcome their forces of mutual repulsion:[30] The release of this unitive power is contingent on the emergence of a unifying personal *center:* the Christ-Omega.

The end-point of evolution, as we have seen, is conceived by Teilhard as a humanity that has become "totally reflexive," both individually and communally. In an earlier phase of human evolution, individual consciousness crossed the threshold into actual thought through a process of "centration." Inevitably, in a further phase of reflection—a super-centering—humanity itself will sooner or later awaken to a common consciousness.[31] This total reflexivity will mark the attainment of the "Ultra-human." Today's experts seem to agree, Teilhard notes, that humanity has already attained the peak of its evolution and has no further to go. Incorrect, he says; rather, at the present time the evidence suggests that we are at the threshold of a phase of "super-humanization." This new phase of superconcentration of humanity upon itself will require the gravitational force of a central star—the emergent Christ-Omega.[32] This image, for someone who has seen the dramatic photographs from the new space telescopes, suggests a still more powerful image, faithful to Teilhard's vision of this quantum leap in human consciousness. We can imagine humanity as a prestellar cloud of gas and dust contracting into a more and more dense mass until it attains the psychic temperature required for the onset of nuclear reaction—when it awakens to a brilliant new life. At this point, the vision carries us beyond the human condition as we know it into something like a global recurrence of the first Eastertime.

ii. The Second Axial Time: Ewert Cousins

Ewert Cousins, following the thought both of Karl Jaspers and of Teilhard, has conceived our present moment of globalization as the beginning of a "second Axial time."[33] German philosopher Karl Jaspers[34] identified the Axial period as the time, roughly the first millennium B.C.E., when a breakthrough in human consciousness occurred at several different points around the earth. Cousins describes this Axial period, with its center about 500 B.C.E., as the transition from a tribal, mythic, and ritualistic consciousness to an individual consciousness that would develop into the analytical, critical, and—fundamentally—self-reflective consciousness that has become so highly developed in the West.

> "Know thyself" became the watchword of Greece; the Upanishads identified the Atman, the transcendent center of the self. The Buddha charted the way of individual enlightenment; the Jewish prophets awakened individual moral responsibility. This sense of individual identity, as distinct from the tribe and from nature, is the most characteristic mark of Axial consciousness. From this flow other characteristics: consciousness that is self-reflective, analytic, and that can be

> applied to nature in the form of scientific theories, to society in the form of social critique, to knowledge in the form of philosophy, and to religion in the form of mapping an individual spiritual journey.[35]

Axial consciousness, however, exacted a cost from the developing human person and community. The organic relation with nature and with the tribal community was broken; human participation in "the matrix of being and life" was endangered.

Our present dominant forms of consciousness and present world religious traditions originated, writes Cousins, in that Axial period. He then goes on to describe a "second Axial period," which is to be distinguished by the emergence of a new form of consciousness which, integrating the personal consciousness attained from the time of the first Axial revolution, has now become *global.* He starts from Teilhard's observation of the contemporary signs of socialization or planetization and his thesis of a shift in the course of evolution during the past hundred years from divergence to convergence. We must align ourselves with this cosmic movement, Cousins writes, and this means acquiring a global consciousness.

> Having developed self-reflective, analytic, critical consciousness in the First Axial Period, we must now, while retaining these values, appropriate and integrate into that consciousness the collective and cosmic dimensions of the pre-Axial consciousness. We must recapture the unity of tribal consciousness by seeing humanity as a single tribe. And we must see this single tribe related organically to the total cosmos. This means that the consciousness of the twenty-first century will be global from two perspectives: 1) from a horizontal perspective, cultures and religions are meeting each other on the surface of the globe, entering into creative encounters that will produce a complexified collective consciousness; 2) from a vertical perspective, they must plunge their roots deep into the earth in order to provide a stable and secure base for future development. This new global consciousness must be organically ecological, supported by structures that will insure justice and peace.

In the historical era which is now dawning, writes Cousins, the attainment of this "twofold global consciousness," which implies a collective ecological awareness and the creation of social structures ensuring justice and peace, is absolutely necessary for human survival.[36]

Teilhard and Cousins expand our field of view to the scale of planet Earth and of the entire evolutionary narrative. They point toward the changes in human consciousness, relationships, and social dynamics that will characterize the new phase of human history that we are entering. While both writers look on cosmos and history from a Christian perspective, Teilhard is the visionary who introduces to our age[37] a bold Christocentric synthesis of planetary evolution, of a convergent human history, and of the unitive transformation of a humanity gathered around an emerging personal center. With the next view that I shall present, that of Karl Rahner, our focus narrows to contemporary Christian experience, and we shift to a Roman Catholic ecclesial perspective, which is distinguished precisely by its new openness to the whole of our world.

iii. The World Church: Karl Rahner

We have noted the highly original three-stage history of the church that Karl Rahner proposed in his theological interpretation of the Second Vatican Council.[38] Now let us look further at this view from our present standpoint at the global threshold. Rahner proposes that, theologically, the church's history consists of three great periods, the third of which has been officially initiated by the Second Vatican Council. The first period is the short era of Judeo-Christianity. In the second period, the church is confined to " a particular cultural group, that of Hellenism and European culture and civilization." In the third period, "the Church's living space is from the very outset the whole world."[39] The theological significance of Vatican II, he concludes, is that it is the first *council of the world church.* At Vatican II, for the first time in history, the plurality of world cultures was truly represented by the presence of native bishops, and the church deliberated and acted with a new scope, as if in a new and larger field of consciousness that embraced the whole world. The church broke out of its confinement within a European and North American perspective.

In a second article,[40] Rahner draws out the implications of this conception of a world church. The circle of consequence widens swiftly. The abolition of the use of Latin as the common liturgical language of the universal church means that a variety of local liturgies will develop. From this change there will, in turn, evolve autonomous regional churches.[41]

With Vatican II, the church adopts a new way of relating to the world, renouncing the use of power to constrict the freedom of others, even "in the service of faith." Speaking more generally, we can say that at this moment in history the church recognizes the claim of the human person, of the various spheres of human activity, and of the secular world itself to function and to realize themselves according to their intrinsic principles.

With Vatican II, the church undergoes something like an ecumenical conversion. Before the council, the Roman Catholic Church regarded non-Catholic churches and communities simply as heretical organizations. The church, further, viewed non-Christian religions as dark and largely futile gropings toward God on the part of unredeemed human beings. All this has changed. As we look toward a unification of the Christian churches, we can expect non-Catholic communities to bring with them "a positive heritage from the history of Christianity." We recognize in the non-Christian religions valid means of salvation. It has now been declared, irreversibly, that this inclusive view belongs to the true mind of the church.[42]

More generally, the council represents the turning point at which the Roman Church abandons its Augustinian pessimism regarding the history of the world and the salvation of those outside its own visible limits. In the view that Western Christianity had inherited from Augustine,

> world-history remained the history of the *massa damnata* from which, in the last resort, by a rarely granted grace of election, only a few were saved. For him [Augustine] the world was dark and only weakly illuminated by the light of God's grace, a grace that can be seen by its rarity to be unmerited . . . on the whole the outcome of world-history is to be found in hell.[43]

Before the time of the council, if theologians pondered how many people are to be saved from the general disaster of world history, today we wonder whether all may be saved. This, writes Rahner, expresses "a more mature Christian awareness that has grown over a long period and is slowly coming to terms more closely with the ultimate basic message of Jesus on the victory of God's kingdom."[44]

In Rahner's concluding paragraph, the expression "world church" takes on a further dimension of meaning: for the first time, the church, as if standing on a common ground, turns to address the world with an affirmative spirit, in confident love. The church tells the world that, despite all the tragedies of the past and uncertainties of the future, it is embraced by a loving God who "in his self-communication offers himself to the world as ground, power, and goal, and of himself makes this offer effective in the freedom of history."

> The church became new at this Council, since it had become a world-church and as such it gives the world a message which, though always the heart of the message of Jesus, is today proclaimed more uncondi-

> tionally and courageously than formerly and therefore in a new way. In both respects, in the messenger and his message, something new has happened, something irreversible, something that remains.[45]

Karl Rahner's three-stage scheme of the history of the church recalls that of Joachim of Flora.[46] Rahner also proclaims a third age, and one which in this new pluralism and confident openness might be called the age of the Spirit. We can feel here the wave of optimism of the time of the council, which was also the time of the emergence of Pentecostalism within the Catholic and other mainstream churches. We shall need to reflect on the significance of this pivotal moment in history; its expansive spirit and all-embracing light are indispensable to our quest for a new Christian wisdom that knows both the unitive ground and the newness of the Spirit.

It is as if, in fully accepting the existence of a world—a humanity, a reality—outside our limited collective identity (the visible church), we remove a stubborn partition within ourself and come back into unity with ourself. We feel ourselves emerging into the world of freedom and spontaneity that opened up in Paul's passionate words to the Galatian Christians (see Gal 3:1–5:15). In conceding to *the whole* a right to existence, and in consenting to the essential integrity or internal relatedness of the whole, I step into a place of both external and internal nonduality. For I am the world; I am that which I had been shutting out. In this exodus from the regressive confinement of exclusive religion into a whole which is unbounded and within which the church—and ourselves—live, we relax into the *gestalt,* the fullness and wholeness also of our own being. This is the natural undividedness of being which cannot be objectified but which expresses itself in freedom and spontaneity, an ability to breathe freely the common air under an open sky.

Our three authors—Teilhard, Cousins, and Rahner—have led us through three concentric circles of focus: cosmic evolution, universal human history, and the history of the Catholic Church. In each of these three perspectives we encounter the threshold of a global consciousness. Each of these three visions is dynamic rather than static, and proceeds toward a new unity of humanity. Teilhard (more clearly in his other writings) and Cousins further envision a new relationship between humans and the Earth. These are three expressions of a single awakening to the process of divine incarnation taking place in history, an awakening that, in our time, has been dramatically accelerated. This global threshold is a central feature of the context in which a new sapiential Christianity will emerge.

3. Toward a Global Consciousness

i. Simone Weil's "New Holiness"

Twentieth-century French intellectual Simone Weil (1909-1943) offers us her very personal version of global consciousness from the "outsider" position which she adopted toward the Roman Catholic Church. She insisted that catholicity means an unconditioned universality. Weil refused to be baptized into the church because of its exclusiveness: because it rejected, condemned as heretical, or despised too many things that she respected and loved. Her insistence that the church be completely catholic meant that it must be open "to all vocations" and to all intellectual positions. Again and again she will firmly distinguish between two orders, which seem at times almost two different churches: a spiritual order of complete universality, and a "cultural" or institutional order of particularity, of partiality, of inclusions and exclusions. The true church, she insisted, belongs only to the first, the spiritual order.

Simone Weil concluded that God did not want her in the church.

> Christianity being catholic by right but not in fact, I regard it as legitimate on my part to be a member of the Church by right but not in fact, not only for a time, but for my whole life if need be.[47]

Upon the universality of the church depends the success of the historical process of incarnation. She understands that her personal obligation "is to show the public the possibility of a truly incarnated Christianity. . . ."

> But everything is so closely bound up together that Christianity cannot be really incarnated unless it is catholic in the sense that I have just defined. How could it circulate through the flesh of all the nations of Europe if it did not contain absolutely everything in itself? Except of course falsehood. But in everything that exists there is most of the time more truth than falsehood. . . .[48]

She has been brought to Christ by many things—beautiful and true—that apparently have nothing to do with Christianity, yet belong to its true nature. And so, "The love of those things that are outside visible Christianity keeps me outside the Church."[49]

Weil envisions a "new saintliness" proper to our time, a holiness that is distinguished by its universality.

> We have to be catholic, that is to say, not bound by so much as a thread to any created thing, unless it be to creation in its totality. Formerly, in the case of the saints, it was possible for this universality to be implicit,

> even in their own consciousness. They were able implicitly to give the rightful place in their soul, on the one hand to the love due only to God and to all his creation, on the other to their obligations to all that is smaller than the universe. I think that Saint Francis and Saint John of the Cross were like this. That was why they were both poets.[50]

Our times, Weil writes, have no precedent, and now "universality, which could formerly be implicit, has to be fully explicit. It has to permeate our language and the whole of our way of life." The new era demands a new kind of holiness, itself without precedent.

> A new type of sanctity is indeed a fresh spring, an invention. If all is kept in proportion and if the order of each thing is preserved, it is almost equivalent to a new revelation of the universe and of human destiny. It is the exposure of a large portion of truth and beauty hitherto concealed under a thick layer of dust. More genius is needed than was needed by Archimedes to invent mechanics and physics. A new saintliness is a still more marvelous invention.[51]

ii. Thomas Merton's "Final Integration"

In a late essay,[52] Thomas Merton reviews the work of innovative Persian psychologist Reza Arasteh.[53] The "final integration" that Arasteh envisions transcends the aims of ordinary psychoanalysis and psychotherapy to include "the final and complete maturing of the human psyche on a transcultural level." This goes far beyond the adjustment to the norms of one's own culture which conventional psychoanalysis may achieve, writes Merton.[54] It is evident that he has found expressed in this work, which today might be labeled "transpersonal psychology," an ideal toward which his own thought and life have been moving. This transcultural aspect of final integration is relevant to our present subject. Here, from a psychological perspective, is another contemporary view of global consciousness.

Final integration might be called a "third birth," following physical birth and the second birth, which is a growth from infancy to responsible adulthood. Arasteh studies this third phase of growth in three concrete individuals: the Sufi poet Rumi, the modern Western writer J. W. Goethe, and a contemporary young Turkish man.[55]

Merton describes, in glowing language, this state of final integration that corresponds so perfectly to his own personalist ideal of the attainment of the "true self."[56] Final integration—very different from adjustment to one's social environment—is a "transcultural maturity" in which the person, having transcended the ego and all cultural limitations, lives from within, having become somehow cosmic and universal. At this point the person has been opened to a capacity to "be identified with everybody."

> He has attained to a deep interior freedom—the Freedom of the Spirit which we read of in the New Testament. He is guided not just by will and reason, but by "spontaneous behavior subject to dynamic insight."[57]

The person who has arrived at final integration has transcended cultural boundaries and the limiting forms of particular ways of life, while integrating that which is most valid within them, "finally giving birth to a fully comprehensive self. . . ."

> He is fully "Catholic" in the best sense of the word. He has a unified vision and experience of the one truth shining out in all its various manifestations, some clearer than others, some more definite and certain than others. He does not set these partial views up in opposition to each other, but unifies them in a dialectic or an insight of complementarity. With this view of life he is able to bring perspective, liberty and spontaneity into the lives of others. The finally integrated man is a peacemaker, and that is why there is such a desperate need for our leaders to become such men of insight.[58]

After sketching the process of disintegration (*fana*) and reintegration (*baqa*) that is involved, according to the Sufis and Arasteh, in the journey toward this integration,[59] Merton suggests the surmounting of a decisive threshold in our time—which recalls Simone Weil's demand for a new holiness characterized by universality. While in former times final integration was limited to a privileged few, "it is now becoming a need and aspiration of mankind as a whole."[60] Both Weil and Merton are idealistic individualists. Both visions tend to achieve their universality at the cost of concrete particularity; this is more evident in Simone Weil as she rejects a Catholic identity that would not be sufficiently catholic. Merton has evolved from a narrow "convert" mentality to a universalist perspective that accords with his appreciation for Asian nonduality. Weil embodied her universalism in her life more visibly with her radical witness as a Catholic outsider, as well as a factory-worker intellectual, while Merton attempted to integrate everything outside while remaining inside, the emphatic "inside" that was his Trappist monastic cloister.

iii. Bede Griffiths's "Universal Wisdom"

Bede Griffiths understood the problems of the contemporary world to have arisen mainly as a result of the widespread abandonment—especially in the West—of the universal wisdom or perennial philosophy, centered in a unitive consciousness, which he found at the heart of each of the great world religions. During his final years, he reflected on the urgent need to recover this common sapiential heritage so that the world religions could put aside their divisive teachings and belligerent postures and, through a new in-depth understanding of one another, lead humanity into the unity which is essential to its survival and its further progress.

This perennial philosophy, which each religion expresses in its own way, originates in an experience of ultimate reality.

> This reality which has no proper name, since it transcends the mind and cannot be expressed in words, was called Brahman and Atman (the Spirit) in Hinduism, Nirvana and Sunyata (the Void) in Buddhism, Tao (the Way) in China, Being (*to ōn*) in Greece and Yahweh ("I am") in Israel, but all these are but words which point to an inexpressible mystery, in which the ultimate meaning of the universe is to be found, but which no human word or thought can express. It is this which is the goal of all human striving, the truth which all science and philosophy seeks to fathom, the bliss in which all human love is fulfilled.[61]

This universal wisdom arose in the Axial period, and in each of the great religious traditions it evolved into a complex philosophical system; but beneath the external differences these systems maintain the original unity. Griffiths continues to write of it as a single, pervasive philosophy that subsisted everywhere in the world. In the fifteenth-century West, however, it began to be swiftly replaced by a new philosophical development based on the rationality and empiricism of Western science. As this modern rationalistic philosophy itself begins to disintegrate in the face of more recent scientific discoveries, the contemporary world is left without a coherent intellectual framework, "in danger of losing all sense of meaning and purpose in human existence." Meanwhile Western technology threatens the planetary environment on which human life depends. It is in this grave predicament that the need for a universal wisdom becomes evident:

> It can be seen that the need of a philosophy, a universal wisdom, which can unify humanity and enable us to face the problems created by Western science and technology, has become the greatest need of humanity today. The religions of the world cannot by themselves

> answer this need. They are themselves today part of the problem of a divided world. The different world religions—Hinduism, Buddhism, Judaism, Christianity and Islam—have themselves to recover the ancient wisdom, which they have inherited, and this has now to be interpreted in the light of the knowledge of the world which Western science has given us.[62]

While Simone Weil insists on the need for a consciousness and a way of life which is "unprecedented" in the face of our unprecedented global situation, Thomas Merton has adopted the view of Arasteh that through the centuries it has been possible for exceptional individuals to attain to a transcultural level of consciousness, a "final integration" which is the total spiritual liberation of the human person. Both writers are looking primarily at the development of the individual person to a level of universality which involves, first of all, the transcending of cultural differences. Bede Griffiths, on the other hand, boldly affirms the objective existence of a unitive—and universal—spiritual and philosophical *tradition* within the world religions and looks toward its general recovery. The point of convergence of these three very different spiritual writers is a universal or global consciousness.

4. Resistance to Incarnation

These two thousand years of Christian history, as we look back over them from our present global threshold, resemble a protracted struggle between two opposing forces: on the one hand, a process of incarnation and diffusion of the original divine gift; on the other hand, a continual resistance to the incarnational process.

Superstructures

> *The stone rejected by the builders has become the cornerstone. It is the Lord's work, and marvelous in our eyes.* (Mark 12:10-11; cf. Ps 118:22; Matt 21:42)

During much of its history, the Christian religion appears to have been elevated above its beginnings and its reality, the body of Christ. The church and its leaders have built upward, away from the ground, away from the "stone." Once the persecutions were over, the public building began on several different levels.

From the home churches worship moved into more imposing structures. Priests became Roman officials. Spirituality became an ascending ladder. Theology became a Platonized superstructure, ascending away from earth, body, woman, and incarnation. "The church" gradually ceased to be understood as the people themselves, becoming rather a clerical structure, a structure of authority and power, built above the people and mediating God or grace to them. This vertical progress would continue through the centuries, especially in the centers of civil and ecclesiastical power, until, at the end of the Middle Ages, the structure of mediation began to topple, and was largely demolished in northern Europe by the Protestant Reformation.

Hierarchy of some kind and degree is required for the efficient functioning of any human society; it is a question of the relation of hierarchy to the vital values of the gospel. The successive "poverty movements" and egalitarian reforms in the churches and in the world have been attempts to restore the original New Testament spirit of equality and communion and the gospel's principle of leadership as service. Our fourth movement—responding to actual events and movements in the world and in the churches—is a movement toward the rediscovery of the cornerstone of incarnation, the foundation and totality, the divine-human matrix which is the body of Christ.

This chronic resistance to the process of incarnation is not only a matter of institutional structures. We shall look at some of its expressions in the worlds of (1) theology, of (2) spirituality, and of (3) church structures.

1. Theological Superstructures

Let us look first at the soteriological theory of St. Anselm of Canterbury (1033–1109), which was followed by St. Thomas Aquinas and then by much of the Catholic tradition. This theology of redemption ascends away from the more sacramental and mystery-centered soteriology of the patristic church. Anselm's theory of redemption is a juridical one. God has suffered a divine offense, an injury of infinite magnitude, in the sin of the first humans, which can only be atoned for by an infinite atonement, offered by an infinite or divine-human person. This is Jesus' role in human salvation. The justification is essentially extrinsic. This theory can be called a superstructure for two reasons. First, the satisfaction takes place "over our heads": not only outside us but above us, on a level of divine honor, justice and reparation to which we cannot attain. But "superstructure" has a deeper meaning here. The theory is constructed "above" the actual mystery of incarnation and justification by divine-human union in the *body* of Christ. This theological doctrine is built on a level of rationality superior to the physical reality of redemptive incorporation in Christ, which it no longer recognizes.

Another example of theological superstructure is the doctrine of the divine Trinity itself, insofar as it has been separated from the Incarnation and closed in upon itself, the immanent Trinity suppressing the economic Trinity.[63] In this way, through the centuries, the power of the Christ-event became concealed. Christians, no longer aware of their baptismal divinization in the body of Christ, returned to modes of worship that often came to resemble those of Israel before Christ. When Christian life had come to be understood no longer as participation in God through Word and Spirit, the trinitarian God seemed to be accessible only to intellectual speculation or to the mystical experience of a few contemplative souls. The speculation itself proceeded, in the West, along the path of interiorization initiated by St. Augustine.

A third theological superstructure is *the supernatural order*. While this, or an equivalent, is a necessary concept in Christian theology, it is particularly susceptible to misunderstanding: to an extreme dualism and externalization. When the supernatural is set above the merely natural as a superior or divine level of being, the universal, transforming divine presence *within* nature itself is negated, and the freedom and subtle pervasiveness of the Holy Spirit are excluded. In Catholicism there has often been a tendency to restore the pre-Christian separation of sacred and profane by declaring certain persons, objects and rituals to be the vessels of divinity, and only the orthodox believers to be participants in the divine grace thus mediated, while the rest of humanity and of creation remained outside this circle of light in the darkness of sin.[64] This too is a largely Augustinian legacy in the West. Post-Reformation Catholic ecclesiology maintained the unique superiority of the church with conceptions of this kind, and within the church itself the primacy of communion in the body of Christ was obscured by the exaltation of clergy and religious above the laity.

A negative correlative to the separate supernatural is the *depression of nature* implicit in the Augustinian doctrine of an original sin that affects the whole creation and in a particular way vitiates humanity. Too often, both in the Platonic East and in the Augustinian West, the Christian order was understood as ascending above nature and moving away from it. Along with the depression of nature has gone the depression of *the feminine, of woman*. From a patriarchal viewpoint (and in the light of the Genesis narrative), woman has been seen as the weak point in human nature through which temptation and sin have gained entry.

2. Spiritual Superstructures

Christian spiritual theology has often borrowed the conceptual structures offered by classical philosophy, developing along the ascending trajectory which is so appealing to the human ego and allowing baptismal initiation to fade from view. With the introduction of Platonic and Neoplatonic paradigms into Christian spirituality (by Clement, Origen, Evagrius, and their successors), the spiritual life became conceived as an *ascent* away from the body and the ordinary things of human existence. Spiritual theology became an architecture of ladders and of ascending gradations of virtues and spiritual states. Monastic interpretations of the series of "senses of Scripture" and Guigo II's "ladder of contemplatives"[65] exemplify this consistent tendency in the medieval West. This mental context corresponded to the cosmological paradigm of the ancient world, with its great chain of being.[66]

3. Institutional Superstructures

While a divinely sanctioned authority and elementary orders of ministry appear already within the New Testament, these *hierarchical elements*, in the course of the centuries, came to predominate over the ecclesial communion to such an extent that the church was transformed. The institutional model became the dominant conception of the church within Catholicism.[67] As the sense of personal participation and of ecclesial communion diminished, the experience of Catholic identity was itself transformed. A deep alienation had imperceptibly grown and would burst forth with the ripening of time. The Protestant Reformation and the progressive dechristianization of modern Europe did not suffice to awaken leaders of the Roman Catholic Church to the real nature of the problem, however, until the time of Vatican II. I have already mentioned the elevation of clerical office above the status of the common Christian people. Priests were elevated to the status of Roman officials by Constantine and became separated from the laity by something like a code of ritual purity through the law of celibacy. From the time of the Council of Elvira (ca. 306), celibacy gradually became the norm not only for monks and religious, but for priests, and through the reform of Gregory VII it became a fundamental element in the institutional structure of the church.

The liturgy itself became a clerical superstructure. The eucharist was separated from and elevated above the people so that—again in this way—they no longer experienced themselves as the body of Christ, the eucharistic body. Through the manner of celebration as well as through solemn paraliturgical eucharistic devotions, the eucharistic body of Christ became objectified and separated from the ecclesial body of Christ constituted by the faithful themselves.

* * *

Two primal distortions threatened the integrity of Christian faith already within the New Testament period: first, the *Judaizing* current, which insisted on retaining full observance of the Jewish law, and, second, the Gnostic current, which explicitly rejected the divine descent that was the incarnation. These two aberrations seem contrary, the former a materializing of the Christian faith and the latter a spiritualizing of the faith. Both, however, can be seen as rejections of incarnation: the latter explicitly and from above, the former more subtly and from below. Both of them insist on the necessity of a separation from the common body, from ordinary Christian existence, failing to recognize the unitive event which is incarnation. Both identify true religion with something added to human life or raised above human life ("law" or "spirit") rather than with an interior transformation of the whole of human life. We have seen later distortions, later superstructures, moving away from the mystery of incarnation as they developed in both of these directions: an externalizing elevation and an interiorizing elevation: institutional superstructures and spiritual superstructures. Both have been supported by the rationalizing superstructures of theology.

The institutional church, while extolling the Christian virtue of humility to the faithful, has consistently been inclined to exalt itself on the basis of its divine mandate. This has been true especially of the Roman Church, with its tradition of papal supremacy; Roman centralization has promoted the overdevelopment of superstructures. The central authority was asserted with a new and greater insistence after the eleventh-century Gregorian reform and the separation from Eastern Christianity, and again following the challenge of the Protestant Reformation. The church seemed to become at the same time ever more institutional and ever more supernatural, raising itself up and away from an unreceptive and despicable world—and simultaneously becoming less and less human—until the decisive turn of Vatican II.

This refusal of incarnation can be seen as a failure of the church to communicate the full, participated reality of the divine incarnation. The Roman Catholic Church has stood boldly and faithfully on the faith and the confession of Peter, proclaiming the divinity of Jesus Christ. It has been much less successful, however, in communicating the good news of the divinization of those who believe and are baptized into Christ. This consistent teaching of Pope Leo the Great[68] has seldom been heard in the Roman Church during recent centuries. The outer boundary of incarnation has been drawn tightly around Christ alone or, a little more widely, around Christ and the institutional church, with the Christian people—and all else—outside it. At most, incarnation has been extended to include faithful Catholics. But to withhold knowledge of the divine gift—incarnation and divinization—from the Christian people is to limit severely the church's ability to communicate the divine gift to the world.

The official motives for this arrest of the incarnational process are as worthy as were the motives of the scribes and Pharisees who condemned Jesus for associating with the prostitutes and tax collectors and for healing the crippled on the Sabbath. Who can deny the obvious necessity of maintaining a distinction between the holy and the profane, the clean and the unclean? Ever present too is the need for control, which requires clear distinctions, levels, and lines of authority. But these necessities almost invariably evoke a compulsive effort to control the Holy Spirit, to program an uncontrollable process, to mediate the immediacy of the mystery, to administer a mystery which lives beneath the level of administration and rationalization, to build up and away from the cornerstone of incarnation, which is the body of Christ. Without doubt, the masculine tendency has had much to do with this reversal of incarnation: if the voice of woman had been heard, would this split—at once horizontal and vertical—have become so grave?

Once we cleave the mystery of incarnation in this way, perhaps we are doomed to be faithful to our initial error and to follow the logic of the failure consistently in all of our theology and spirituality: with the ladders, the multistorey buildings, the structures of mediation, the return to the dominance of law. We have seen a few of these superstructures, which vitiate their usefulness to the extent that they obscure or even replace the mystery. The attempt to rationalize the mystery into an efficient form always seems to lead to these surrogates for incarnation. Reliable and static structures imperceptibly supplant the uncontrollable, living incarnational process.

5. The Descent of History

i. The Downward Curve

Incarnational movements arose again and again within the Catholic Church. One conspicuous example is the birth of the medieval religious orders that succeeded monasticism, descending from the monks' pursuit of contemplative interiority to move outward into the world. Around the same time, in the twelfth and thirteenth centuries, a parallel descent begins to take place in Christian thought. The transition from a Platonic to an Aristotelian philosophy and theology is an incarnational movement that further parallels the transfer of the intellectual center from monastery to university and city. In fact, a descending movement is perceptible already in the West during the patristic period in the cultural transition from the contemplative theology and spirituality of the Greeks to the moral and practical teaching of the Latins, the Western Europeans. No doubt, the inundation of the Roman Empire and classical civilization by the new peoples of the West, the "barbarians," played a major role in the popularization of religion, but the incarnational descent is already evident in the writings of St. Augustine.

In the unfolding of the modern age and with the emergence of a secular world free from the supervision of ecclesial authority, the ecclesial wineskin was broken and the wine spilled forth, pouring downward in a kind of secular incarnation. From that point we can recognize in the West two great complementary yet opposed pseudo-incarnations, each one, and both together, incomplete: institutional church and secular humanity.

Secular Western culture, freed from the direction of the church, continued to descend, as we have seen in chap. 4. We can observe the descent in the further movement from Aristotelian to Newtonian thought, and onward to the reductionism of Marx and Freud and the deconstructionism of Derrida. We have seen this incarnational direction already in the series of European revolutions described by Rosenstock-Huessy.[69] In a descending movement within society and politics, active participation is extended, at least in principle, at each stage to a new, larger, and less privileged class of people.

As we have also seen, the incarnational movement in history is manifested in the modern West particularly through an empowerment of the human person in which the *mirabilia Dei* seem to come about through human activity rather than by direct divine intervention in the world. Through science and technology, the creative intelligence and expansive energy of the West, a transformation of the world is taking place, a humanization of the world, which is not cancelled by the more glaring instances of dehumanization. A striking further example of secular incarnation is the late emergence and acceptance of the implications of gospel values regarding universal human rights, civil rights without racial distinction, the universal dignity of the human person, the injustice of slavery, the freedom and equality of women, etc. We may ask why it has taken so long for these fruits to emerge. Was it necessary for history to proceed until the immanent divine force of incarnation had outrun not only the grip of the old social order but also the conservatism of a Christian religion of privilege? When we recall that the church had assumed the responsibilities abandoned by the dying Roman Empire, it is not hard to understand how the church clung to the binding of Christian office to secular privilege. Whatever the precise chain of causality, the incarnational movement of Western history had to move outside the church to achieve these results.

A parallel cultural example of incarnational descent appears in the history of Western literature recounted by Erich Auerbach.[70] The story progresses from a literature governed by the classical principle that only eminent persons—kings, nobles, exceptional heroes—can be the subject of serious writing, to the social realism of nineteenth-century novels which deliberately portray the ordinariness of life, even its squalor, meaninglessness, and alienation. Auerbach attributes this descending line of progression to the continuing influence of the *gospel* on Western culture.[71]

The role of the ecclesial institution in the drama of incarnation is not primarily a negative one, as it might seem from what we have been saying. It is necessary to bring to light this resistance which has been concealed beneath official complacency and denial, and which cannot be dealt with until it has become visible. The church is, first of all, the living body of Christ, the people of God. Second—and still on the level of incarnational reality—it is a sacramental organism[72] that embodies the divine gift and makes it present to people in their everyday life on earth. Perhaps on this level, the immediate problem is more often that the presence of spirit remains inaccessible to consciousness and experience beneath the thick veil of the ordinary. The church seems at once too matter-of-fact, too ordinary, and too exalted in an artificial (and obviously human), rather than a spiritual way. The church often seems a kind of intermediate world of institutional pseudo-reality, sometimes even a solemn and out-of-date world of clerical artificiality, tediously mediating between two realities which are already one: God and humanity. It is this church which is not real but a comic fantasy; the reality is the body of Christ. In summary, *to the extent that the "formal" church (both of East and of West) has resisted incarnation, history has moved beyond it, pursuing its incarnational trajectory.*

ii. Compensatory Movements

The difficulties that have impeded the Christian church from progressing toward full incarnation have drawn forth a series of reactions from below, both inside and outside the church. Successive "poverty movements" in the medieval church of the West sought to witness to the incarnational gospel of Christ in the face of a top-heavy hierarchical institution. Waldensian and Protestant movements in the early modern period moved in the same direction, bringing Christianity down to the ground once again. We have recalled the birth of a secular world in the modern West outside and beneath the sacred institution of the church. Marxism, with its ideology of dialectical materialism, during the twentieth century, was a further ground-level compensatory reaction, a collectivism that positioned itself not only against the capitalist individualism of the secular West but against a Christianity that had failed to incarnate the gospel through social justice and the sharing of material goods. With the collapse of Marxist communism, Islam emerges once again to resume its role of disinherited brother or shadow figure, confronting the Christian and post-Christian West on behalf of those who have been left outside the incarnational process in which the divine gifts brought by Christ—not only spiritual but material gifts—are diffused into humanity.[73] While Marxism, heir to the historical dynamism of Christianity, pressed beyond modern Western individualism toward a classless collectivity, militant Islam has recoiled from modern secular individualism toward the archaic consciousness and mythos of a pre-personal society, a quasi-tribal society.

Today, at the beginning of the postmodern age, a series of liberation movements, arising from below, confront the West and its Christian churches. These movements too give a voice to the elements of human society that have been left outside—and often beneath—the incarnational progress of history. Liberation or self-realization is the personal or subjective side of incarnation. Racial, economic, religious, and gender distinctions have continued to mark out boundaries of inequality. Today, in the words of Paul to the Galatians, we hear not only the proclamation of the gift of divine *koinonia* to the church but a wider message as well: a social, political, and economic imperative that extends to all humanity, and that has become explicit in the social encyclicals of recent popes and in the *Constitution on the Church and the Modern World* of Vatican II.

> There is neither Jew nor Greek, there is neither slave nor free, there is neither male nor female; for you are all one in Christ Jesus. (Gal 3:28)

The church arrives at a new level of maturity, coming to understand its place in the world and to speak in the common language of human existence and human needs, the language of the person. This too is an expression of the historical process of incarnation.

Where did the vertical gap begin? When did the progress of incarnation begin to be arrested, the church first pull itself upward away from the ground and the people of the earth? One root of this disincarnation can already be discerned in the Old Testament with the (however necessary) abolition of the preexisting natural religion, the pagan earth religions, and the elevation and institutionalization of religion within Israel. The vertical polarization is already there: institution opposed to nature. We can theorize that the incarnational process inaugurated by Jesus should have bridged that gap, reaching downward and outward to re-integrate the creation into the religious tradition, but in actuality that happened only partially and hesitantly. Within the New Testament itself, Paul's opposing of "spirit" and "flesh" certainly supported the vertical elevation of Christianity away from ground, nature, body, and ordinary human life. The Greek philosophers had elevated intellect or spirit far above body and material nature, and when Christians appropriated those philosophies—especially Platonism—the imported dualism reinforced the separation inherited from Israel, but now particularly in the direction of spiritual interiority.

6. Global Christianity: The Southern Turn

Ten years after the Second Vatican Council, Walbert Bühlmann, a Swiss Capuchin missionary and scholar, published *The Coming of the Third Church*,[74] a pioneering work in which he announced the advent of a new era of Christianity (at the beginning of the third millennium of Christianity). The Third Church that he saw emerging is the church of the South, destined to assume the dominant position formerly occupied, in turn, by the churches of East and West.[75]

Thirty years later, Philip Jenkins, in *The Next Christendom: The Coming of Global Christianity*,[76] has studied the same Southern turn of Christianity more broadly and more thoroughly, including within his field of view the Protestant churches and the new independent churches. In the Southern movement of Christianity, the new Pentecostal churches play a leading role. His overall evaluation confirms Bühlmann's conclusion: "The era of Western Christianity has passed within our lifetimes, and the day of Southern Christianity is dawning."[77] Jenkins observes that the number of Christians in Africa has increased from ten million in 1900 to 360 million in 2000. By the year 2050, he predicts, only one Christian in five will be a non-Hispanic white person, and the center of gravity of the Christian world will have shifted decisively to the Southern hemisphere.

This momentous global shift within Christianity is unnoticed by most Western observers. Many of these, whose view of Christianity is limited to Europe and North America, have concluded that Christianity is in a phase of decline. In fact the number of Christians continues to grow, and in some regions to grow very dramatically. The largest numbers of new Christians in the churches of the South are to be found among Pentecostals and traditionalist Roman Catholics.

Jenkins specifies the main characteristics of this new Christianity of the South as poverty, conservatism, supernaturalism, and Pentecostalism. In contrast to the relative prosperity of the Christian peoples of Europe and North America, the great majority of the new Christians are *poor*, and many of them are very poor. This is true particularly in Africa. The new churches are more *conservative* than the older churches in terms both of beliefs and of moral teaching: "The churches that have made the most dramatic progress in the global South have either been Roman Catholic, of a traditionalist and fideist kind, or radical Protestant sects, evangelical, or Pentecostal."[78] The new Christians of the South are *supernaturalists* both in their habitual acceptance of spiritual experiences and other extraordinary religious phenomena and in their intense concern with personal salvation, and they are relatively indifferent to the political transformation of society.

While a century ago the *Pentecostals* were "only a handful," they number several hundred million at present, and Jenkins estimates that they will have grown to over a billion by the year 2050.[79] The Pentecostal and independent churches, Jenkins notes, are located in the world's regions of fastest population growth. They may possibly, within a few decades, constitute a majority of all Christians in the world.

At present, the Christian South remains divided into two great separate regions, Africa and Asia, with little communication between them. But Jenkins foresees a time when the Southern Christian movement will become truly global, as these two clusters of churches begin to relate to each other and to attain something of a common sense of Christian identity. "Once that axis is established, we really would be speaking of a new Christendom, based in the southern hemisphere."[80] The two great religions that will dominate the global future, Jenkins believes, are Christianity and Islam; and there is the danger of a return to the state of ongoing Christian-Muslim conflict that characterized the Middle Ages.

This striking phenomenon of the Southern shift of Christianity can be understood as a further expression of the *incarnational* dynamic—the downward and outward flow—of the Christ-event as it unfolds in the course of history. In general, we discover something like a recurrence of the New Testament phenomenon: a movement from formalized (and now rationalized) religion to a simpler, more popular religion that has become one with human life—this simplicity and unity being particularly manifest under the pressure of poverty, hardship, and persecution.

Several incarnational aspects of the shift toward a Southern Christianity can be distinguished: (1) a shift toward lower economic and social status; (2) a liberation of worship from (a modern Western) confinement within the individual person's mind and heart, as the communal dimension of religion is rediscovered; (3) a recovery by the people of participatory worship; (4) a descent of religion into the physicality of the person: not only a return to song and dance as essential elements of celebration, but a new awareness of the presence of the Spirit in the whole of bodily life and activity.

Our first reaction to the Southern revolution, from the viewpoint of a sapiential theology, might be dismay at the rigid structure of belief which is so prevalent among the new Christian churches. The fresh start from the initial Christian experience, however, which is exemplified by the new churches of the South, offers the possibility of a *sapiential rebirth,* if the spiritual and theological development can be guided away from the rigid and literalist tendencies of the fundamentalisms of both the Protestant biblical and the Catholic institutional kinds.

Sapiential theology is part of the consciousness and culture of the earliest Christian communities. It is explicit in Paul and in the Johannine writings, as well as the patristic writings of the first two centuries of Christianity. There is great promise for the renewal of Christian sapiential theology (or rather theologies) in an experiential *return to the beginning* like that known by the early Christian communities who, with the new catechumens in their midst, celebrated the paschal mysteries and the sacraments of initiation during the Easter vigil.

As the wisdom of early Christian communities grew from the sacramental experience of baptism and eucharist, so may a new sapiential consciousness and theology develop from participation in the sacramental depths of the mystery of Christ, the perennial generative core of Christian faith. Similarly the Scriptures of both Testaments, which the new Christians find endlessly attractive and enlightening, can be opened by a sapiential exegesis to the power of the mystery that lies within them, as was done by the fathers of the early centuries. A primary need, therefore, will be for a mystagogical exegesis both of the sacraments of initiation and of the Old and New Testaments. A sapiential, that is, participatory, unfolding of the mystery can, today as well as in those first days, enable Christians to participate consciously in the life of Christ as they experience both the new intimacy and the new exile that belong to his disciples.

Our four movements suggest the gifts that a sapiential Christianity can bring to the new churches: (1) a deep, organic, and participatory theological understanding of the mystery of Christ as it has emerged freshly in the work of the council, and in which the "wisdom of God" as well as the "power of God" is known in Christ (1 Cor 1:22-24); (2) a unitive understanding of the mystery and of the new divine identity that underlies the experience of "baptism in the Holy Spirit"; (3) growth in personal autonomy, rationality, freedom, self-realization; the capacity for critical reflection; an understanding of human creativity and progressive history as fruits of the event of Christ; a developmental understanding of the life of faith;[81] (4) an expansive sapiential understanding of the mystery of Christ in its plurality, of the "breadth and length and height and depth" (Eph 3:18) which, sustaining the new freedom that is the Spirit's gift, allows the gospel to unfold to the fullness of its global and cosmic dimensions.[82]

7. Christian Nonduality II: Incarnation

We have already touched upon the quest for a Christian *advaita*, or nonduality,[83] as a point of convergence between the Asian traditions (and specifically, Hindu Vedanta) and Christianity. Now, in our fourth movement, it is time to look at this problem again in the light of the mystery of *incarnation*.

It was Jules Monchanin, the first of the three fathers of Shantivanam, who set forth the spiritual goal of the ashram as a contemplation or understanding of the Christian Trinity in the light of Hindu *advaita*. Bede Griffiths recalled, "the founder of Saccidananda Ashram, Father Monchanin, once said that our aim is *advaita* and the Trinity, nonduality and the Trinity."[84] We have already reviewed the responses of these three men to the challenge of reconciling Trinity and *advaita*.[85] On the right side, stood Monchanin with his "Greek" thinking, a man of ideas mistrustful of the apophatic way. A scrupulous and exact theologian, he came to the conclusion that Trinity and *advaita* are incompatible. On the left, we find Abhishiktananda, who abandoned the conceptual schemes of Christian theology entirely as he plunged into the advaitic depths, into nonduality. Between the two, Griffiths approached the problem with his characteristic synthetic confidence. He saw no contradiction, rather "harmonious tension," between Trinity and *advaita*, while Monchanin turned back and Abhishiktananda plunged forward into the *advaitin* experience.

The goal, from a Christian perspective, was set too high. The crucial task, I believe, is to not to find the meeting point between nonduality and Trinity, but between nonduality and *incarnation*. In the New Testament we do find abundant evidence of nonduality, as we have already seen.[86] In the event of Christ, however, the divine nonduality becomes present in a new way. *Nonduality has become a human being*.[87] And in this human being all things in heaven and on earth are to be gathered together. A single line from John's prologue has become the central column, the backbone of Christian faith and theology: "the Word became flesh and dwelt among us. . . ." (John 1:14). The event of Christ brings nonduality down to earth. The divine Wisdom has come to dwell in the bodiliness of humanity.

Through the course of the centuries, an increasingly objectifying theology progressively closed the divine Trinity in upon itself—like a hinged triptych of icons—leaving Christians outside and below, worshiping the three divine persons.[88] We have seen, however, that the Christ-event, the event of the cross, is the fusion of Trinity and creation in the body of Christ. The divine Absolute, divine nonduality, becomes incarnate, becomes a bodily human being. The problem of Christian nonduality is not resolved on the level of pure spirit, of pure contemplation; its solution is to be found on the human level. From the moment of divine incarnation, however, human life becomes centered in the divine identity, and it is newly illumined from within by the nondual divine light. The Christ-event is a descent of the "center"[89] from the metaphysical level of *Atman, Nous,* or the nondual Absolute, the One, (a) into the whole human person: body, soul, and spirit; (b) into the human center—the heart, where body, soul, and spirit are one. This takes place first in Jesus and then in those who accept his gift.

Within the symbol of the cross, as it appears in the New Testament and in early Christianity, there persists a strange tension. The body of the baptized person is signed with the cross (the four-membered figure) and with the names of the three divine persons. Four and three: beneath this awkward nonequivalence is hidden the central mystery, the event of Christ and its plenitude of meaning. The figure and mystery of the cross is completed when the human person—in whom the created world is present—is joined to the three divine persons in the paschal event of Christ and in the sacramental event of baptism.[90] The baptismal seal that marks this completion, this fullness, is at once the threefold divine name, the figure of the cross, and the Holy Spirit.[91] The seal is inscribed upon the body, the fourth, henceforth "crucified in Christ."[92]

> For in him all the fullness of God was pleased to dwell, and through him to reconcile to himself all things, whether on earth or in heaven, making peace by the blood of his cross. And you, who once were estranged and hostile in mind, doing evil deeds, he has now *reconciled in his body of flesh* by his death, in order to present you holy and blameless and irreproachable before him. . . . (Col 1:19-22)
>
> . . . But now in Christ Jesus you who once were far off have been brought near in the blood of Christ. For he is our peace, who has made us both one, and has broken down the dividing wall of hostility, by abolishing *in his flesh* the law of commandments and ordinances, that he might create in himself one new man in place of the two, so making peace, and might *reconcile us both to God in one body* through the cross, thereby bringing the hostility to an end. (Eph 2:13-16)

The reconciliation, the union, takes place through and in the physical body of Christ: it is in the unitive divinity that the body of Christ takes on this power of unification. Nondual divinity has become embodied—first in the individual person of Jesus, and then in those who are "in Christ" through faith and baptism. The eucharist makes this incarnation of unitive divinity sacramentally present—visible, tangible, even edible—in the midst of the community through the ages.

A central question throughout this study has been: *what has become of wisdom*, and where are we to find it once again? Within these New Testament texts lies, I believe, an answer to this question: *divine Wisdom has become incarnate*, and not only in the historical Christ-event itself but also in the history that follows upon this event. It is in the prologue of John's Gospel and in the Pauline letter to the Colossians that the embodiment of Wisdom is most explicit.

> that their hearts may be encouraged as they are knit together in love, to have all the riches of assured understanding and the knowledge of God's mystery, *of Christ, in whom are hid all the treasures of wisdom and knowledge.* (Col 2:2-3)
>
> See to it that no one makes a prey of you by philosophy and empty deceit, according to human tradition, according to the elemental spirits of the universe, and not according to Christ. For *in him the whole fullness of deity dwells bodily,* and you have come to fullness of life in him, who is the head of all rule and authority. (Col 2:8-10)

The key to a true Christian nonduality is here: nondual divinity descends into what we are and then opens us to its own fullness from within ourselves.

Emile Mersch, the French Jesuit theologian of the last century, understood the unitive power of the mystery of Christ as the center of Christian theology; he has provided the basic documentation for a theology of Christian nonduality without ever using that language.[93] At the conclusion of his long treatise on the doctrine of Christ's Mystical Body in Scripture and in tradition, he briefly recapitulates this doctrine of bodily unity in Christ.

> The message is this: in the Church, which is the continuation of Christ, there exists between the incarnate Word and each Christian more than any bond of love, however ardent, more than a relation of resemblance, however close, more than the bond of total dependence that binds to their one Saviour all men who have received the grace of pardon and sanctification. There is something more than the union of subjects to any king, more than the insecure incorporation of members in an organism, more than the closest possible moral union. There is a "physical" union, we should say, if the very term itself did not appear to place this bond in the category of mere natural unions. At all events it is a real, ontological union, or, since the traditional names are still the best, it is a mystical, transcendent, supernatural union whose unity and reality exceed our powers of expression; it is a union that God alone can make us understand, as He alone was able to bring it into being.[94]

This theological nonduality may evolve from a personal initiatory experience into a dimension of faith—a faith, however, which becomes more and more luminous as we live in its mysterious light. While related to the "metaphysical" nonduality of the Asian traditions (which may also be experienced by Christians in their own way),[95] it is unlike it. Mersch would prefer to call it a *physical* union. Something has happened: the divine unity embraces created reality in an event of incarnation and then in a continuing historical process of incarnation. This is a decisive historical change, which, of course, will hardly seem credible from other than a Christian perspective. From the moment of the incarnation in Christ, the divine nonduality dwells within the world in a new way—embodied and particularized—then to manifest itself in all the dimensions of human existence. From the perspective of a quaternary anthropology, these four expressions can be distinguished:[96]

I. Closest to the nondual experience of the classical Asian traditions is the experience of *baptismal initiation* and the unitive contemplative experience in which the same nondual identity is consciously realized from time to time.[97]
II. Unitive *wisdom,* a personal participation in the divine Word or Wisdom.[98]
III. *Koinonia* (communion), as a participation in the Holy Spirit (Rom 5:5; 1 Cor 12:4-13, 31; 13:1-13; 1 John 4:16-21).
IV. The *sacramental* dimension of Christian life; bodily expression and experience of the unitive reality—in the eucharist, in ordinary life and work, in action and in suffering (Matt 25:31-45; Mark 10:38-39; Acts 9:1-5; 1 Cor 6:15; 12:27; 2 Cor 4:7-12; Col 1:24).

As, in the Second Vatican Council, the consciousness of Western Christianity opens once again to the unitive Christology and ecclesiology of the New Testament and of Irenaeus, the overall movement of history appears as a *unitive incarnation.*

> For God's Word, by Whom all things were made, was Himself made flesh so that as perfect man He might save all men and sum up all things in Himself. The Lord is the goal of human history, the focal point of the longings of history and of civilization, the center of the human race, the joy of every heart and the answer to all its yearnings. He it is Whom the Father raised from the dead, lifted on high and stationed at His right hand, making Him judge of the living and the dead. Enlivened and united in His Spirit, we journey toward the consummation of human history, one which fully accords with the counsel of

> God's love: "To re-establish all things in Christ, both those in the heavens and those on the earth."[99]

Western monasticism, following the patristic theologians (especially Augustine), developed a sapiential spiritual theology with a trinitarian structure and an ascending movement—away from the world to union with God. If this once seemed appropriate to those who had left the world to seek God, today it neither corresponds to personal experience nor appears to be compatible with the Christ-event and its incarnational, descending movement. The phenomenon of globalization and the descending movement of history challenge us to a new view of our relation to the world, to the body, to matter.[100] *We are* world, body, and matter, and in Jesus Christ this cosmic stuff has become one with God. Many Christian theologians today occupy themselves with the problem of a Christian cosmology, a theology of matter and body, sometimes joining the issues of ecology with those of social justice and liberation of the oppressed, and the concerns of feminism.[101]

One possible sapiential response to this challenge is by way of a quaternary theology, joining the paradigm of Paul and of Irenaeus with the universal symbol of the mandala as developed, for example, in the thought of C. G. Jung.[102] Incarnation is the "event of nonduality" in this world. Further, our nondual baptismal identity is "identical" with the event of incarnation. Incarnation is also the principle of history, or of the intelligibility of history. The converse of incarnation is divinization, or "birth in God," which is experienced as the awakening of the person. Therefore, our two principles or dimensions (horizontal and vertical)—history and identity—intersect or coincide at this point of incarnation, which becomes the center of a cross or mandala figure.

Incarnation achieves unity beneath the level of culture and cultures; culture is a differentiating objectification of that which remains one on the level of the body. The incarnation which took place in Jesus and continues throughout humanity is the transmission of the gift of divinity, of the One, at a depth transcending consciousness and thought. The seed has gone into the ground.

8. The Incarnation of Wisdom

Beneath the numbing multiplicity and diversity of the phenomena of postmodernity moves the single, massive process of global convergence. The globalization that we see everywhere around us—and which often casts a sinister shadow over the less advantaged people of the world and over the earth itself—is only the visible tip of a much larger—and a necessary—historical event. As the dominance of the West begins to be vigorously challenged by the other peoples of the world and our Eurocentric view of reality begins to give way, we enter a new era in which the unification of humanity becomes the central issue. The secular and material elements of this unification are essential to its progress, and these, as well as the descending movement of Western culture which has brought them forth, derive principally from the event of Christ. I would like to quote at greater length Karl Rahner's bold affirmation of this continuity.[103]

> . . . the Christian is completely capable of regarding the planetary unification of world-history under a positively Christian aspect—indeed, from an aspect necessarily demanded by Christianity. In other words, if the universality of the Church is to be or become something real, and is not to be merely something belonging to the basic definition of Christianity, then this can be achieved by Christianity in the concrete only in, together with and by the creation of this globally unified history. The Christian will not be surprised to learn, therefore, that this fusion of the history of every nation into one had its real starting point in the very birth of Christianity and in the place where Christianity first took roots in the world and in history, viz. in the Western world. If this world and and history of the future is a world of rational planning, a demythologized world, a world secularized by the creature in order that it may serve as the raw material for man's activity, then this whole modern attitude—no matter what particular elements in it we may be able and ought to criticize—is basically a Christian one.[104]

Rahner sees both the secular modern world and the unification of humanity which it brings about, as deriving from the one great historical event which is the incarnation. He draws a bold, continuous line from the event of Christ through the Christian religion and the civilization of the West, through the rationalized and demythologized secular world, and finally to a unified humanity. At this point we may feel the intellectual vertigo produced by one of the synthetic equations of modern physics. Meanwhile in the back of our mind lurks our old, obsessive question: how does this relate to the sapiential, the unitive consciousness? *Where has wisdom gone?*

We have already considered Rahner's vision of a dawning *world church*, inaugurated in the time of the Second Vatican Council; in those essays he spelled out in greater detail the features of the transformation of the Roman

Catholic Church which are to accompany the movement into a truly global human world. In larger perspective, we also glanced at Teilhard's idea of an evolutionary stage of human *planetization*, as well as Cousins's related concept of a "second Axial time" characterized by the emergence of a global consciousness. As Rahner sees a convergent world history from a Christocentric perspective, so Teilhard views this new convergent phase of evolution as centered in and energized by an emerging Christ-Omega. I believe that Cousins's second Axial period can be seen theologically in the same way, as centered in Christ,[105] and as actualizing the body of Christ.

These convergent views offer us a good position from which to ask the sapiential question once again here in our fourth movement. Where, in this new global world, is the place of Christian wisdom? And what will be its nature? Our three contemporary spiritual writers—Simone Weil, Thomas Merton, and Bede Griffiths—together with Ewert Cousins—have offered us some elements for a response to these questions. From one perspective, the three are proposing—or demanding—the same thing: an inclusive, or *universal consciousness.* For Weil, this is her definition of "catholicity" and the key to a new spirituality. For Merton, it is the final stage of psychological and spiritual integration. For Bede Griffiths, it is the "universal tradition," the wisdom at the heart of every religion, which is essentially nondual consciousness. Griffiths found it breaking forth in the (first) Axial time, in the tradition of the Upanishads. This is what we discovered at the heart of the Asian traditions in our second movement, the Eastern turn. This nondual consciousness is present at the crest of the Western development as well, and it is implicit, I believe, nearly everywhere in the thought of Karl Rahner. It is an essential element of what we are seeking, but not yet the whole of it. For at this point we cannot simply return to a wisdom of the beginning; we must follow the movement of the Spirit forward, toward a wisdom of the *end.*

Ewert Cousins's proposal of a second Axial time, which demands a new global consciousness, points forward by pointing *downward.* The vertical component of Cousins's global consciousness is the recovery of a participatory relationship with the Earth: "organically ecological, supported by structures that will insure justice and peace."[106] Cousins repeats these words in a later article, adding:

> The voices of the oppressed must be heard and heeded: the poor, women, racial and ethnic minorities. These groups, along with the earth itself, can be looked upon as the prophets and teachers of the Second Axial Period.[107]

In the oppressed—the poor, women, minorities—and on the Earth itself, the shadow of the West becomes visible, clearly outlined. Jesus' words in the Gospel become audible—the beatitudes, first of all—and Jesus' little parable of the seed falling into the earth (John 12:23-24), as he looks forward to his own death and burial in the ground, and to the new blossoming of that ground which is at once earth and humanity.

I have hardly touched on these urgent questions of poverty and oppression, social justice and ecology, which are at last receiving much attention from theologians in our time. They have suddenly become central issues as we arrive at this global threshold. They must also be central issues for a new Christian wisdom. Whereas the earlier Christian sapiential tradition followed the prophets and the New Testament writers in relating faith in God and participation in Christ immediately to a personal responsibility for justice and for generosity toward the poor, today we awaken to a shared responsibility for all of humanity and for the transformation of society.

If it seems that this practical and even political imperative has little to do with a sapiential consciousness, one has merely to remember Gandhi or Merton. Unitive wisdom becomes incarnate as the essential divinity of the person and the essential oneness of humanity are actualized in the works of justice and love—and in the structures of society. As the nonduality at the core of our person and of our consciousness is actualized in this way, the one great event of incarnation runs forward toward its completion. One broad task of a new sapiential theology will be to make clear this continuity between the nondual One and concrete existence in a world of inequality and exploitation—the continuum of incarnation.

Our fourth movement, therefore, brings wisdom down to earth. The destination toward which we look is also the mystery within which we live and act, that is, *the body of Christ.* But *what is new* in our vision of this body of Christ that was not so evident to the sapiential theologians of the early centuries? First, we begin to see the body of Christ in its global totality and moving toward full realization beneath the events of our time; second, we awaken to its nondual nature and to the illumination of the whole body by its unitive interior sun. Third, we become aware of the dynamic actuality of the growth and integration of this great organism that pervades the entire course of history; and fourth, we come to realize our own vocation as active and creative participants in this global process. These lessons remain from our journey through the four movements.

We can look at the entire historical process as *an incarnation of divine Wisdom in the whole of humanity.* From this perspective, it should not surprise us that our wisdom—mystical experience, nondual consciousness, sapiential theology—has gone into eclipse again and again through the centuries and continues to disappear. At our fourth station, however, we need to make a special profession of ignorance. We really do not know what the future will unfold. We seem at times to be once again in the situation of Jesus' first disciples, for whom the fall of Jerusalem was hardly distinguishable from the end of the world.[108] The end of a chapter—as the era of the West gives way to a global era—can look like the end of the book. We do not know what further conflicts, turnings, beginnings, and endings lie in the future. We do know, however, that from now on the story is, irreversibly, *one* story, and that the story will be understood, finally, in the light of its one, central event.

Epilogue

HAVING BEGUN WITH AN INQUIRY INTO THE PUZZLING ECLIPSE OF CHRISTIAN sapiential theology many centuries ago and its nearly total absence during recent centuries, we have at length arrived at the hypothesis of a strong emergent theological wisdom capable of comprehending our present situation as well as the intervening history.[1] In this mood of sapiential optimism, we can imagine the centuries-long encounter of wisdom with history moving toward a reconciliation between history and a new sapiential theology in which wisdom becomes embodied and history becomes transparent. While history will continue to flow forward, downward, and outward as incarnation, a perennial spiritual wisdom will continue to swim back, upward, and inward toward its unitive source. The gift of our time is an opportunity to see the whole living picture and to orient ourselves consciously within it.

Wisdom has completed another cycle, has passed through its dark quadrant (or night), and awakens to a new dawn. Medieval wisdom, as it moved toward its eclipse, lived still in the morning light of the East. Now, as the hyperrational Western world approaches its sunset on the global horizon, the time arrives for a new, late, and distinctly Western theological wisdom to emerge. This paradoxical wisdom of incarnation must integrate the distinctly Western developments—the free and creative individual person *in this world,* and the unprecedented historical movement that has arisen from the confluence of new personal energies. Reborn out of the critical purification of recent centuries, Christian wisdom finds its essential principles differentiated and clarified. It awakens to new potencies, which include a theological interpretation of history and culture. Along with the historical consciousness that has arisen everywhere in the Western thought of recent centuries (and along with the emerging sciences of change and of process, from the calculus to evolutionary biology), this historical *gnosis* emerges late in the day to open the historical process itself to theological understanding. From the new perspective historical change becomes reflexively conscious, transparent to itself. For seven centuries, Christian wisdom has remained still as a seed in the ground, bare as a tree in winter, while a new world sprang up and flourished in the strong light of Western rationality. Now, when the widespread branches of this historical movement have borne their fruit and the dazzling rational light is itself declining, the dawn of a deeper awakening can already be sensed. The main currents of this new wisdom will no longer be monastic. But the light in which it unfolds—in which person, world, and history become newly transparent to the central mystery—will ultimately be, as always, the *uncreated* light in which contemplative life is at home.

The wisdom of Christianity, however, does not find itself quite at home among the other sapiential traditions of the world. The unitive wisdom which has become manifest in Christ disappears into—more boldly, we might say *metamorphoses* into[2]—an immanent historical dynamism that transforms all created reality. The eclipse corresponds to the sunset of Jesus' own life on earth. God came newly into the world in Christ, to be consumed by the world and then gradually to emerge as the heart of the world and its development. It is thus that Christian wisdom has lost itself, to rediscover itself after centuries as it emerges, deeper and larger than before, from this historical process that gradually reveals itself to be the embodiment of divine Wisdom.

A basic conviction that has crystallized in the writing of this book is that the event of Christ, through baptismal initiation, has endowed us with a unitive divine light in which everything—the world, history, and our own being—can become newly transparent, that is, intelligible. The apparent eclipse of Christian wisdom by history is an optical illusion, since history itself is an unfolding of the event of Christ and eventually opens itself to sapiential understanding. Christian sapiential understanding is able to be reborn again and again, and in our time it comes forth into the new scope and freedom with which history has favored us.

I have suggested that the mystery of Christ in its quaternary expression can be compared with the central equations of modern physics,[3] which bring together radically disparate aspects of cosmic reality (mass, energy, light, space, and time) in a single quantitative fabric of relationship. As the mystery reemerges in its native simplicity and power from the confinement and accretions of the centuries, we find that it unites within itself all reality—matter, psyche/consciousness, and divine spirit—interacting in the progressive movement of human history. The center of this comprehensive unity is Jesus, the divine-human person, and we discover that, in him, we too are at the center. The work of a new theology, again like that of the sciences, will not be concluded on the plane of speculation. As physics has penetrated the atomic nucleus to release the transcendent energies hidden there, a new theology must light a path toward the discovery of the divine energies that dwell within human hearts and bodies, waiting to be released so that they may converge into a single flame.[4] If the light of the mystery of Christ becomes visible once again in its simple fullness, at this time of global awakening and of the Second Vatican Council, we have reason to infer that the *energy* of the Christ-event is also strongly—and newly—present at this time. Our experience of the years during and immediately following the council encourages us in this belief.

We have said little of the Holy Spirit, little of woman, or the feminine, and little of the human psyche and its intuitive knowing.[5] A serious exploration of these intimately related themes would require another book. We should need to reflect on the complementarity and interaction of Word and Spirit, of masculine and feminine, of rationality and feeling, thought and imagination. In pursuing this inquiry, we would also be seeking to overcome one of the limitations of the present work, which despite its attempt at comprehensiveness remains still largely within the *logos* of theo*logy.* A new Christian wisdom needs to recognize not only the right hand but also the left hand of God, the presence and work of the immanent divine Spirit everywhere in humanity, outside the lighted circle of the Word and its Western penumbra.

Sapiential consciousness and theology are not of merely aesthetic interest; they are organic components of spiritual life. Let us recall, here at the end of our inquiry, a few of the benefits that we may expect from their recovery. First, a new Christian wisdom theology can help to make the *sources* of wisdom accessible by opening our contemporary understanding to the dimensions of consciousness and reality that have been excluded for centuries by the dominant rationalist epistemology of the West. Further, a healthy sapiential theology becomes a *mystagogy,* inseparable from our personal participation in the sources themselves: in (1) the absolute nondual mystery that we call God, and in (2) the dynamic event that we call the mystery of Christ. Our first two movements have been attempts to recover, or to liberate, these two primary sources. A second, related function is *developmental;* this proceeds in the direction of the spiritual theology of early and medieval monastic writers (e.g., Evagrius, Cassian, Bernard, William of St. Thierry). The personal transformation is to be understood now, however, as an immediate and creative participation in the event of Christ as it continues to unfold in living *history.* A third function of a new sapiential theology today is to interpret the whole historical process through this same opening of the spectrum of consciousness and through the application of these same two sapiential principles: the nondual mystery and the Christ-event. It is especially in the third and fourth movements that we have confronted this challenge of historical understanding.

The objective toward which we look, finally, is not the renewal of a particular discipline—sapiential theology or even Christian theology—but, more generally, a liberation of the vision of Christian faith through an awakening to its multidimensional and dynamic fullness, the "breadth and length, height and depth" (Eph 3:18). If this prospect seems grandiose, it is no more so than the vision that Paul himself has opened before us. And the "word of the cross" (1 Cor 1:18-25), along with the sobering experience of life, will suffice, if we are attentive, to keep us from weaving another triumphalistic illusion, and will bring us back to earth once again. In looking toward a rebirth of sapiential Christianity, this book should not be understood as projecting a new golden age of Christian wisdom, a contemplative return to Paradise. In reality, a new sapiential consciousness, with its depth, its breadth, and its power, may prove to be a vital need in the face of the tremendous challenges toward which we are being borne by history.

Contemplative consciousness, with its intrinsic interiority, simplicity, and unity, evolves in the course of history, moving outside the monastic walls and assuming new modalities. As its understanding of the mystery of Christ matures, contemplative wisdom begins to respond consciously to the the incarnational dynamism of this mystery. The dynamic principle and the incarnational principle, at length, also break out of the enclosure of the *individual* spiritual life and manifest themselves in the unfolding of human history. This is what we have observed in the evolution of the West during the past thousand years and in our encounter today with the threshold of a global humanity.

Major limitations of the present work derive from an isolation which is partly a matter of personality and partly a matter of circumstances, especially the monastic context from which the work comes forth. Much of life and human experience has been left out, and it may appear that the perspective turns in upon itself to the point of a circularity in which the original premises are continually verified. It is for the reader to judge whether any apparent success of the demonstration is the result of a real and significant convergence or whether it merely reflects the circularity of wishful thinking.

In attempting to trace the inner structure of the Christ-mystery's historical unfolding, we are moving on a different plane than that of historical-critical New Testament scholarship. Nevertheless, I am encouraged by the words with which Raymond E. Brown qualified his theoretical model of the development of the Johannine community: "I warn the reader that my reconstruction claims at most probability; and if sixty percent of my detective work is accepted, I shall be happy indeed."[6] In the present case as well, 60 percent will be very gratifying. Flying high above the ground, one may gain a panoramic view of geological features that remain obscure from a lower altitude. But one may also sometimes mistake a shadow for a solid prominence, a river valley for a mountain ridge. At the level of generalization from which we have sought to discern the inner shape and meaning of history, it is possible to make some impressive errors. But a "strong" Christian sapiential vision cannot realize itself in our time without breaking through thick, centuries-old walls. The force of a full swing, even if not aimed with exactness, is sometimes needed. The freedom to hypothesize, and possibly to be wrong, must be recovered if we are to recover our sapiential birthright. A contemporary physicist writes of the cosmological vision proposed by a fellow scientist, "Even if many of the details later turn out to be wrong, the picture is a big step toward understanding. Progress in science is often built on wrong theories that are later corrected. It is better to be wrong than to be vague."[7] In our present situation, it is often better to be wrong than to be timid. We move forward by successive approximations. What is proposed here, obviously, makes no claim to finality. It is an invitation to resume the long-interrupted game with a renewed keenness and on a larger field than before.

In this book I have proposed a perspective from which a rebirth of sapiential theology can be envisioned. This effort has brought forth what amounts to an outline of one possible model of such a theology, and involved as well the development of one more theological interpretation of history. I have gradually become aware that the value of this work may be measured, finally, in its success in outlining *the space of opportunity* that lies before us, inviting the creation of new theologies. We have looked at some of the major discontinuities that await a new and stronger synthetic vision, and we have sought to bring to clarity the few great principles from which new syntheses will come forth. Late in the day, our sapiential quest brings us, once again, to the threshold of a new beginning.

Notes

1. Introduction

1. Matt 13:44. The Revised Standard Version is used for biblical texts. Changes from the RSV text to inclusive language will be indicated by brackets, e.g. [child].

2. Exceptions include the writings of Louis Bouyer on Christian *gnosis*, and of Cipriano Vagaggini on the *gnosis-sapientia* of patristic times. See Bouyer, *The Spirituality of the New Testament and the Fathers*; Vagaggini, *Theological Dimensions of the Liturgy*.

3. See Richard Smoley and Jay Kinney, *Hidden Wisdom*.

4. Aldous Huxley, *The Perennial Philosophy*.

5. Ibid., vii.

6. The texts are reproduced here as Huxley has quoted them, with no attempt to replace the original translations with more accurate ones.

7. Ibid., 5.

8. Ibid., 6.

9. Ibid., 10.

10. Ibid., 12.

11. Ibid.

12. Ibid., 14.

13. Ibid., 127.

14. Ibid., 141.

15. Bede Griffiths, *Return to the Center*, 25.

16. Thomas Merton, *Contemplative Prayer*, 119.

17. Wallace Stevens, "Notes toward a Supreme Fiction," in *The Collected Poems of Wallace Stevens*, 382.

18. See Smoley and Kinney, *Hidden Wisdom*.

19. Jean Leclercq, *The Love of Learning and the Desire for God*, 256–58, 263–70.

20. On "spiritual understanding," see Henri de Lubac, *The Sources of Revelation*, 1–84, esp. 11–31.

21. Louis Bouyer, *The Spirituality of the New Testament and the Fathers*, 237–55, esp. 237–45.

22. Major collections of the patristic texts in their original languages include the Patrologia Graeca (PG; 168 vols.) and Patrologia Latina (PL; 222 vols.) of J. P. Migne (Paris: 1844–1866); the extensive and growing Corpus Christianorum (CC; Belgium: Brepols); Corpus Scriptorum Ecclesiasticorum Latinorum (CSEL; Vienna); and the Corpus of Greek Fathers (GCS; Berlin). We shall cite Sources Chrétiennes (SC; Paris: Éditions du Cerf), which now exceeds four hundred volumes.

English translations of the patristic writings include the two nineteenth-century series Ante-Nicene Fathers (ANF) and Nicene and Post-Nicene Fathers (NPNF) (reprinted: Grand Rapids, Mich.: Eerdmans); The Fathers of the Church (FOC; Washington, D.C.: Catholic University of America Press); The Library of Christian Classics (LCC; Philadelphia: Westminster Press); and Ancient Christian Writers (ACW; New York: Newman/Paulist).

Smaller selections of short texts, following the liturgical year, include *The Liturgy of the Hours* (*LH;* 4 volumes; in the second readings for the Office of Readings; New York: Catholic Book Publishing Co., 1975–1976); *A Word in Season: Monastic Lectionary for the Divine Office,* 6 vols. (English edition of the Benedictine Lectionary; Augustinian Press, 1987–1995), and *Christ Our Light: Patristic Readings on Gospel Themes*, 2 vols., translated and edited by Friends of Henry Ashworth, vol. 1 (Riverdale, Md.: Exordium Books, 1981); vol. 2 (Ambler, Pa.: Friends of Henry Ashworth, 1985); and (following the old calendar) *Patristic Homilies on the Gospels: The Sunday Sermons of the Fathers*, translated and edited by M. F. Toal, 4 vols. (London: Longmans Green, 1954). The continuing series Classics of Western Spirituality (CWS; New York: Paulist Press) includes a number of patristic and monastic sapiential works. Numerous monastic texts from both the medieval and patristic periods will be found in the Cistercian Fathers Series (CF) and the Cistercian Studies Series (CS); (both Kalamazoo, Mich.: Cistercian Publications).

23. "Paschal mystery" refers to the death and resurrection of Jesus Christ, which is the central and decisive event of Christian faith. See chap. 2, section 3.

24. From an Easter homily, chaps. 2–7, 100–103 (Sources Chrétiennes [SC] 123:60–64, 120–22). From *Liturgy of the Hours* [*LH*], 2:554.

25. Augustine, *Tractates on the Gospel of John,* tractate 124, nos. 5, 7, from *LH* 2:947–49. For an English translation of the entire sermon, see *The Fathers of the Church* [*FOC*] (1995), 92:82–94.

26. Maximus the Confessor, *Ambigua* (PG 91:1360), quoted in Olivier Clément, *The Roots of Christian Mysticism*, 40.

27. See Dogmatic Constitution on the Church (*Lumen Gentium*), 1–5; Constitution on the Sacred Liturgy (*Sacrosanctum Concilium*), 2, 5–6; Dogmatic Constitution on Divine Revelation (*Dei Verbum*), 1–6, 17, in *Vatican Council II: The Conciliar and Post Conciliar Documents,* ed. Austin Flannery, O.P., 350–53; 1–2, 3–4; 750–53, 760.

28. See Karl Rahner, "Man (Anthropology)," in *Sacramentum Mundi,* ed. Karl Rahner et al., 3:366–67.

29. Leclercq, *The Love of Learning*, 271–77.

30. Ibid., 111–38.

31. *Sermon 42*: PL 194:1831–32. From *LH* 1:856–58.

32. "Animal" is equivalent to St. Paul's *psychikos* (1 Cor 2:14). For the threefold anthropology in Paul, see 1 Thess 5:23.

33. William of St. Thierry, *The Golden Epistle,* 25–27, nn. 41, 43–44.

34. See Karl Rahner, "Theology and Anthropology," 28–45.

35. On the decline of sapiential thought in the West, see Seyed Hossein Nasr, *Knowledge and the Sacred,* 34–48; Henri de Lubac, *Sources of Revelation,* 49–84. For a detailed history of the evolution of biblical interpretation, see Beryl Smalley, *The Study of the Bible in the Middle Ages.*

36. See chap. 4, section 4, iii through vii.

37. Chap. 4, section 4, iii.

38. See Bede Griffiths, *The Golden String*, 9–12.

39. See Louis Bouyer, *Spirituality of the New Testament and the Fathers*, 211–55; Cipriano Vagaggini: *Theological Dimensions of the Liturgy*, 619–25, 945 (s.v. *gnosis)*; Nasr, *Knowledge and the Sacred*, 1–24; Griffiths, *Return to the Center*; Huxley, *The Perennial Philosophy*.

40. Peter Brown, *Augustine of Hippo*, 40–42.

41. See P. Vrajaprana, "Regaining the Lost Kingdom: Purity and Meditation in the Hindu Spiritual Tradition," in *Purity of Heart and Contemplation*, ed. Bruno Barnhart and Joseph Wong, 27–38. Vrajaprana summarizes the teaching of Vivekananda on the four yogas. See below, chap. 3, section 1, iii.

42. See Sara Grant, *Toward an Alternative Theology: Confessions of a Non-Dualist Christian*. The works of Merton, Abhishiktananda, and Griffiths are well known and will be cited below. Other women sapiential writers include Beatrice Bruteau and Sister Vandana. Among contemporary sapiential writers I shall often cite Merton and Griffiths.

43. On the Axial time, see Karl Jaspers, *The Origin and Goal of History*, 1–6; Ewert Cousins, *Christ of the 21st Century*, 4–7.

44. See chap. 5, section 2, ii.

45. See chap. 4, sections 4, 5, 6. "Western Axial period" is not a commonly recognized expression.

46. See chap. 5, passim.

47. See the Vatican II decree on the renewal of religious life, *Perfectae Caritatis*, n. 2, in Flannery, ed., *Vatican Council II*, 612–13.

48. As mentioned in section 1 above, these four movements will provide the structure for our theological journey throughout this book.

49. The basic quaternity of Father, Word, Spirit, and creation appears clearly in Irenaeus, e.g., *Against the Heresies*, 4.20, n. 1–3, SC 100 (1965), 624–26. The usual Pauline version of this quaternity is: God, Jews, Gentiles (or "Greeks"), and humanity (or the creation): See Eph 2:11-18; Col 1:19-22. See Bruno Barnhart, *Second Simplicity*.

50. Henri de Lubac, *Histoire et Esprit*.

51. See Bede Griffiths, *The Marriage of East and West*, 51–55, 57–59.

52. See Karl Rahner, "Man (Anthropology), III. Theological," 368–69.

2. Movement 1: The Sapiential Awakening

1. See Bede Griffiths, *The Golden String*, 10.

2. William Blake, *Jerusalem*.

3. Merton's dissertation for the Master's Degree at Columbia University was a study of Blake's theories of art from the perspective of Thomist aesthetics as interpreted by Jacques Maritain: "Nature and Art in William Blake: An Essay in Interpretation," 385–453.

4. Bede Griffiths, *Pathways to the Supreme*, ix. See Shirley du Boulay, *Beyond the Darkness: A Biography of Bede Griffiths*, 140–41.

5. See Peter Brown, *Augustine of Hippo*, 41–42.

6. See chap. 1, section 7 above.

7. See Constitution on the Sacred Liturgy, 2, 5–10; Dogmatic Constitution on the Church, 1–8; Dogmatic Constitution on Divine Revelation, 1–6: Flannery, ed., *Vatican Council II,* 1–6; 350–58; 750–52.

8. The paschal mystery of Christ, the historical core of the Christ-mystery, includes these events at the end of his earthly life through which the divine life has been communicated to humanity. The central importance of the paschal mystery re-emerges in the documents of Vatican II, particularly as the key to the theological meaning of the Christian liturgy.

9. Constitution on the Sacred Liturgy, 5; Flannery, ed., 3.

10. Decree on the Training of Priests (*Optatum Totius*), 14; Flannery, ed., 717–18.

11. *Optatam totius,* 16; Flannery, ed., 719–21.

12. Henri de Lubac, *Medieval Exegesis.*

13. Henri de Lubac, *Histoire et Esprit.* The conclusion of this book was republished as the first chapter of *The Sources of Revelation.* See pp. 80–81.

14. De Lubac, *Sources of Revelation,* 82–83.

15. Ibid., 84.

16. Ibid.

17. Ibid., 50.

18. Ibid., 53.

19. Ibid., 54.

20. Ibid.

21. Ibid., 55.

22. Ibid., 67–72.

23. Ibid., 69.

24. Ibid., 71.

25. Jean Leclercq, *The Love of Learning and the Desire for God* (see chap. 1, section 4 above). Particularly relevant here is chap. 9, "Monastic Theology."

26. Ibid., 3.

27. A similar distinction began to appear much earlier, however, in the theology of the Christian East; for example, between the Alexandrians (Origen et al.) and the writers of the school of Antioch (e.g., Theodore of Mopsuestia).

28. Ibid., 2.

29. Ibid., 8–9.

30. See Andrew Louth, *Discerning the Mystery.*

31. Leclercq, *The Love of Learning,* 246–47.

32. Ibid., 266.

33. Ibid., 278–79.

34. Cipriano Vagaggini, O.S.B., *Theological Dimensions of the Liturgy.*

35. Ibid., 619–25.

36. See Vagaggini's extensive article "Teologia."

37. Ibid., 1607–32.

38. Ibid., 1633–47.

39. Ibid., 1650.

40. See Irenaeus of Lyons, *Contre les Hérésies,* 3.11.8 (SC 211:160–70); 4.20.1–4 (SC 100:624–36); 5.17.4 (SC 153:234); *Démonstration de la Prédication Apostolique (*SC 406:130–32; Engl. trans. *Proof of the Apostolic Preaching* (Ancient Christian Writers [ACW] 16:69–70.

41. Irenaeus, *Against Heresies*, 3.11.8.
42. See Catherine M. LaCugna, *God for Us: The Trinity and Christian Life.*
43. See Owen Barfield, *Saving the Appearances.*
44. T. S. Eliot, *Four Quartets*, "Burnt Norton," I, 190.
45. Jean Leclercq, introduction to Thomas Merton's *Contemplation in a World of Action*, ix.
46. Ibid., xx.
47. In contrast to the more "objective" theology of the Black Monks; see Leclercq, *The Love of Learning and the Desire for God*, 271–77.
48. See "Poetry and Contemplation: A Reappraisal," in Thomas Merton, *The Literary Essays of Thomas Merton*, 338–54.
49. The value connoted by the word "secular" in Merton's writings varies from neutral, as in *Contemplation in a World of Action*, 143–56, to negative, as in *The Inner Experience*, 51–56.
50. See Anne E. Carr, *A Search for Wisdom and Spirit: Thomas Merton's Theology of the Self*, esp. "The Story of the Self," 121–40.
51. A glaring exception is Thomas Merton, *Ascent to Truth*, a book that Merton later disliked.
52. Robert Lowell, quoted in George Kilcourse, *Ace of Freedoms*, 44.
53. Armand Viellieux, OCSO, "Monk on a Journey," 263.
54. See *Conjectures of a Guilty Bystander.*
55. Merton's extensive writings on contemplation include *What Is Contemplation?*; *Seeds of Contemplation*; *The Ascent to Truth; The Inner Experience*; *New Seeds of Contemplation*; *Contemplative Prayer.*
56. See William H. Shannon, *Merton's Dark Path*, 3–4.
57. Compare, for example, *Seeds of Contemplation* (1949) with *Conjectures of a Guilty Bystander* (1966).
58. Merton's note: "Vivian de Sola's essay in *Mansions of the Spirit* brings this out well."
59. Thomas Merton, "Baptism in the Forest," 99.
60. See Robert Imperato, *Merton and Walsh on the Person.*
61. "Baptism in the Forest," 99–100.
62. Ibid., 100.
63. Wallace Stevens, " Adagia," in *Opus Posthumous*, ed. Milton J. Bates, 198.
64. The most revealing study of this development is George Kilcourse's *Ace of Freedoms.*
65. These authors will be found in the pages of *Conjectures* and of *Literary Essays* as well as in the volumes of Merton's journals and letters. They include, among many others, Jacques and Raïssa Maritain, T. S. Eliot, Karl Barth, Dietrich Bonhoeffer, Louis Massignon, contemporary poets Czeslaw Milosz, Louis Zukofsky, and George Oppen as well as Latin American poets (in particular the Chilean antipoet Nicanor Parra, who inspired Merton's own anti-poetry), and the novelists Albert Camus, Boris Pasternak, and William Faulkner.
66. Graphically representative of this awakening to human solidarity is Merton's well-known "Fourth and Walnut" narrative in *Conjectures of a Guilty Bystander*, 140–42.
67. The sense of a solidarity in human sinfulness appears, e.g., in *Conjectures*, 51–113.

68. See *Conjectures,* 57–59.

69. Thomas Merton,"Louis Zukofsky: The Paradise Ear," 128.

70. Armand Viellieux, in *Thomas Merton Monk,* 263. The final two lines of verse are from T. S. Eliot, *Four Quartets,* "Burnt Norton," I, 191.

71. For Rahner's transcendental method in theology, see his "Reflections on Methodology in Theology," 68–114, esp. 84–101; and William V. Dych, "Theology in a New Key," 1–16.

72. On transcendence, see Karl Rahner, *Foundations of Christian Faith,* 31–35.

73. Dych, "Theology in a New Key," 14.

74. Ibid., 7.

75. Ibid.

76. Harvey Egan, in his preface to Karl Rahner, *The Content of Faith,* xi.

77. The participated mystery for Rahner, however, is not directly that experienced in the "mysteries" of Christian initiation but the mystery of personal existence, of the experience of the transcendent and historical *subject.*

78. Karl Rahner, "The Concept of Mystery in Catholic Theology," 36–37.

79. Karl Rahner, *Foundations of Christian Faith,* 30.

80. Ibid., 31.

81. Ibid., 33.

82. Ibid., 61.

83. Ibid., 60.

84. Ibid., 57.

85. Ibid., 62.

86. David Loy, *Nonduality.*

87. See Karl Rahner, "The Experience of God Today," 64–65.

88. See Karl Rahner, *Spirit in the World.*

89. Dych, "Theology in a New Key," 14.

90. Karl Rahner, "Man (Anthropology)," 3:369.

91. See above, chap. 1, section 11, "Spirit and History."

92. See *Foundations of Christian Faith,* 141–42.

93. Charles Taylor, *Sources of the Self,* 491.

94. This historical awakening appears, for example, in the development of Western anthropology as recounted by Rahner, "Man (Anthropology)," 3:365–68.

95. Karl Rahner, "Christianity and the 'New Man,'" 152–53.

96. Karl Rahner, "Basic Theological Interpretation of the Second Vatican Council," 77–89; and idem, "Abiding Significance of the Second Vatican Council," 90–102. See chap. 5, section 2, iii below.

97. We have seen this "spiritual understanding" of the patristic writers as presented by Henri de Lubac in chap. 2, section 4 above.

3. Movement II: The Eastern Turn

1. See chap. 3, section 13, below.

2. The quaternary scheme, which will recur throughout the book, was introduced in chap. 1, section 8, and further developed in chap. 2, section 7.

3. Chap. 1, section 8.

4. *Hatha* yoga, the integrative discipline of the body, hardly finds a counterpart in a Christian tradition which has emphasized a domination and disciplining of the body through renunciation and asceticism.

5. Chap. 2, section 7.

6. See Ingrid Fischer-Schreiber, Franz-Karl Erhard, Kurt Friedrichs, and Michael S. Diener, *The Encyclopedia of Eastern Philosophy and Religion: Buddhism, Hinduism, Taoism, Zen,* s.v. *yoga, dhyana, jnana, bhakti, karma.*

7. See, for example, the four "functions" of Carl Jung's typology: intuition, thinking, feeling, sensing (C. Jung, *Psychological Types*).

8. See Hugo Rahner, "The Christian Mystery and the Pagan Mysteries," 337–401, esp. "The Mystery of the Cross," 369–87.

9. See Col 1:19-22; Eph 1:10; 2:13-16; see also the Hugo Rahner article cited in the preceding note.

10. See chap. 2, section 7 and the texts of Irenaeus cited in the notes there.

11. See Bruno Barnhart, *Second Simplicity.*

12. This contrast between East and West within Christianity seems to be foreshadowed in the contrast between the two disciples of Jesus, the Beloved Disciple and Peter, in the final chapter of John's Gospel (21:19-22). When Jesus has told Peter, *"follow me,"* he says of the other disciple, "If it is my will that he *remain* until I come. . . ."

13 See chap. 5, section 7.

14. David Loy, *Nonduality,* 3.

15. *Brihadāranyaka* Upanishad II.iv.14, in *The Upanishads, A New Translation,* 3:183. Nikhilananda's additions are bracketed. Quoted by Loy, *Nonduality,* 26.

16. *Iśa* Upanishad, 7, in *The Upanishads,* 1:206. Quoted by Loy, *Nonduality,* 26.

17. Shankara, *The Crest Jewel of Discrimination (Viveka-Chudamani),* 99–100.

18. Lao Tzu, *Tao Teh Ching,* 3.

19. *Tao Teh Ching,* chap. 4, p. 9.

20. *Chuang-tzu,* with commentary by Kuo Hsiang, trans. Fung Yu-Lan, 46. Quoted in Loy, *Nonduality,* 34.

21. Chuang Tzu, *Chuang Tzu, Basic Writings,* 36.

22. Ibid., 42.

23. Asvaghosha, *The Doctrine of Suchness,* 248–51. Asvaghosha was a first-century poet and Mahayana philosopher, writing in Sanskrit.

24. Ibid., 248–49.

25. Ibid., 249.

26. Ibid., 250.

27. Daisetz T. Suzuki, "Zen as Chinese Interpretation of the Doctrine of Enlightenment," 68.

28. D. T. Suzuki, "On Satori—The Revelation of a New Truth in Zen Buddhism", 230.

29. Ibid., 231.

30. Shantivanam is an ashram in Tamil Nadu (Southern India) where an Indian inculturation of Christian monasticism was initiated.

31. Abhishiktananda, *Saccidananda,* 94–95.

32. From the spiritual diary of Abhishiktananda, *Ascent to the Depth of the Heart,* entry for April 24, 1972 (p. 347). See *Brihadāranyaka* Upanishad, 1,4,1.

33. See Judson Trapnell, "Two Models of Christian Dialogue with Hinduism: Bede

Griffiths and Abhishiktananda," (I) 101–10, (II) 183–91, (III) 243–54. This late quotation from James Stuart's *Swami Abhishiktananda,* 349, is reproduced in part III of Trapnell's essay, 248.

34. Trapnell, "Two Models of Christian Dialogue with Hinduism," (II) 189–90.

35. Sten Rodhe, "Christianity and Hinduism: A Comparison of the Views Held by Jules Monchanin and Bede Griffiths," 173.

36. From a letter written by Monchanin in 1957; quoted by Sten Rodhe in "Christianity and Hinduism," 172.

37. Ibid., 173.

38. Bede Griffiths, *A New Vision of Reality,* 220.

39. These metaphors, "beginning" and (especially) "end," are only approximate and provisory but useful to denote the two differing forms of nondual experience in Christianity. We shall have more to say of the "end" as we continue, particularly in our fourth movement (chap. 5).

40. See chap. 5, section 8.

41. The *ego eimi* ("I am") statements of Jesus are related to the use of the verb *einai* ("to be") in the prologue, and particularly in 1:18 (see Exod 3:14, Septuagint translation, *ho ōn*). In John 14, the unitive meaning is found particularly in the images of house and indwelling; in John 15, it is particularly in the vine and the branches; in John 16, it is both in the mysterious mother and child and in the new immediacy which is promised in Jesus' words to the disciples in 16:25-27. In the great prayer of John 17, a final crescendo of unitive meaning can be heard in Jesus' repeated reference to the impartation of the divine Name (to be understood as the Name of Exod 3:14 and in relation to his own "I am" statements), and in his insistent prayer that the disciples may be *one* as he and the Father are one.

42. See the passage from Eckhart's *Sermon 16* quoted in chap. 4, section 4, vi, below, from *Meister Eckhart: Sermons and Treatises,* 1:138.

43. See Daisetz T. Suzuki, *Mysticism, Christian and Buddhist,* 5–38.

44. See chap. 1, section 11, "Spirit and History."

45. See the "transcendence" and "historicity" of Karl Rahner's anthropology, in chap. 2, section 11 above.

46. See Kilian McDonnell, "Jesus' Baptism in the Jordan," 209–36; and idem, *Jesus' Baptism in the Jordan.*

47. See Evelyn Underhill, *Mysticism,* 415.

48. See chap. 2, section 7 above.

49. Emile Mersch, *The Theology of the Mystical Body,* 37.

50. Constitution on the Church, n. 1.

51. Here I am bypassing the question of the precise authorship of Colossians and Ephesians and assuming that these two letters represent Pauline theology. On the authorship question, see Raymond E. Brown, *An Introduction to the New Testament,* 610ff. (Colossians), 627ff. (Ephesians).

52. Irenaeus, *Against the Heresies,* 3.16.6 (SC 211:312–14).

53. Meister Eckhart, Sermon 57, in *Meister Eckhart: Sermons and Treatises,* 2:85.

54. See chap. 2, section 6 (Vagaggini on the anthropocentric and subjective turn of the new theology), and Karl Rahner, "Theology and Anthropology," 28–45.

55. The biblical sources include, first of all, the two accounts of the creation of the human person: (1) as the "image and likeness of God" (Gen 1:26-27), and (2) as molded from clay and infused with the spirit of life by the divine breath (Gen 2:7).

56. These philosophical structures include the three-level anthropology of body, soul, and spirit and the three-pole psychology of *nous* (intellect), *thymis* (irascible faculty), *and epithymia* (concupiscible faculty). The Greek philosophical conceptions of the human person are generally marked by a strong "intellectualist" bias and a relative neglect of psyche and body.

57. See chap. 2, section 11.

58. See Karl Rahner, "Anthropology, III, Theology," *Sacramentum Mundi*, 3:369–70.

59. See Olivier Clément, *On Human Being*, chap. 3.

60. Clément, *On Human Being*, 30–31.

61. Karl Rahner, *Christian at the Crossroads*, 11.

62. See Anne E. Carr, *A Search for Wisdom and Spirit;* and Robert Imperato, *Merton and Walsh on the Person.*

63. See above, chap. 2, section 11.

64. See Karl Rahner, "Theology and Anthropology," *Theological Investigations* 9:28–45; and idem, "Man (Anthropology) III, Theological," *Sacramentum Mundi* 3:365–70.

65. "Transcendence," in Karl Rahner and Herbert Vorgrimler, *Dictionary of Theology*, 509.

66. See above, chap. 2, section 11.

67. "Person," in Rahner and Vorgrimler, *Dictionary of Theology*, 378.

68. "Anthropology," in Rahner and Vorgrimler, *Dictionary of Theology*, 18.

69. See chap. 1, section 11.

70. Guigo II, *The Ladder of Monks*. Guigo's ladder ascends through *lectio, meditatio,* and *oratio* to *contemplatio.*

71. See Henri de Lubac, *Sources of Revelation*, 42–55.

72. See Bernard McGinn, ed., *Meister Eckhart and the Beguine Mystics*, 12–14.

73. See *The Martyrdom of Saint Polycarp*, n.15, SC 10 *bis*, p. 228; Engl. trans. in James A. Kleist, ACW 6 (1948), 98; Ignatius of Antioch, *To the Romans*, 4, SC 10 *bis*, p. 110; Engl. trans. in James A. Kleist, ACW 1 (1946), 82.

74. This interpretation, obviously, does not exhaust the meaning of Jesus' washing the feet of his disciples in John 13. The removal of his clothes, as well as the pouring of the water over the disciples' feet, suggests further symbolic meaning here, as does the strong thread of baptismal symbolism that runs throughout John's Gospel.

75. Beatrice Bruteau, *The Holy Thursday Revolution*; see esp. 51–66.

76. Adolphe Tanquerey, *The Spiritual Life*, 649.

77. Ibid., 649.

78. Thomas Merton, *Zen and the Birds of Appetite*, 23–24.

79. See section 10 of this chap. 3, above, and chap. 2, section 11, on the fundamental human dimension of transcendence in the anthropology of Karl Rahner.

80. For the ongoing debate between "perennialists" and "constructivists" or contextualists, see Robert K. C. Forman, *Mysticism-Mind-Consciousness* (with bibliography); and *Mysticism and Language*, ed. Steven T. Katz.

81. Here I have not distinguished the ascending and descending components of this history and their complex interactions. We shall attend to these movements in chap. 3.

4. Movement III: The Western (Modern) Turn

1. Cf., e.g., Georg Wilhelm Friedrich Hegel, *The Philosophy of History*; Pierre Teilhard de Chardin, *The Future of Man*; Pitirim Sorokin, *Social and Cultural Dynamics*; Lewis Mumford, *The Transformations of Man*, chap. 6, "New World Man"; Jacques Barzun, *From Dawn to Decadence*, e.g., xix; Charles Murray, *Human Accomplishment*.

2. See especially the Constitution on the Church in the Modern World, *Gaudium et Spes*.

3. See *From Modernism to Postmodernism: An Anthology*, ed. Lawrence Cahoone, 11–13.

4. Karl Rahner and Pierre Teilhard de Chardin, among others, point in this direction.

5. Roughly equivalent to these two "hemispheres" of the human person are the "transcendent" and "historical" dimensions of Karl Rahner's anthropology. See *Sacramentum Mundi* 3:369.

6. Karl Rahner, "Basic Theological Interpretation of the Second Vatican Council," *Theological Investigations* 20:82–83.

7. See chap. 2, section 11 and chap. 5, section 2.

8. Rahner, "Basic Theological Interpretation of the Second Vatican Council," 20:82–83.

9. A parallel can be seen in the unification of the world achieved by the Roman Empire around the beginning of the Christian era. See Christopher Dawson, *Religion and World History*, 250–52.

10. See Christopher Dawson, *The Making of Europe*, esp. 218–44.

11. See Pierre Teilhard de Chardin, "A Great Event Foreshadowed: The Planetisation of Mankind," *The Future of Man*, 127.

12. Ibid., 284–88.

13. K. Rahner, "Christianity and the New Man," *Theological Investigations* 5:152.

14. Karl Löwith, *Meaning in History*.

15. See Marjorie Reeves, *Joachim of Fiore and the Prophetic Future*.

16. Pitirim Sorokin, *Social and Cultural Dynamics*, 27–28.

17. Ibid., 28–29.

18. Pitirim Sorokin, *The Crisis of Our Age*, 7.

19. Sorokin offers a theory to explain the alternation of phases in chap. 9 of *Social and Cultural Dynamics*, "The Why and How of Sociocultural Change," chaps. 38–42.

20. See Marie-Dominique Chenu, *Nature, Man, and Society in the Twelfth Century*, 1–4.

21. Denys Hay, "The Idea of Renaissance," *Dictionary of the History of Ideas*, 4:121–29.

22. Colin Morris, *The Discovery of the Individual 1050–1200*, 158.

23. See Eugen Rosenstock-Huessy, *Out of Revolution*, 545, 552; Christopher Dawson, *Religion and the Rise of Western Culture*, e.g. 19–22.

24. Chenu, *Nature, Man, and Society in the Twelfth Century*.

25. Ibid., chapters 5, 6, 7.

26. Ibid., 238.

27. Ibid., 236.

28. See Sorokin's ideational (spiritual) and sensate modes of consciousness.

29. The cultural expressions that we are referring to in Western history have been, until very recently, attributed almost entirely to *men*; very few women are credited with major accomplishments. See Tarnas, *Passion of the Western Mind*, 441–45; Murray, *Human Accomplishment*, 265–93.

30. Chenu, *Nature, Man, and Society in the Twelfth Century*, 239–69.

31. Ibid., 202–3.

32. See Leclercq, *The Love of Learning and the Desire for God*, 237–59; Chenu, *Nature, Man, and Society*, 270–309.

33. De Lubac, *The Sources of Revelation*, 51–57.

34. Ewert Cousins, *Bonaventure and the Coincidence of Opposites*, 3, 46f., 49–51, 59–66; Ewert Cousins, *Christ of the 21st Century*, 135–55.

35. Ewert Cousins, *Bonaventure and the Coincidence of Opposites*, 161–97.

36. A mandala (Sanskrit, "circle") is a centered and symmetrical figure that combines circular form with quaternity—circle with square, that is—and holds tightly within itself the tension between unity and multiplicity. It is thus a compact, formal image of both the cosmos and the person. See Carl Jung, "Concerning Mandala Symbolism," 355–84.

37. Cousins, *Bonaventure and the Coincidence of Opposites*, 190.

48. Ibid., 191.

39. See chap. 2, section 7.

40. See chap. 4, section 4, ii.

41. Cousins, *Bonaventure and the Coincidence of Opposites*, 193f.

42. See chap. 4, sections 3 and 4 in this volume.

43. See Karl Rahner, "On Recognizing the Importance of Thomas Aquinas," 3–12, esp. 10–11.

44. See Etienne Gilson, *The Christian Philosophy of St. Thomas* Aquinas, 84–95.

45. See chap. 4, section 6 below.

46. See Rahner, "On Recognizing the Importance of St. Thomas Aquinas," 11.

47. See chap. 5, section 2, iii, below, and Karl Rahner, "The Abiding Significance of the Second Vatican Council," 99–100.

48. See Daisetz T. Suzuki, *Mysticism, Christian and Buddhist*, 5–38.

49. See Bernard McGinn, "Meister Eckhart on God as Absolute Unity," in *Neoplatonism and Christian Thought*, 128–39; idem, *The Mystical Thought of Meister Eckhart*, 170–72.

50. See *Meister Eckhart: The Essential Sermons, Commentaries, Treatises, and Defense*, "Introduction II: Theological Summary," by Bernard McGinn, 24–61; McGinn, *The Mystical Thought of Meister Eckhart*, 35–161.

51. McGinn, introduction to *Meister Eckhart: The Essential Sermons*, 31.

52. Meister Eckhart, *Sermon 16*, in *Meister Eckhart: Sermons and Treatises*, trans. and ed. Maurice O'C. Walshe, 1:138.

53. This unitive baptismal initiation is signified in Mark's Gospel—the first of the Gospels to be written—by the baptism of Jesus with which the story begins, the empty tomb (symbolically equivalent to the baptismal font) with which it ends, and by the transfiguration of Jesus at its center.

54. Hans Urs von Balthasar, *The Glory of the Lord: A Theological Aesthetics*, 3:9–34.

55. See also Erich Auerbach, *Dante, Poet of the Secular World*.

56. Paul O. Kristeller, "Introduction to Pico della Mirandola," 221.

57. See Daniel Boorstin, *The Discoverers*; idem, *The Creators*; idem, *The Seekers*; Charles Murray, *Human Accomplishment.*

58. See respective entries in *The Encyclopedia of Eastern Philosophy and Religion.*

59. See chap. 3, section 2 above, and David Loy, *Nonduality.*

60. See Tarnas, *Passion of the Western Mind*, 248–61, 416–19; Thomas Kuhn, *The Copernican Revolution.*

61. Owen Barfield, *Saving the Appearances.*

62. Bede Griffiths, *A New Vision of Reality*, 276–81.

63. Charles Taylor, *Philosophical Arguments,* vii–xii, 1–19.

64. See chap. 4, section 4, ii.

65. Charles Taylor, *Sources of the Self.*

66. Ibid., ix.

67. Ibid., x.

68. Ibid., chap. 8, 143–58.

69. See chap. 4, section 4, ii.

70. Taylor, *Sources of the Self*, 456–93.

71. Ibid., 151, 156–57.

72. See section 8 below.

73. See Tarnas, *Passion of the Western Mind*, 375–422, esp. 416–22; Richard Tarnas, *Cosmos and Psyche,* 11–49.

74. See Tarnas, *Passion of the Western Mind,* 395–413, 416–22.

75. Nicolas Berdyaev, *The Meaning of History,* 110.

76. Ibid., 125.

77. See Gal 3:23–5:13. The whole of the Letter to the Galatians is concerned with the movement from the heteronomy of the old Judaic law to the freedom of the Holy Spirit, conferred by Christ.

78. See John 1:1. See also the variant of John 1:18 often preferred in contemporary translations: "The only *God,* who is in the bosom of the Father. . . ."

79. While the term "nonduality" will not, of course, be found in Rahner's writings, I have proposed above that the "transcendence" which is the basis of Rahner's epistemology is a true Western equivalent of the nondual consciousness that is central to the great Asian spiritual traditions. See chap. 2, section 11.

80. Karl Rahner, "True Freedom," 203–64.

81. Ibid., 205.

82. Ibid., 226–27.

83. Ibid., 257–58.

84. Simone Weil, *Oeuvres Completes,* 1:189–90; quoted in H. L. Finch, *Simone Weil and the Intellect of Grace,* 33.

85. Quoted in *Integrities* (Watsonville, Calif.), June 1998, 14.

86. Eugen Rosenstock-Huessy, *Out of Revolution.*

87. Ibid., 485–515, esp. 502.

88. Ibid., 516–61.

89. Ibid., 359–450.

90. Ibid., 126–256.

91. Ibid., 35–125.

92. See chap. 3, section 1, iii.

93. Taylor, *Sources of the Self*, 395.

94. Ibid., 130–31, 176–78.

95. This image is very imperfect. Ascending and descending movements are, of course, concurrent as well as successive.

96. Chap. 3, section 12 (VI).

97. Authors who have conceived historical movement as analogical to the cycle of organic life include Johann Herder, Oswald Spengler, and Arnold Toynbee.

98. Chap. 2, section 9.

99. This corresponds both to the release of stored creative energies described by Berdyaev (*The Meaning of History*, 128f.) and to the reversal that Barfield points out from slavish "original participation" to creative "final participation" (*Saving the Appearances*, 169–86). See also Owen Barfield, "Philology and the Incarnation," in *The Rediscovery of Meaning and Other Essays*, 235.

100. See chap. 4, section 5, i.

101. *Saving the Appearances*, 132.

102. Ibid., 109.

103. See chap. 3, sections 3–13 above.

104. See Barfield, *Saving the Appearances*, 126–32.

105. See chap. 3, section 4 above.

106. *Saving the Appearances*, 195–96.

107. A new sapiential sensibility appears in the German Idealist philosophers Fichte, Schelling, and Hegel, and in the English Romantic poets Blake, Wordsworth, Coleridge, Shelley, and Keats.

108. See M. H. Abrams, *Natural Supernaturalism*, esp. 141–95.

109. "Poetry is, above all, an approach to the truth of feeling . . ."; Muriel Rukeyser, *The Life of Poetry*, 8.

110. See Taylor, *Sources of the Self*, 419ff.

111. Wallace Stevens, "Adagia," in Wallace Stevens, *Opus Posthumous*, 190.

112. It is tempting here to speak of the interaction and cooperation of a *masculine* and a *feminine* principle of mind. See Bede Griffiths, *The Marriage of East and West*, 8, 150–71.

113. See also chap. 3, section 12 above.

114. See Löwith, *Meaning in History*.

115. See *From Modernism to Postmodernism*, ed. L. Cahoone, 11–13.

116. Second Vatican Council, Constitution on the Church in the Modern World, 10.

117. See Augustine, *De Genesi ad litteram*, 4.22.31; *De Civitate Dei*, 12.7.20; Thomas Aquinas, *Summa Theologica*, I, 58, arts. 6, 7.

118. See chap. 4, section 3 above.

119. See chap. 3, section 12 above: "The Trajectory of Life . . . "

120. See Karl Rahner, "Basic Theological Interpretation of the Second Vatican Council," 77–89; see also chap. 5, section 2, iii in this volume.

121. See chap. 4, section 3 above.

122. See Bede Griffiths, *The Golden String*, foreword to 1980 edition, 7–8; see also 178–79; Bede Griffiths, *A New Vision of Reality*, 276–79.

123. See, e.g., Bede Griffiths, "Spirit as Mother," in *The One Light: Bede Griffiths' Principal Writings*, ed. Bruno Barnhart, 108–12.

124. See chap. 4, section 4, ii, above.

125. See Arthur Lovejoy, *The Great Chain of Being*.

126. See Paul's Letter to the Galatians, *passim*.

127. See chap. 2, section 7, and the Irenaeus texts cited there.

128. See Fritjof Capra, *The Tao of Physics*; Gary Zukav, *The Dancing Wu Li Masters*; Bede Griffiths: *A New Vision of Reality*; Ken Wilber, *Sense and Soul*.

129. See chap. 4, section 2 above.

130. See Tarnas, *Passion of the Western Mind*, 441–45, and Murray, *Human Accomplishment*, 265–93.

131. Use of the terms "masculine" and "feminine" to denote particular internal components of the human person requires caution and discrimination, and is often not welcomed by feminist critics today.

5. Movement IV: The Global (Postmodern) Turn

1. See Paul Lakeland, *Postmodernity*.

2. Some of the confusion surrounding postmodernity results from the ambiguity of the term *modern* itself. Its meaning can vary from a particular cultural phenomenon of the late nineteenth and early twentieth century ("modernism") to the whole modern world which has come into being during the past four or five centuries as a result of Western advances in rational thought, science, and technology (see Lakeland, *Postmodernity*, xi). The understanding of postmodernity that I shall presuppose here is based upon the latter, wider, sense of the term "modern."

3. See David Loy, *Nonduality*, 248–59.

4. See Vatican II, Declaration on the Relation of the Church to Non-Christian Religions *(Nostra Aetate)*, esp. n. 2. See also chap. 3, section 1 above.

5. See Vatican II, Constitution on the Church and the Modern World *(Gaudium et Spes)*.

6. See Jorge Ferrer, *Revisioning Transpersonal Theory*, 151–57.

7. Tarnas, *The Passion of the Western Mind*, 407.

8. See Taylor, *Sources of the Self*, 456–93; and Jacques Maritain, *Creative Intuition in Art and Poetry*, 214–23.

9. See Morris Berman, *The Twilight of American Culture*; Lakeland, *Postmodernity*, 1–11; Tarnas, *Passion of the Western Mind*, 395–402.

10. See Fritjof Capra, *The Turning Point*.

11. Among the major critics of the Western philosophical tradition as a whole are Friedrich Nietzsche, Martin Heidegger, and Jacques Derrida. See Tarnas, *Passion of the Western Mind*, 398–401.

12. See below, chap. 5, section 2, iii.

13. The term "explicate" is borrowed from David Bohm, who contrasts the "implicate order" and the "explicate order." See his *Wholeness and the Implicate Order*.

14. Karl Rahner understands these historical movements in this way, from within a theological sense of the unfolding Christ-mystery. See chap. 5, section 9 below.

15. See Oswald Spengler, *The Decline of the West*, 1:31–50, 292–95; Sorokin, *Social and Cultural Dynamics*, 699–704.

16. See Rahner's interpretation of Vatican II as the beginning of a "world church,"

chap. 5, section 2, iii below. "European" should be understood here as including North America."

17. The essays dealing with "planetization" are largely collected in Pierre Teilhard de Chardin, *The Future of Man*.

18. Ibid., 113.

19. Ibid., 228–31.

20. Ibid., 257–59.

21. Ibid., 124.

22. Ibid., 128.

23. Ibid., 114.

24. Ibid., 93–94.

25. Ibid., 133.

26. Ibid., 253.

27. Ibid., 19.

28. Ibid., 124–25.

29. Ibid., 119.

30. Ibid., 235–36.

31. Ibid., 133.

32. Ibid., 279.

33. Cousins, *Christ of the 21st Century*, 7–10.

34. Jaspers, *The Origin and Goal of History*. See chap. 1, section 9 above in this volume.

35. Cousins, *Christ of the 21st Century*, 6.

36. Ibid., 10.

37. The relation of Teilhard's Christocentric cosmic vision to the Pauline vision which appears in the letters to the Colossians and Ephesians is demonstrated by Robert Hale in *Christ and the Universe*.

38. Karl Rahner, "Basic Theological Interpretation of Vatican II." See chap. 2, section 11 and chap. 4, section 2 in this volume.

39. Ibid., 82–83.

40. Rahner, "The Abiding Significance of the Second Vatican Council."

41. Ibid., 92.

42. Ibid., 98–99.

43. Ibid., 99–100.

44. Ibid., 101.

45. Ibid., 102.

46. See chap. 4, section 3, i, 1 in this volume.

47. *The Simone Weil Reader*, ed. George Panichas, "Spiritual Autobiography," 20.

48. Ibid., 21.

49. Ibid., 111.

50. Ibid., 113.

51. Ibid., 114.

52. Thomas Merton, "Final Integration: Toward a Monastic Therapy," 205–17.

53. Reza Arasteh, *Final Integration in the Adult Personality*.

54. Merton, "Final Integration," 208–9.

55. Ibid., 210.

56. See Robert Imperato, *Merton and Walsh on the Person*; Anne E. Carr, *A Search*

for Wisdom and Spirit; William H. Shannon, "Person," in *The Thomas Merton Encyclopedia,* ed. W. H. Shannon, et al., 356–57; William H. Shannon, "Self," in ibid., 417–20.

57. Merton, "Final Integration," 211.
58. Ibid., 212.
59. Ibid., 214.
60. Ibid., 216.
61. Bede Griffiths, *Universal Wisdom,* 8.
62. Ibid., 10.
63. See Catherine M. LaCugna, *God for Us.*
64. See chap. 5, section 2, iii above.
65. (1) On the scheme of the four senses of Scripture, see Henri de Lubac, *The Sources of Revelation,* 42–84, 217–29; idem, "On an Old Distich: The Doctrine of the 'Fourfold Sense' in Scripture," 109–27; (2) The "Ladder of Contemplatives"; see Guigo II, *The Ladder of Monks.*
66. See Arthur Lovejoy, *The Great Chain of Being.*
67. See Avery Dulles, *Models of the Church.*
68. Leo the Great insists again and again in his sermons for the great liturgical feasts, on the participation of all the members of the body of Christ in the successive phases of Jesus' own journey, by virtue of the taking up of human nature into his own divine-human person. A number of these texts will be found in the *Liturgy of the Hours.* See, e.g., the famous *Sermo 51* on the transfiguration, *Liturgy of the Hours* 2:149–50 (Second Sunday of Lent; full text in *Léon le Grand: Sermons* III, SC 74, ed. R. Dolle [1961], 13–21); *Sermo 1 de Ascensione, LH* 2:898–99 (Wednesday of the sixth week of Easter); *Sermo 2 de Ascensione, LH* 2:937 (Friday of sixth week of Easter).
69. See chap. 4, section 6, iii above.
70. Erich Auerbach: *Mimesis.*
71. Ibid., 151–55, 247–48, 323, 555.
72. See Vatican II, Constitution on the Church, 1, 5, 7.
73. See chap. 5, section 7 below.
74. Walbert Bühlmann: *The Coming of the Third Church.*
75. Bühlmann: *The Coming of the Third Church,* ix.
76. Philip Jenkins: *The Next Christendom.*
77. Ibid., 3.
78. Ibid., 7.
79. Ibid., 8.
80. Ibid., 12.
81. See James Fowler, *Stages of Faith.*
82. New Christians are often tempted to the same "judaizing" regression against which Paul so passionately warned the new Christians of Galatia, withdrawing into a rigid cultural shell which is closed to everything outside. See the Letter to the Galatians, *passim.*
83. See chap. 3, section 3 above.
84. Bede Griffiths, in *A Human Search,* 92.
85. See chap. 3, section 3 above.
86. See chap. 3, sections 4, 7, 8.
87. More accurately, a *divine-human* person. Here I am not using the word *person,* however, in the technical sense of the Christological definitions of the Council of Chalcedon. Once again, our language is analogical, "as if."

88. See chap. 5, section 4 above, and C. LaCugna, *God for Us.*

89. I am using the word "center" here approximately in the sense in which Raimon Panikkar employed it as he defined the "monastic archetype" in *Blessed Simplicity*, 14–19.

90. See chap. 2, section 7 above.

91. See G. W. H. Lampe, *The Seal of the Spirit.*

92. Ibid., 269; see Rom 6:3-8.

93. The texts from the New Testament and the theological tradition will be found in Emile Mersch, *The Whole Christ.* Mersch presents the "whole Christ" as unitive center in his *Theology of the Mystical Body* (see chap. 3, section 7 above).

94. Mersch, *The Whole Christ*, 584.

95. Christian meditative and contemplative experience may resemble the Asian nondual experience. See above, chap. 3, section 13.

96. See chap. 3, section 8.

97. See chap. 3, sections 4, 5, 13.

98. See John 1:1-18; 1 John 1:1-3; 2:20-21, 27; 5:20. See also texts such as Eph 3:4-19, on the Pauline *gnosis* of the mystery.

99. Second Vatican Council, Pastoral Constitution on the Church in the Modern World *(Gaudium et Spes)*, 45, quoting Eph 1:10.

100. See Peter Brown, *The Body and Society*; Adrian Hastings, "Body," in *The Oxford Companion to Christian Thought*, 77–78.

101. See Sallie McFague, *Life Abundant.*

102. I have already suggested a quaternary theological pattern several times in the course of our four movements. See chap. 1, section 8; chap. 2, section 7; chap. 3, section 1, iii; chap. 4, section 5, ii; section 6, iv; and in the present section 8 of chap. 5. This figure corresponds, I believe, to the inner structure of the New Testament. See the texts quoted above: Col 1:19-22; Eph 2:13-16. In these passages the crucified Jesus is depicted as uniting in himself all reality: heaven and earth (God and creation), Jews and Gentiles (the first people to receive God's word and all humanity). Quaternity appears as the differentiated obverse "face" of unity.

103. See chap. 4, section 2 above.

104. Karl Rahner, "Christianity and the 'New Man,'" 152–53.

105. Above, in chap. 5, section 7, iii, 9, I have also suggested that the Christ-event may be considered the "noonday" between first and second Axial times, or between personal and global consciousness.

106. See chap. 5, section 2, ii above, and Cousins, *Christ of the 21st Century*, 10.

107. Ewert Cousins, "The World Religions: Facing Modernity Together," in the online *Global Dialogue Institute Anthology: Envisioning a Global Ethic*, http://astro.temple.edu/-dialogue/Antho/ewert_an.htm, p. 8.

108. See Jesus' "eschatological discourse" in Mark 13:3-37, and Paul's expectation of the proximate return of the Lord (e.g., in 1 Cor 7:29-31; 1 Thess 4:13-17).

Epilogue

1. This comprehension, deriving from faith and from the operation of a strongly intuitive rationality, will be of a different order than the rational-empirical certainty of Western science.

2. Again speaking analogically, "as if. . . ."

3. See *It Must Be Beautiful: Great Equations of Modern Science,* ed. Graham Farmelo; Michael Guillen, *Five Equations that Changed the World*; David Bodanis, $E=mc^2$.

4. See Pierre Teilhard de Chardin, *Human Energy.*

5. See Bede Griffiths, *The Marriage of East and West,* 7–12, 150–71.

6. Raymond E. Brown, preface to *The Community of the Beloved Disciple,* 65.

7. Freeman Dyson, *The New York Review of Books,* May 13, 2004, 16.

Bibliography

Abhishiktananda. *Ascent to the Depth of the Heart: The Spiritual Diary of Swami Abhishiktananda.* Edited by Raimon Panikkar. Translated by David Fleming and James Stuart. Delhi: I.S.P.C.K., 1998.

———. *Saccidananda: A Christian Approach to Advaitic Experience.* Delhi: I.S.P.C.K., 1974.

Abrams, M. H. *The Mirror and the Lamp: Romantic Theory and the Critical Tradition.* New York: Oxford University Press, 1953.

———. *Natural Supernaturalism: Tradition and Revolution in Romantic Literature.* New York: W. W. Norton, 1971.

Arasteh, Reza. *Final Integration in the Adult Personality.* Leiden: E. J. Brill, 1965.

Asvaghosha: "The Doctrine of Suchness." In *World of the Buddha: A Reader.* Edited by Lucien Stryk, 248–51. Garden City, N.Y.: Doubleday, 1968.

Auerbach, Erich. *Dante, Poet of the Secular World.* Translated by T. Silverstein. Edited by R. Manheim. Chicago: University of Chicago Press, 1961.

———. *Mimesis: The Representation of Reality in Western Literature.* Translated by W. R. Trask. Princeton: Princeton University Press, 1953/1974.

Balthasar, Hans Urs von. *The Glory of the Lord: A Theological Aesthetics.* III, *Studies in Theological Style: Lay Styles.* Translated by A. Louth, J. Saward, M. Simon, and R. Williams. Edited by John Riches. San Francisco: Ignatius Press, 1986.

Barfield, Owen. *Saving the Appearances: A Study in Idolatry.* New York: Harcourt Brace Jovanovich, 1983.

Barnhart, Bruno. *Second Simplicity: The Inner Shape of Christianity.* New York: Paulist, 1999.

———, and Joseph Wong, eds. *Purity of Heart and Contemplation: A Monastic Dialogue between Christian and Asian Traditions.* New York: Continuum, 2001.

Barzun, Jacques. *From Dawn to Decadence: 500 Years of Western Cultural Life.* New York: HarperCollins Perennial, 2001.

Berdyaev, Nicholas. *The Meaning of the Creative Act.* New York: Collier, 1962.

———. *The Meaning of History.* London: Geoffrey Bles, 1936.

———. "Salvation and Creativity." In *Historical Roots, Ecumenical Routes.* Edited by Matthew Fox, 115–39. Notre Dame, Ind.: Fides, 1979.

Berman, Morris. *The Twilight of American Culture.* New York: Norton, 2000.

Bodanis, David. *$E=mc^2$: A Biography of the World's Best Known Equation.* New York: Walker, 2000.

Bohm, David. *Wholeness and the Implicate Order.* London: Routledge and Kegan Paul, 1980.

Boorstin, Daniel. *The Creators.* New York: Random House, 1992.

———. *The Discoverers.* New York: Random House, 1983.

———. *The Seekers.* New York: Random House, 1998.

Bouyer, Louis. *The Spirituality of the New Testament and the Fathers.* New York: Desclée, 1963.

Brown, Peter. *Augustine of Hippo.* Berkeley: University of California Press, 1969.

———. *The Body and Society: Men, Women and Sexual Renunciation in Early Christianity.* New York: Columbia University Press, 1988.

Brown, Raymond E. *The Community of the Beloved Disciple.* New York: Paulist Press, 1979.

———. *An Introduction to the New Testament.* New York: Doubleday, 1997.

Bruteau, Beatrice. *The Holy Thursday Revolution.* Maryknoll, N.Y.: Orbis Books, 2005.

Bühlmann, Walbert. *The Coming of the Third Church: An Analysis of the Present and Future of the Church.* Maryknoll, N.Y.: Orbis Books, 1978.

Cahoone, Lawrence, ed. *From Modernism to Postmodernism: An Anthology.* Cambridge Mass.: Blackwell, 1996.

Calati, Benedetto. *Sapienza Monastica: Saggi di Storia, Spiritualità e problemi Monastici.* Edited by A. Cislaghi and G. Remondi. Introduction by I. Gargano. Studia Anselmiana 117. Rome, 1994.

Capra, Fritjof. *The Tao of Physics: An Exploration of the Parallels between Modern Physics and Eastern Mysticism.* Berkeley: Shambala, 1975.

———. *The Turning Point: Science, Society and the Rising Culture.* New York: Simon & Schuster, 1982.

Carr, Anne E. *A Search for Wisdom and Spirit: Thomas Merton's Theology of the Self.* Notre Dame, Ind.: University of Notre Dame Press, 1988.

Cary, Phillip. *Augustine's Invention of the Inner Self: The Legacy of a Christian Platonist.* New York: Oxford University Press, 2000.

Chenu, Marie-Dominique. *Nature, Man, and Society in the Twelfth Century: Essays on New Theological Perspectives in the Latin West.* Selected, edited, and translated by J. Taylor and L. K. Little. Chicago: University of Chicago Press, 1968.

Chuang Tzu. *Chuang Tzu, Basic Writings.* Translated by Burton Watson. New York: Columbia University Press, 1964.

Clément, Olivier. *On Human Being: A Spiritual Anthropology.* New York: New City, 2000.

Cousins, Ewert. *Bonaventure and the Coincidence of Opposites.* Chicago: Franciscan Herald Press, 1978.

———. *Christ of the 21st Century.* Rockport, Mass.: Element Books, 1992.

———. "The World Religions: Facing Modernity Together." In the online Global Dialogue Institute Anthology: *Envisioning a Global Ethic.* http://astro.temple.edu/-dialogue/Antho/ewert_an.htm.

Daniélou, Jean. *From Shadows to Reality: Studies in the Biblical Typology of the Fathers.* Translated by W. Hibberd. London: Burns & Oates, 1960.

Dawson, Christopher. *The Making of Europe: An Introduction to the History of European Unity.* New York: Meridian, 1956.

———. *Religion and the Rise of Western Culture.* Garden City, N.Y.: Doubleday Image, 1957.

———. *Religion and World History.* Edited by J. Oliver and C. Scott. New York: Doubleday Image, 1975.

de Lubac, Henri. *Corpus Mysticum: Essai Historique.* Paris: Aubier-Montaigne, 1944.

———. *Histoire et Esprit: l'intelligence de l'Ecriture d'après Origène*. Coll. "Théologie" 16. Paris: Aubier-Montaigne, 1950.

———. *Medieval Exegesis*, vols. 1 and 2, "The Four Senses of Scripture," translated by M. Sebanc and E. M. Macierowski. Grand Rapids, Mich.: Eerdmans, 1998, 2000.

———. "On an Old Distich: The Doctrine of the 'Fourfold Sense' in Scripture." In H. de Lubac, *Theological Fragments*, translated by R. H. Balinski. San Francisco: Ignatius Press, 1989.

———. *The Sources of Revelation*. Translated by Luke O'Neill. New York: Herder & Herder, 1968.

della Mirandola, Pico. "On the Dignity of Man." In *The Renaissance Philosophy of Man*. Edited by E. Cassirer, P. O. Kristeller, and J. H. Randall, 223–54. Chicago: University of Chicago Press, 1948.

du Boulay, Shirley. *Beyond the Darkness: A Biography of Bede Griffiths*. New York: Doubleday, 1998.

———. *The Cave of the Heart: The Life of Swami Abhishiktananda*. Maryknoll, N.Y.: Orbis Books, 2005.

Dulles, Avery. *Models of the Church*. Garden City, N.Y.: Doubleday, 1974.

Dych, William V. "Theology in a New Key." In *A World of Grace: An Introduction to the Themes and Foundations of Karl Rahner's Theology*. Edited by Leo J. O'Donovan, 1–16. New York: Crossroad, 1981.

Eckhart, Meister. *Meister Eckhart: The Essential Sermons, Commentaries, Treatises and Defense*. Translated and with an introduction by Edmund Colledge and Bernard McGinn. New York: Paulist, 1981.

———. *Meister Eckhart: A New Translation*. Translated and edited by R. B. Blakney. New York: Harper & Row, 1941.

———. *Meister Eckhart: Sermons and Treatises*. 3 vols. Translated and edited by Maurice O' C. Walshe, Rockport, Mass.: Element Books, 1987–1991.

———. *Meister Eckhart: Teacher and Preacher*. Edited by Bernard McGinn, F. Tobin, and E. Borgstadt. New York: Paulist, 1986.

Eliot, T. S. *Four Quartets*. In *Collected Poems 1909–1962*. London: Faber & Faber, 1963.

Farmelo, Graham, ed. *It Must Be Beautiful: Great Equations of Modern Science*. London: Granta Books, 2002.

Ferrer, Jorge. *Revisioning Transpersonal Theory: A Participatory Vision of Human Spirituality*. Albany: State University of New York Press, 2002.

Finch, H. L. *Simone Weil and the Intellect of Grace*. Edited by M. Andic. New York: Continuum, 2001.

Fischer-Schreiber, Ingrid, Franz-Karl Erhard, Kurt Friedrichs, and Michael S. Diener. *The Encyclopedia of Eastern Philosophy and Religion: Buddhism, Hinduism, Taoism, Zen*. Boston: Shambhala, 1994.

Flannery, Austin et al., eds. *The Conciliar and Postconciliar Documents*. New York: Costello Publishing Co. 1975.

Forman, Robert K. C. *Mysticism-Mind-Consciousness*. Albany: State University of New York Press, 1999.

Fowler, James. *Stages of Faith: The Psychology of Human Development and the Quest for Meaning*. San Francisco: HarperCollins, 1981.

Gilson, Etienne. *The Christian Philosophy of St. Thomas Aquinas*. New York: Random House, 1956.

Grant, Sara. *Toward an Alternative Theology: Confessions of a Non-Dualist Christian.* Bangalore: Asian Trading Corporation, 1991.

Griffiths, Bede. "Eastern Religious Experience." In *Monastic Studies* 9 (1972): 153–60.

———. *The Golden String.* Springfield, Ill.: Templegate, 1954/1980.

———. *A Human Search: Bede Griffiths Reflects on His Life, An Oral History.* Edited by John Swindells. Liguori, Mo.: Triumph Books, 1997.

———. *The Marriage of East and West.* Springfield, Ill.: Templegate, 1982.

———. *A New Vision of Reality: Western Science, Eastern Mysticism and Christian Faith.* Springfield, Ill.: Templegate, 1989.

———. *Pathways to the Supreme.* Edited by Roland Ropers. London: HarperCollins, 1995.

———. *Return to the Center.* Springfield, Ill.: Templegate, 1976.

———. "Spirit as Mother." *The Tablet,* June 9, 1979. Reprinted in *The One Light: Bede Griffiths' Principal Writings.* Edited by Bruno Barnhart, 108–12. Springfield, Ill., Templegate, 2001.

———. *Universal Wisdom: A Journey through the Sacred Wisdom of the World.* Edited by Roland Ropers. San Francisco: HarperCollins, 1994.

Guigo II. *The Ladder of Monks: A Letter on the Contemplative Life and Twelve Meditations.* Edited and translated by Edmund Colledge and James Walsh. Kalamazoo, Mich.: Cistercian Publications, 1981.

Guillen, Michael. *Five Equations That Changed the World: The Power and the Poetry of Mathematics.* New York: MJF Books, 1995.

Hale, Robert. *Christ and the Universe: Teilhard de Chardin and the Cosmos.* Chicago: Franciscan Herald Press, 1973.

Hastings, Adrian, Alistair Mason, and Hugh Pyper, eds., *The Oxford Companion to Christian Thought.* Oxford: Oxford University Press, 2000.

Hay, Denys. "The Idea of Renaissance." In *Dictionary of the History of Ideas.* Edited by P. P. Wiener, 4:121–29. New York: Scribner's Sons, 1973.

Hegel, Georg Wilhelm Friedrich. *The Philosophy of History.* Translated by J. Sibree. New York: Dover, 1899/1956.

Holy Bible, Revised Standard Version 1952. © 1946, 1952, 1973, Division of Christian Education of the National Council of Churches of Christ in the United States of America.

Huxley, Aldous. *The Perennial Philosophy.* New York: Harper & Row, 1944.

Ignatius of Antioch. *To the Romans: Ignace d'Antioche, Lettres.* Edited by T. Camelot. Sources Chrétiennes (SC) 10 *bis,* 106–17. English trans., *The Epistles of St. Clement of Rome and St. Ignatius of Antioch,* translated by J. A. Kleist. Ancient Christian Writers 1:80–84. Westminster, Md.: Newman, 1946.

Imperato, Robert. *Merton and Walsh on the Person.* Brookfield, Wis.: Liturgical Publications, 1987.

Integrities, June 1998. Special issue on Eugen Rosenstock-Huessy. Watsonville, Calif.

Irenaeus of Lyons. *Irénée de Lyon, Contre les heresies.* Edited by A. Rousseau and L. Doutreleaux. I: Sources Chrétiennes 264 (1979); II: Sources Chrétiennes 294 (1982); III: Sources Chrétiennes 211 (1974); IV: Sources Chrétiennes 100 (vol. 2, 1965); V (edited by A. Rousseau, L. Doutreleaux, and C. Mercier): Sources Chrétiennes 153 (1969). Paris: Éditions du Cerf, 1965–1982. Engl. trans. of vols. I–V, *The Ante-Nicene Fathers,* American edition, vol. 1, 315–567. Grand Rapids, Mich.: Eerdmans, 1885.

———. *Irénée de Lyon, Demonstration de la predication apostolique.* Edited by A. Rousseau, Sources Chrétiennes 406. Paris: Éditions du Cerf, 1995. English trans., *Proof of the Apostolic Preaching,* translated by J. F. Smith. Ancient Christian Writers 16. New York: Newman (Paulist), 1952.

Isaac of Stella. *Sermo 42.* Patrologia Latina 194, 1831–32. Extract in *Liturgy of the Hours,* 2:856–57.

———. *Sermons on the Christian Year,* vol. 1. Translated by Hugh McCaffery. Kalamazoo, Mich.: Cistercian Publications, 1979.

Jaspers, Karl. The *Origin and Goal of History.* New Haven: Yale University Press, 1953.

Jenkins, Philip. *The Next Christendom: The Coming of Global Christianity,* New York: Oxford University Press, 2002.

Jung, Carl. "Concerning Mandala Symbolism." In Carl Jung, *The Archetypes of the Collective Unconscious,* translated by R. F. C. Hull. Collected Works 9/1, 355–84. 2nd ed. Princeton: Princeton University Press, 1968.

———. *Memories, Dreams, Reflections.* Edited by A. Jaffé. Translated by R. and C. Winston. New York: Random House, 1961, 1965 (2nd ed.).

———. *Psychological Types.* Translated by H. G. Baynes and R. F. C. Hull. Collected Works 6. Princeton: Princeton University Press, 1971.

Katz, Steven T., ed. *Mysticism and Language.* New York: Oxford University Press, 1992.

Kilcourse, George. *Ace of Freedoms: Thomas Merton's Christ.* Notre Dame, Ind.: University of Notre Dame Press, 1993.

Kristeller, Paul O. "Introduction to Pico della Mirandola." In *The Renaissance Philosophy of Man.* Edited by Ernst Cassirer, Paul Kristeller, and John H. Randall, 215–22. Chicago: University of Chicago Press, 1948.

Kuhn, Thomas. *The Copernican Revolution: Planetary Astronomy in the Development of Western Thought.* Cambridge, Mass.: Harvard University Press, 1957.

LaCugna, Catherine M. *God for Us: The Trinity and Christian Life.* New York: HarperCollins, 1991.

Lakeland, Paul. *Postmodernity: Christian Identity in a Fragmented Age.* Minneapolis, Minn.: Fortress Press, 1997.

Lampe, G. W. H. *The Seal of the Spirit: A Study in the Doctrine of Baptism and Confirmation in the New Testament and the Fathers.* London: S.P.C.K., 1967.

Lao Tzu. *Tao Teh Ching.* Translated by John C. H. Wu. Boston: Shambhala, 1989.

Leclercq, Jean. *The Love of Learning and the Desire for God: A Study of Monastic Culture,* translated by Catharine Misrahi. New York: Fordham University Press, 1961.

Leo the Great. *Sermo 51.* Extract in *Liturgy of the Hours,* 2:149–50. Full text in *Léon le Grand: Sermons* III, Sources Chrétiennes 74:13–21. Edited by R. Dolle. Paris: Éditions du Cerf, 1961.

———. *Sermo 1 de Ascensione.* Extract in *Liturgy of the Hours,* 2:898–99.

———. *Sermo 2 de Ascensione.* Extract in *Liturgy of the Hours,* 2:937.

Liturgy of the Hours according to the Roman Rite, 4 vols. New York: Catholic Book Publishing Co., 1975.

Louth, Andrew. *Discerning the Mystery: An Essay on the Nature of Theology.* Oxford: Oxford University Press, 1983.

Lovejoy, Arthur. *The Great Chain of Being: A Study of the History of an Idea.* Cambridge, Mass.: Harvard University Press, 1936.

Löwith, Karl. *Meaning in History.* Chicago: University of Chicago Press, 1949.

Loy, David. *Nonduality: A Study in Comparative Philosophy.* New Haven: Yale University Press, 1988.

Maritain, Jacques. *Creative Intuition in Art and Poetry.* New York: Meridian, 1957.

Marsili, Salvatore. *Giovanni Cassiano ed Evagrio Pontico: Dottrina sulla caritá e contemplazione.* Studia Anselmiana 5. Rome: Herder, 1936.

McDonnell, Kilian. "Jesus' Baptism in the Jordan." *Theological Studies* 56 (1995): 209–36.

———. *Jesus' Baptism in the Jordan: The Trinitarian and Cosmic Order of Salvation.* Collegeville, Minn.: Liturgical Press, 1996.

McFague, Sallie. *Life Abundant: Rethinking Theology and Economy for a Planet in Peril.* Minneapolis: Fortress Press, 2001.

McGinn, Bernard. *The Growth of Mysticism.* New York: Crossroad, 1994.

———. "Meister Eckhart on God as Absolute Unity." In *Neoplatonism and Christian Thought.* Edited by Dominic J. O'Meara, 129–39. Albany: State University of New York Press, 1982.

———. *The Mystical Thought of Meister Eckhart.* New York: Crossroad, 2001.

———, ed. *Meister Eckhart and the Beguine Mystics.* New York: Continuum, 1997.

Mersch, Emile. *The Theology of the Mystical Body.* St. Louis, Mo.: B. Herder, 1952.

———. *The Whole Christ: The Historical Development of the Doctrine of the Mystical Body in Scripture and Tradition.* Milwaukee: Bruce, 1938.

Merton, Thomas. *Ascent to Truth.* New York: Harcourt, Brace, 1951.

———. "'Baptism in the Forest': Wisdom and Initiation in William Faulkner." In *The Literary Essays,* 92–116.

———. *Conjectures of a Guilty Bystander.* Garden City, N.Y.: Doubleday, 1966.

———. *Contemplation in a World of Action.* Garden City, N.Y.: Doubleday, 1971.

———. *Contemplative Prayer.* New York: Herder & Herder, 1969. Published also as *The Climate of Monastic Prayer.* Kalamazoo, Mich.: Cistercian Publications, 1969.

———. "Final Integration: Toward a Monastic Therapy." In *Contemplation in a World of Action,* 205–17.

———. *The Inner Experience: Notes on Contemplation.* Edited by William H. Shannon. San Francisco: HarperCollins, 2003.

———. *The Literary Essays of Thomas Merton.* Edited by Bro. Patrick Hart. New York: New Directions, 1981.

———. "Louis Zukofsky: The Paradise Ear." In *The Literary Essays,* 128–33.

———. "Nature and Art in William Blake: An Essay in Interpretation," (dissertation for the Master's Degree at Columbia University, 1939). In *The Literary Essays of Thomas Merton,* 385–453. New York: New Directions, 1981.

———. *New Seeds of Contemplation.* New York: New Directions, 1962.

———. "Poetry and Contemplation: A Reappraisal." In *The Literary Essays,* 338–54.

———. *Seeds of Contemplation.* New York: New Directions, 1949.

———. *Zen and the Birds of Appetite.* New York: New Directions, 1968.

Mitchell, Donald W., and James Wiseman, eds. *The Gethsemani Encounter.* New York: Continuum, 1998.

Monchanin, Jules. *Jules Monchanin (1895–1957) as Seen from East and West: Acts of the Colloquium Held in Lyon-Fleurie, France, and in Shantivanam-Tannirpalli, India (April-July 1995).* Vol. I. Lyon-Fleurie. Translated by Thomas Matus et al. Delhi: I.S.P.C.K., 2001. Vol. II. Shantivanam-Tannirpalli. Delhi: I.S.P.C.K., 2001.

Morris, Colin. *The Discovery of the Individual 1050–1200.* Toronto: University of Toronto Press, 1972/1987.

Mumford, Lewis. *The Transformations of Man.* New York: Collier, 1962.

Murray, Charles. *Human Accomplishment: The Pursuit of Excellence in the Arts and Sciences, 800 BC to 1950.* New York: HarperCollins, 2003.

Nasr, Seyed Hossein. *Knowledge and the Sacred.* New York: Crossroad, 1981.

Panichas, George, ed. *The Simone Weil Reader.* New York: David McKay, 1977.

Panikkar, Raimon. *Blessed Simplicity: The Monk as Universal Archetype.* New York: Seabury, 1982.

———. *Christophany: The Fullness of Man.* Translated by Alfred DiLascia. Maryknoll, N.Y.: Orbis Books, 2004.

Polycarp, St. *Martyre de Polycarpe.* Edited by T. Camelot. Sources Chrétiennes 10 *bis,* 210–39. Paris: Cerf, 1998. English trans., *The Martyrdom of St. Polycarp.* Edited by J. A. Kleist. Ancient Christian Writers 6:90–102. Westminster, Md.: Newman Press, 1948.

Rahner, Hugo. "The Christian Mystery and the Pagan Mysteries." In *Papers from the Eranos Yearbooks. II, The Mysteries.* Edited by Joseph Campbell, 337–401. Princeton: Princeton University Press, 1955.

Rahner, Karl. "The Abiding Significance of the Second Vatican Council." *Theological Investigations* 20:90–102. New York: Seabury, 1981.

———. "Basic Theological Interpretation of the Second Vatican Council." *Theological Investigations* 20:77–89. New York: Seabury, 1981.

———. *Christian at the Crossroads.* New York: Seabury, 1975.

———. "Christianity and the 'New Man.'" *Theological Investigations* 5:135–53. London: Darton, Longman & Todd, 1966.

———. "The Concept of Mystery in Catholic Theology." *Theological Investigations* 4:36–73. London: Darton, Longman & Todd, 1966.

———. *The Content of Faith: The Best of Karl Rahner's Theological Writings.* Edited by Karl Lehmann and Franz Raffelt. Translation editor Harvey Egan. New York: Crossroad, 1994.

———. "The Experience of God Today." *Theological Investigations* 11:149–65. New York: Seabury, 1974.

———. *Foundations of Christian Faith: An Introduction to the Idea of Christianity.* Translated by William V. Dych. New York: Seabury, 1978.

———. *Hearers of the Word.* Montreal: Palm Publishers, 1969.

———. "Man (Anthropology), III. Theological." In *Sacramentum Mundi* 3 (1969): 365–70.

———. "On Recognizing the Importance of Thomas Aquinas." *Theological Investigations* 13:3–12. New York: Seabury, 1975.

———. "Reflections on Methodology in Theology." *Theological Investigations* 11:68–114. New York: Seabury, 1974.

———. *Spirit in the World.* Montreal: Palm Publishers, 1968.

———. *Theological Investigations.* 23 vols. London: Darton, Longman & Todd, 1961–1992. New York: Seabury/Crossroad, 1974–1992.

———. "Theology and Anthropology." *Theological Investigations* 9:28–45. London: Darton, Longman & Todd, 1972.

———. "True Freedom." In *Grace and Freedom,* 203–64. Montreal: Palm Publishers, 1969.

———et al., eds. *Sacramentum Mundi: An Encyclopedia of Theology*. 6 vols. New York: Seabury Press, 1968–1970.

———, and Herbert Vorgrimler. *Dictionary of Theology*. 2nd ed. New York: Crossroad, 1981.

Reeves, Marjorie. *Joachim of Fiore and the Prophetic Future: A Medieval Study in Historical Thinking*. Second revised edition. Stroud, Gloucestershire: Sutton Publishing, 1999.

Rodhe, Sten. "Christianity and Hinduism: A Comparison of the Views held by Jules Monchanin and Bede Griffiths." In *Jules Monchanin (1895–1957) as Seen from East and West*, 1:169–81. Delhi: I.S.P.C.K, 2001.

Rosenstock-Huessy, Eugen. *Out of Revolution: Autobiography of Western Man*. Providence, R.I.: Berg, 1938/1993.

Rukeyser, Muriel. *The Life of Poetry*. Ashfield, Mass.: Paris Press, 1996.

Vatican Council II. *Dei Verbum*. Dogmatic Constitution on Divine Revelation. November 18, 1965. Pages 750ff. in Flannery, ed. *The Conciliar and Postconciliar Documents*.

———. *Gaudium et Spes*. Pastoral Constitution on the Church in the Modern World. December 7, 1965. Pages 903ff. in Flannery, ed. *The Conciliar and Postconciliar Documents*.

———. *Lumen Gentium*. Dogmatic Constitution on the Church. November 21, 1964. Pages 350ff. in Flannery, ed. *The Conciliar and Postconciliar Documents*.

———. *Nostra Aetate*. Declaration on the Relation of the Church to Non-Christian Religions. October 28, 1965. Pages 738ff. in Flannery, ed. *The Conciliar and Postconciliar Documents*.

———. *Optatum Totius*. Decree on the Training of Priests. October 28, 1965. Pages 707ff. in Flannery, ed. *The Conciliar and Postconciliar Documents*.

———. *Perfectae Caritatis*. Decree on the Up-to-date Renewal of Religious Life. October 28, 1965. Pages 611ff. in Flannery, ed. *The Conciliar and Postconciliar Documents*.

———. *Sacrosanctum Concilium*. Constitution on the Sacred Liturgy. December 4, 1963. Pages 1ff. in Flannery, ed. *The Conciliar and Postconciliar Documents*.

Schuon, Frithjof. *The Transcendent Unity of Religions*. Wheaton, Ill.: Theosophical Publishing House, 1984.

Shankara. *The Crest Jewel of Discrimination (Viveka-Chudamani)*. Translated by Swami Prabhavananda and Christopher Isherwood. Hollywood, Calif.: Vedanta Press, 1947, 1978.

Shannon, William H. *Merton's Dark Path: The Inner Experience of a Contemplative*. New York: Penguin, 1982.

———, Christine M. Bochen, and Patrick F. O' Connell. *The Thomas Merton Encyclopedia*. Maryknoll, N.Y.: Orbis Books, 2002.

Smalley, Beryl. *The Study of the Bible in the Middle Ages*. Oxford: Basil Blackwood, 1952; Notre Dame, Ind.: University of Notre Dame Press, 1962.

Smoley, Richard, and Jay Kinney. *Hidden Wisdom: A Guide to the Western Inner Traditions*. 2nd ed. Wheaton, Ill.: Quest Books, Theosophical Publishing House, 2006.

Sorokin, Pitirim. *The Crisis of Our Age: The Social and Cultural Outlook*. London: Angus & Robertson, 1942.

———. *Social and Cultural Dynamics*. Revised one-volume edition. Boston: Porter Sargent, 1957.

Spengler, Oswald. *The Decline of the West.* Translated by Charles F. Atkinson, 2 vols. New York: Knopf, 1926–1928.

Stein, Murray. *Jung's Treatment of Christianity: The Psychotherapy of a Religious Tradition.* Wilmette, Ill.: Chiron, 1986.

Stevens, Wallace. *The Collected Poems of Wallace Stevens.* New York: Knopf, 1954.

———. *Opus Posthumous: Poems/Plays/Prose.* Revised second edition. Edited by Milton J. Bates. New York: Knopf, 1989.

Stewart, Columba. *Cassian the Monk.* New York: Oxford University Press, 1998.

Stolz, Anselm. *L'Ascèse Chrétien.* Chevetogne: Éditions des Benedictines d'Amay, 1948.

———. *Doctrine of Spiritual Perfection.* Translated by Aidan Williams. St. Louis: B. Herder, 1938.

Stuart, James. *Swami Abhishiktananda: His Life Told Through His Letters.* Delhi: I.S.P.C.K., 1989.

Suzuki, Daisetz T. *Mysticism, Christian and Buddhist.* New York: Harper & Row, 1971.

———. "On Satori—The Revelation of a New Truth in Zen Buddhism." In *Essays in Zen Buddhism, First Series,* 229–66. New York: Grove Press, 1949, 1951 (2nd ed.).

———. "Zen as Chinese Interpretation of the Doctrine of Enlightenment." *Essays in Zen Buddhism, First Series,* 39–117. New York: Grove Press, 1949, 1951 (2nd ed.).

Tanquerey, Adolphe. *The Spiritual Life: A Treatise on Ascetical and Mystical Theology.* 2nd ed. Tournay: Desclée, 1930.

Tarnas, Richard. *Cosmos and Psyche: Intimations of a New World View.* New York: Viking Penguin, 2006.

———. *The Passion of the Western Mind: Understanding the Ideas That Have Shaped Our World View.* New York: Harmony Books, 1991.

Taylor, Charles. *Philosophical Arguments.* Cambridge, Mass.: Harvard University Press, 1989.

———. *Sources of the Self: The Making of the Modern Identity.* Cambridge, Mass.: Harvard University Press, 1989.

Teilhard de Chardin, Pierre. *Activation of Energy.* New York: Harcourt Brace Jovanovich, 1970.

———. *The Future of Man.* Translated by Norman Denny. London: Collins, 1964.

———. *Human Energy.* New York: Harcourt Brace Jovanovich, 1969.

———. *The Phenomenon of Man.* Translated by Bernard Wall. New York: Harper, 1961.

Toal, M. F. *Patristic Homilies on the Gospels: The Sunday Sermons of the Fathers,* 4 vols. London: Longmans Green, 1954.

Trapnell, Judson. *Bede Griffiths: A Life in Dialogue.* Albany: State University of New York Press, 2001.

———. "Two Models of Christian Dialogue with Hinduism: Bede Griffiths and Abhishiktananda." *Vidyajyoti:* 60, nos. 2–4 (February-April 1996): I (101–10); II (183–91); III (243–54).

Underhill, Evelyn. *Mysticism.* New York: Meridian, 1955.

The Upanishads, A New Translation, 4 vols. Translated and edited by Swami Nikhilananda. New York: Ramakrishna-Vivekananda Society. I:1949, 1990 (5th ed.); II:1952, 1990 (3rd ed.); III:1956, 1990 (3rd ed.); IV: 1959, 1979 (2nd ed.).

Vagaggini, Cipriano. "Teologia." In *Nuovo Dizionario di Teologia.* Edited by G. Barbaglio and S. Dianich. Rome: Edizioni Paoline, 1979.

———. *Theological Dimensions of the Liturgy.* Translated by L. J. Doyle and W. A. Jurgens. 4th ed. Collegeville, Minn.: Liturgical Press, 1976.

Viellieux, Armand. “Monk on a Journey.” In *Thomas Merton Monk.* Edited by Patrick Hart, 263. 2nd ed. Kalamazoo Mich.: Cistercian Publications, 1983.

Vrajaprana. “Regaining the Lost Kingdom: Purity and Meditation in the Hindu Spiritual Tradition.” In *Purity of Heart and Contemplation: A Monastic Dialogue between Christian and Asian Traditions.* Edited by B. Barnhart and J. Wong. New York: Continuum, 2001.

Weil, Simone. *Oeuvres Completes.* Edited by A. Devaux and F. De Lussy. Paris: Gallimard, 1988–.

Wilber, Ken. *Sex, Ecology, Spirituality: The Spirit of Evolution.* Boston: Shambhala, 1995.

William of St. Thierry. *The Golden Epistle: A Letter to the Brethren at Mont Dieu.* Translated by Theodore Berkeley. Kalamazoo, Mich.: Cistercian Publications, 1971.

Zukav, Gary. *The Dancing Wu Li Masters: An Overview of the New Physics.* New York: William Morrow, 1979.

Index